Ex Auditu

I0887516

An Annual of the Frederick Neumann Symposium on Theological Interpretation of Scripture. Princeton Theological Seminary, Princeton, New Jersey.

Ex Auditu is published annually by Pickwick Publications, 4137 Timberlane Drive, Allison Park, Pennsylvania, 15101, U.S.A.

Subscriptions:

Individuals
- U.S.A. - $15.00
- Canada - $12.00 (in U.S. Funds)
- All other countries - $15.00
- Students - $10.00

Institutions and/or Libraries (includes one membership of the Symposium)
- U.S.A. - $25.00
- Canada - $20.00 (in U.S. Funds)
- All other countries - $25.00

Indexed in Religion Index One: Periodicals, published by the American Theological Library Association, Chicago, Illinois, available online in the ATLA Religion Database through BRS Information Technologies (Latham, New York) and DIALOG Information Services (Palo Alto, California); Internationale Zeitschriftenschau für Bibelwissenschaft und Grenzgebeite.

Please address all subscription correspondence and change of address information to Pickwick Publications.

ISSN 08883-0053

EX AUDITU

The Editorial Consultants represent various disciplines and denominations. Theological Interpretation of Scripture is a task to be taken seriously by scholars who are committed to the Christian faith and tradition. However, as one editorial consultant stated it: "let people gradually get used to the idea that a sane hermeneutics is both oriented in advance toward agreement/consent and is simultaneously exigent, discriminating, critical."

EX AUDITU

Volume III 1987

CONTENTS

INTRODUCTION

THOMAS W. GILLESPIE

The Second Annual Frederick Neumann Symposium on Theological Interpretation of Scripture was held at Princeton Theological Seminary on October 16-19, 1987, under the able leadership of the committee of faculty members responsible for its planning and chaired by Dr. Karlfried Froehlich, the Benjamin B. Warfield Professor of Ecclesiastical History. Again the Symposium brought together scholars from a broad ecumenical, international, and disciplinary spectrum. We were privileged to have as our special guest, Dr. Edith Neumann, the benefactor of the Symposium that bears the name of her late husband.

The biblical theme addressed from a variety of perspectives on this occasion was "Creation" as attested in the Scriptures of the Old and New Testaments and reflected upon in the theological tradition of the Church. Although the issue of the relationship between faith and science, or, more precisely, between the biblical witness and modern scientific cosmology surfaced in the discussions of the Symposium and was addressed brilliantly in an opening address by Dr. Stanley L. Jaki, this was not the burden of the papers presented. What emerges from these presentations rather is the clear recognition that the term *creation* in this context is employed by the biblical authors to interpret the reality of the universe in its relation to its transcendent Creator and the reality of human life in such a world so understood. Your horizons will be expanded, I am sure, by a careful reading of these papers in their published form.

Looking ahead to the Third Annual Frederick Neumann Symposium, scheduled for October 14-17, 1988, here at Princeton Seminary, the theme to be addressed is "The Church and Israel (Romans 9-11)." Plans for this event are well under way, and it is hoped that many subscribers to *Ex Auditu* will be able to attend. The fourth Symposium has been set for October 13-16, 1989, when the theme will be "The Theological Center of Scripture."

The Ecological Crisis as a Challenge for Biblical Theology*

Peter Stuhlmacher

The biblical theology which we have begun under the banner of "Ex Auditu" does not operate in a vacuum. On the contrary, the purpose of biblical theology is to serve the church, by interpreting the Holy Scriptures of both Old and New Testaments, so that the original witness of the Bible can be understood as a message relevant for today. In order to accomplish this purpose, we must carefully consider three questions. First, what are the challenges confronting the church today? Second, what, if anything, does the Bible have to say about these challenges? And, third, what modern applications can be drawn from an examination of the biblical texts?

As a model of this threefold agenda, the following discussion focuses on the ecological problem in Europe today. The attempt will be made to understand this ecological problem as a challenge which makes biblical theology both fruitful and practical.

I. The Ecological Problem

Since the end of the Second World War, Central Europe has experienced incredibly rapid economic growth. Thanks to the Marshall plan, the devastation caused by the war, which in some places was enormous, could be relatively quickly removed in Western Europe; destroyed cities could be rebuilt; factories could be renovated; and industrial production could be reactivated. The post war restoration of East Germany and also of Austria took much longer than in the West, but in effect the process was similar. Never before in its history has Central Europe had such a high standard of living as it does today. I have personally witnessed this development, first for a short time in East Germany and then, since 1947, in West Germany.

After the war, we were deeply grateful just to have a roof over our heads, food on the table, and clothes on our backs. At the same time, however, we young people were fascinated with the new models of cars and planes, machines and ships, which came off the assembly lines every year; we were amazed at the sudden development of European agriculture into a high capacity, surplus-producing industry. Nevertheless, for sometime now our initial thankfulness and enthusiasm have waned, and given way to an increasing anxiety in not a few men and women of my generation. This turnabout has nothing to do with anti-Americanism! Rather, we have had to realize that the land mass of Europe is too small and too sensitive to be an ever escalating process of industrialization; it simply cannot survive it in the long run. The rapid

**Translated by James M. Scott, Tübingen*

growth, which we formerly welcomed with open arms, has now gone so far as to threaten the basis of our very existence, as well as that of the generations to come. Instead of quoting (well-known) abstract statistics, I would like to present three concrete examples of the deleterious effects of industrialization in both eastern and western portions of Central Europe.

In Saxony, where I grew up (and which is now part of East Germany), the area around Leipzig used to be known for its fertility and for its rustic charm. Saxony also possessed a densely-forested resort known throughout Europe, the so-called "Erzgebirge" or "Ore Mountains." An unpleasant shock awaits anyone visiting my hometown and the Erzgebirge today; for these two regions have been radically changed. Because of the scarcity of alternative energy sources and the lack of money to import oil or coal, the East German government is forced utterly to exploit its own brown-coal resources by strip mining the area around Leipzig. Every year, more and more villages and farm land are sacrificed for the coal which lies just below them. Whether or not the ravaged countryside can ever be restored to arable land is very uncertain. As for the Erzgebirge, only a few isolated woods remain in the region which was once celebrated for its forests. Literally hundreds of square miles of this forest have been destroyed by unfiltered emissions from the heavy industry not only of East Germany itself, but especially of neighboring Czechoslovakia. Part of the ground has been so polluted by acid rain that it is impossible to plant new trees. This once magnificent mountain range, for whose conservation my own father fought in the 1930's, has now become largely a barren wasteland.

Two years ago a friend of mine from Switzerland told me that in the near future many Alpine valleys would have to be closed off and the inhabitants evacuated. This is because the destruction of the Alpine trees and vegetation has progressed so rapidly that the woods, shrubbery and grasscover will no longer be able to fulfill their age-old function of protecting against flooding, avalanches, and rock slides. This prognosis was confirmed with horrible vividness this summer by the massive landslide in Valtellina in the Tyrolean Alps of Northern Italy. What happened there also threatens the whole range of the Swiss, Bavarian, and Austrian Alps. The forests and vegetation of the Alps have been so damaged by the consistent development of this area for summer and winter tourism, and by the industrial pollution from both the East and the West, that the inhabitants of the entire regions and cities are worried about their future survival.

The industrialization of agriculture also has its price. I will mention here merely one example: the pollution of the ground water with nitrates, which makes the water unfit for human consumption. Whole crops, some of which, like corn, were introduced to Europe from elsewhere, can flourish only if they are simultaneously kept free from insects by liberal use of insecticides and treated with fertilizers to stimulate rapid growth. The residues from these insecticides and fertilizers ruin not only the flora and fauna of the farm lands themselves, but they also pollute the drinking water, when the chemicals penetrate with the rain deep into the soil, reach the ground water, and contaminate the wells. Because of this, entire regions in Germany have had to pipe in drinking water in the last two years from areas which are still free from pollution.

Many other alarming examples of the ecological crisis could be given: the melt-down at Chernobyl; the pollution of the Rhine River by industrial accidents; and the contamination of the North and Baltic Seas by industrial sewage and poisonous wastes from contiguous countries of the East and West. The (mostly contrived) needs of our industrial civilization are wreaking havoc on the environment.[1] At the same time, however, we must not isolate this ecological crisis from other dangers which have been growing in the past few decades in Europe (and which are also characteristic of all other Western industrial nations), including the misuse and overestimation of military power; the irresponsible treatment of human life; and the rapacious desires of consumerism. In other words, the industrial way of life which Europe chose in 1946-47 is turning out to be the way of death.

In view of this horrible situation, the theologian and exegete is immediately reminded of Rom. 1:18-32: Mankind has broken out of the creative order and is now given up to destruction by his own insatiable desires and schemes. Yet Rom. 1:18-32 is by no means the final word of the Apostle Paul on the subject of the world's present condition and its future. Therefore, the question is whether we as Christians should just sit back and watch our world be devastated, or whether there is a way for us to serve life on earth in behalf of God, and thereby thwart the ecological catastrophe. Since, throughout the whole Bible, God's judgments are never an end in themselves, but are always a call to repentence and return to the righteousness which God demands, I hope that this will also hold true in our very dire circumstances. What then are we to do? Let us bring this question to the Holy Scriptures.

II. The Biblical Theology of Creation

For biblical theology, the Old and New Testaments belong together and are mutually interpretative. However, they both have their own historical contexts, and should not, therefore, be too quickly and naively applied to our present-day situation. First we must place ourselves before the Holy Scriptures and hear *their* message.

In examining the question of the testimony of the Scriptures concerning creation and ecology, I focus on the message of Jesus and the teaching of Paul. This serves as the most convenient point of departure into the Scriptures as a whole and into the question of possible Christian service to life and creation.

Jesus' Teaching about Man's Dealings with the Creation

Before we attempt to consider what Jesus had to say about man's dealings with the creation, we must first realize that a consciousness of the ecological crisis is a rather *recent* development. We cannot, therefore, presuppose our own sensitization to the ecological problem for the time of Jesus and the New Testament, although - even if they were not recognized as such - environmental violations were already perpetrated in the ancient world. Herbert Donner writes in his book, *Introduction to Biblical Geography and Archaeology:*[2]

> *Without exception, regions with more than 19 in. of annual rainfall were originally forest areas. Of course, the forests were cut down very early, in order to clear the land for cultivation and to use the wood for building houses, ships, etc. The result of this uncontrolled cutting over the course of thousands of years is the complete denudation of the once lush mountain regions.*

1. Cf. Jürgen Moltmann's analysis in his book *God in Creation: An Ecological Doctrine of Creation.* The Gifford Lectures, 1984-1985; trans. Margaret Kohl (London: SCM Press, 1985), pp. 20-52.

2. Herbert Donner, *Einführung in die biblische Landes- und Altertumskunde* (Darmstadt: Wissenschaftliche Buchgesellschaft, 1976), p. 40.

The following two examples are sufficient to gain a realistic impression of the ancient exploitation of forests which took place in and around Palestine. It is interesting to note that these examples stem from the military sector. Already in the ancient world, ecological exploitation went hand in hand with military exploits. During his seven-month siege of Tyre, Alexander the Great built a causeway which extended 656 yards from the mainland out to the beleaguered island. Upon this causeway Alexander was able to transport over the water a number of siege towers, each 164 ft. tall, and finally conquer the city in 332 B.C. All of the building materials necessary for such an engineering feat, including the lumber, were undoubtedly acquired from the surrounding area. Similarly, Titus exploited the land of Palestine when he besieged Jerusalem and took it by storm in A.D. 70. Josephus reports that during the siege all of the usable wood within a 100-stadia (or 12-mile) radius from Jerusalem was cut down for building barriers and siege ramps (*BJ* V, pp. 552ff.; VI, p. 375.).

Thus exploitation of creation took place already in biblical times, even if its irreparable effects were not recognized. In the time of the New Testament, the unawareness of ecological issues may be attributed, in part, to the early church's expectation of the imminent return of Christ, which goes back to Jesus' preaching of repentance and to his related message of the soon coming of the kingdom of God. Even when these are taken into consideration, however, Jesus' dealings with the creation remain a guide for us today. This assertion is supported by the following reasons.

First of all, Jesus himself was inspired with the *belief in God the Creator,* and he explicitly obligated his disciples to this belief. This is seen not only in Jesus' affirmation of the First Commandment and of the Shema (cf. Mk. 12:28ff. par.), but especially in his familiar Wisdom sayings in Matt. 5:45; 6:26ff./Lk. 12:23ff.; Matt. 10:16/ Lk. 10:3; and Matt. 10:29-31/Lk. 12:6-7, where the disciples are instructed to go out and measure themselves by the conduct of their Heavenly Father, who is the Creator of the world and the Lord over life and death. In so teaching, Jesus affirms the Old Testament creation accounts and creeds without either modifying or retracting them. With Jesus, therefore, many Old Testament passages on creation can be legitimately read and applied without qualification. I refer not only to Gen. 1 and 2; Ps. 19; 104; 147; 148, etc., but also to the Wisdom texts which praise God's creative order (e.g., Prov. 8:22ff.; Wisd. 9; Sir. 24). Since Jesus' (and the New Testament authors') preaching did not wish to establish a new Bible, but rather presupposed the "Holy Scriptures" as well-known and valid, this *relection* of the Old Testament is also legitimate for Christians!

For Jesus, and for his disciples after him, *creation was a source for parables.* This is illustrated by the aforementioned Wisdom sayings and by Jesus' parables using the imagery of growth: the Parable of the Sower (Mk. 4:1-9 par.); the Parable of the Seed Growing Secretly (Mk. 4:26-29); the Parable of the Mustard Seed (Mk. 4:30-32 par.); the Parable of the Rich Fool (Lk. 12:16-21); and the Parable of the Barren Fig Tree (Lk. 13:6-9). Furthermore, Mk. 13:28f. (par.) appeals to the signs of the seasons as an illustration of the signs of the times. For Jesus, creation was a source of parables, because it rests in God's hands. From their personal experience, Jesus and his followers could depend on the creative order, that is, on the Wisdom of God which interweaves creation and sets it in order.

Jesus too, sees himself and his disciples as personally active in creation, in that *they bring about blessing and judgment* in the world. In the account of the feeding of the 5000, Jesus brings about blessing when he feeds the hungry crowd, after having given thanks to God the Creator (cf. Mk. 6:41 par.). In his exorcism and healing, Jesus restores to the kingdom of God the ruinous lives of the sick who had been separated from God. When, by the commission of Jesus, the disciples themselves take part in this exorcism and healing (cf. Matt. 10:8 par.), they work in the name of Jesus, to mend a life which is created by God and which belongs to him alone.

Sometimes Jesus also brings about judgment on the creation, as in the burlesque of the healing of the Gerasene/Gergesene demoniac (Mk. 5:1 13 par.), and in the (symbolic) account of the cursing of the fig tree (= Israel; cp. Mk. 11:12-14, 20-26 par., with Joel 1:7). By virtue of the faith which (metaphorically speaking) is able to cast mountains into the sea (or uproot trees), the disciples participate in the judicial authority of God (cf. esp. Mk. 11:22ff. par.).[3] The judgment carried out by Jesus and his disciples does not revoke the blessing imparted by them in healing and exorcism. The contrast is merely complementary; for the *krisis* which Jesus (and his disciples) pronounce by word and deed is precisely the means by which the saving kingdom of God is finally brought about (cf. Matt. 15:13: "Every plant which my heavenly Father did not plant shall be rooted up.'').

As Mk. 2:23-27 (par.), Luke 6:5, and Mk. 3:1-6 (par.) illustrate, Jesus did not abolish *the commandment to keep the Sabbath,* but vividly illustrated it in his own messianic sense, and instilled it with new meaning. Jesus taught that any deed is allowed on the Sabbath which brings heaven and earth together in a spirit of love and freedom; for such deeds (*e.g.* healing) allow the giver and the receiver to experience God's goodness and mercy. When Jesus healed on the Sabbath, his main concern was to mend a ruined life. In light of Jesus' example, it is advisable to reconsider carefully the Old Testament commandment to keep the Sabbath (especially in the version of Deut. 5:12-15),[4] and to learn from it how we Christians - without impinging on the celebration of Christ's resurrection on Sunday - should sanctify Christian holy days.

As the Messiah, Jesus no longer sees the world in its present state as the only criterion for the belief in creation; *he already looks forward to the New Creation to be consummated by God.* In that day, man will be like the angels (as glorified beings) (cf. Mk. 12:25 par.); "many'' from all peoples will gather together (on Zion) for God's lavish banquet (cf. Matt. 8:11ff./Lk. 13:29, with Isa. 25:6ff.); and Jesus himself (as the glorified, messianic Son of Man) will then "drink (anew) of the fruit of the vine" with his own people (Mk. 14:25 par.). *Jesus' messianic mission and message shares the perspective of Isa. 25:6-8; Jesus lives for the day when the power of death over all creation will come to an end.* Jesus' eschatological expectation in the first part of the Lord's Prayer is based on this view of the New Creation, and the disciples are instructed to pray likewise. For this reason, it is possible and legitimate to see the disciples' commission in light of a

3. In the Old Testament, "to remove mountains" (cf. Job 9:5; Isa. 13:10; Jer. 51:25) and "to uproot (trees)" (cf. Jer. 1:10; 18:7; 31:28; 45:4; Dan. 4:14 LXX) are metaphors for divine judgment. In light of this, Jesus' idea of faith that can remove mountains (and uproot trees) has judicial connotations.

4. Cf. Hartmut Gese, *Essays on Biblical Theology,* trans. Keith Crim (Minneapolis, Minn.: Augsburg Publishing House, 1981), pp. 86-88; Ferdinand Hahn, "Schabbat und Sonntag," *Evangelische Theologie* 46 (1986), 495-507; Patrick D. Miller, Jr., "The Human Sabbath: A Study in Deuteronomic Theology," *The Princeton Seminary Bulletin* N.S. 6 (1985); pp. 81-97; Moltmann, *Creation,* pp. 290-296.

broader theology of creation. As seen in their eschatological greeting of peace upon every house they entered (cf. Lk. 10:5f.), in their preaching, and in their kindness to the sick (Lk. 10:9), the evangelizing disciples are forerunners of the coming kingdom of God and of shalom for the whole creation. Christian teaching about the kingdom of God which ignores this apocalyptic dimension and perspective illegitimately detracts from the missionary commission which the apostles received!

The foregoing view is corroborated by the fact that in the synoptic tradition animals were also associated with Jesus' messianic mission. When, according to Mk. 6:34, Jesus has compassion on the multitude because they seem to him "like sheep without a shepherd," this is a simile which has messianic overtones in view of Num. 27:17. In the Parable of the Lost Sheep (Lk. 15:3ff.; Matt. 18:12ff.), the concern of the shepherd for one lost sheep out of the hundred is used as a metaphor for God's seeking after the lost sinner. Because Jesus illustrates God's seeking after mankind, he also appears in the synoptic Gospels as what John calls "the good shepherd" (Jn. 10:11, 14); his behavior is a model for the disciples.

Mk. 1:12f., however, goes far beyond any such comparisons (cf. also Matt. 6:26/Lk. 12:24; Matt. 10:29/Lk. 12:6). In the very concise Marcan version of Jesus' temptation in the wilderness, we find the remarkable statement:" . . . and he was with the wild animals." As Fritz Neugebauer[5] and Erich Grässer[6] have recently shown, this comment has messianic-eschatological significance: *Jesus appears here in expectation of the culmination of his messianic mission, when he ushers in the time of messianic peace in fulfillment of Isa. 11:1-8.* Thus the messianic expectation of Isa. 11:1ff. is in no way spiritualized in the New Testament; on the contrary, it is Christologically appropriated and confirmed.

The entire ministry of Jesus and of those who work in his name is concerned with the salvation and redemption of the whole creation. *All that Jesus is and does - and all that the disciples say and do in his commission - is intended as a sign of hope for all creation.* This insight is fundamental to an understanding of the disciples' view of creation and of the proper relation of humans to it. For, if the salvation and redemption of creation are integral to that messianic commission, it follows that all the disciples say and do which does not provide a sign of hope for creation fails to live up to Jesus' commission, whether totally or partially. It is interesting to note that Paul confirms this view and develops it.

PAUL'S TEACHING ABOUT MAN'S DEALINGS WITH THE CREATION

As we turn to the letters of Paul with the question of how man should relate to creation, we must once again remind ourselves that a sensitivity to ecological issues is a modern phenomenon which cannot be presupposed for the ancient world. As was suggested above, one reason for this is Paul's expectation of the imminent return of Christ (cf. 1 Cor. 7:31). Just as in the case of Jesus, therefore, we can answer the

5. Fritz Neugebauer, *Jesu Versuchung. Wegentscheidung am Anfang* (Tübingen: J. C. B. Mohr [Paul Siebeck], 1986), pp. 23-25.

6. Erich Grässer, "KAI ĒN 'META TŌN THĒRIŌN (Mk 1,13b). Ansätze einer theologischen Tierschutzethik, in *Studien zum Text und zur Ethik des Neuen Testaments. Festschrift zum 80.Geburtstag von Heinrich Greeven*, ed. Wolfgang Schrage (Berlin/New York: Walter de Gruyter, 1986), pp. 144-157.

question only indirectly by examining Paul's views on creation in general. Although Paul seems to have been somewhat estranged from creation intellectually, his overall perspective on creation offsets this problem.

In 1 Cor. 9:9 (cf. 1 Tim. 5:18), Paul uses Deut. 25:4 allegorically in reference to the financial support of the apostles: "You shall not muzzle an ox while he is threshing." Paul excludes the possiblity that, as Rabbinic exegesis repeatedly attests, the passage actually refers to oxen on the threshing floor; for he goes on to remark: "God is not concerned for oxen, is he?" Furthermore, for a long time the metaphor of ingrafting in Rom. 11:17ff. seemed to provide the other example of Paul's estrangement from creation. As early as Origen (in his commentary on Romans), Paul is said to speak here: "not in the order . . . which is usual among farmers, . . . By changing the proper order, Paul, with true apostolic authority, accommodated more the facts to his line of argumentation, than the line of argumentation to the facts." In his commentary on Romans, Hans Lietzmann cites this statement from Origen and adds in view of Paul's seemingly inaccurate metaphor (from an arboricultural standpoint): "One always grafts the cultivated shoot into the wildling, and not vice versa; otherwise the good tree is spoiled. Paul is a city boy; Jesus came from the country."[7] But Origen and Lietzmann were wrong! A. G. Baxter and J. A. Ziesler[8] have recently shown that in Rom. 11 Paul refers to a method of engrafting which was actually used in the ancient world. By engrafting the scion of a wild olive tree, the orchard keeper was able to rejuvenate an old, unfruitful olive tree (cf. Columella, *De Arboribus,* V 9, 16). Thus, although the Apostle may have had a somewhat aloof relationship to what we call today "the environment," he was better informed about the arboriculture of his day than his ancient and modern commentators believed. *In any case, Paul opens up perspectives in his letters which are of great importance for developing a creation ethic.*

In this connection, the creedal traditions which Paul appropriates should be mentioned first, namely, 1 Cor. 1:30 and 8:6, which are supplemented by the (pre-Pauline?) hymn in Col. 1:15-20. Based on Jewish Wisdom tradition, and materially on Jesus' own appearance as "messianic Teacher of Wisdom,"[9] all three texts speak of Jesus as the mediator of both the original creation and the New Creation. By the sacrificial death of Jesus on the cross and his resurrection from the dead, God has begun to usher in this New Creation. In none of the three texts is God's own position as Creator supplanted by Christ; rather, Jesus stands protologically, soteriologically, and eschatologically in the service of the one true God who created the world (and chose Israel as a people of his own possession). God is mentioned in 1 Cor. 1:30 by the *ex autou* which begins the verse and by the *apo theou* which follows; he is mentioned in 1 Cor. 8:6 in the parallelism; and he is mentioned in Col. 1:15-20 by the *passivum divinum* in v. 16 *(ektisthē)* and by the explicit mention of divine pleroma in v. 19f. The fact that the one true God works in *Christ* to create and redeem the world is fundamental to the understanding

7. Hans Lietzmann, *An die Römer,* 5th ed., Handbuch zum Neuen Testament, 8 (Tübingen: J. C. B. Mohr [Paul Siebeck], 1971), p. 105.

8. A. G. Baxter and J. A. Ziesler, "Paul and Arboriculture: Romans 11.17-24," *Journal for the Study of the New Testament* 24 (1985) pp. 25-32.

9. Cf. Martin Hengel,"Jesus als messianischer Lehrer der Weisheit und die Anfänge der Christologie," in *Sagesse et Religion. Colloque de Strasbourg, Octobre 1976* (Paris: Presses Universitaires de France, 1979), pp. 147-188.

of these creeds. *Through Christ, the believer can know and experience the New Creation for him/herself and anticipate the culmination of the good plan of the one true God for the rest of creation, a creation which presently suffers in wretchedness.*

To put it more concretely: just as in Proto- and Deutero-Isaiah the statements about the creation reinforce and support the soteriological promises (cf., *e.g.* Isa. 37:16-20; 45:6-7 or 46:9-13), so also in the creedal traditions appropriated by Paul. The only difference is that the redemption which God offers in Christ is no longer just a promise; it is already a reality which can be experienced. From Christ, Christians experience redemption through the forgiveness of sins, justification, and reconciliation. It is these things which bind the church together. In early Jewish tradition, we already find forgiveness of sins and new creation closely connected in terminology and content.[10] Likewise, Jesus' comparison of the return of thc prodigal son to being resurrected from the dead is not without good reason: He who was lost has escaped from the dominion of death and has been restored to life in the presence of God (cf. Lk. 15:32). From Jesus and early Judaism, Paul and the rest of early Christianity were able to articulate their encounters with the resurrected Christ - for example, at the call to apostleship, at the hearing of the gospel, at baptism, and at the celebration of the Lord's Supper - as experiences of redemption and new creation (cf., *e.g.* 2 Cor. 5:17; 1 Pet. 2:2). So there is a definite reason why the vision of the early church expanded along the lines of a theology of creation: In the community of believers, Christians saw themselves placed within a cosmos established by God, determined by Jesus, secured for eternity. *Since the redemptive will of God, protologically and eschatologically revealed in Christ, permeated and directed the community of believers, the church could experience and value (anew) its own being and that of all creation, based on Christ and oriented on his return.* The three texts which we have been discussing invite us to pursue a relationship with life and every living creature in the light of Christ, and to hope with creation for the coming redemption of the whole world from the power of death. The Christological interpretation of creation as the object of divine redemption defines what creation is and where it is going in the plan of God.

The fact that 1 Cor. 1:30; 8:6 and Col. 1:15-20 are formulated in the style of a creed and of a hymn, respectively, indicates that they stem from the context of early Christian confession and worship. At the time when these pre-Pauline traditions were written, an article of faith was needed to answer the very difficult and disputed Hellenistic questions of whether life was still worth living, and whether the world was hopelessly lost.[11] The answer which was given them also serves as a guide for us today: In Christ, God affirms his creation; he will not forsake it, but rather lead it through his Son into eschatological peace *(shalom). 1 Cor. 1:30; 8:6 and Col. 1:15-20 do not resort either to replacing God with Christ as the Creator or to speculating about the universe, but--really for the first time in Christian history -open up God's creation to belief in Christ as the sphere for life and faith!* From this point of departure, crucial perspectives for a theology of creation once again follow.

In 1 Cor. 1:21-25, 26-31, Paul mentions that the world, with its self-made wisdom, was neither willing nor capable of truly recognizing and acknowledging God, despite

10. Cf., *e.g.*, IQH 3:19ff.; JosAs 19:5ff. See further Hermann Strack and Paul Billerbeck, *Kommentar zum Neuen Testament aus Talmud und Midrasch*, 5 vols. (Munich: Beck, 1965), 2.; pp. 421-423.

11. Cf. Eduard Schweizer, "Das hellenistische Weldbild als Produkt der Weltangst," in *Neotestamentica. German and English Essays (1951-1963)* (Zürich/Stuttgart: Zwingli Verlag, 1963), pp. 15-27.

the fact that God's Wisdom governs the cosmos (and had done so since creation). God has responded to this failure of the world's wisdom with the "foolishness" of the message of the cross, in order that, through this "foolishness" and the Counter-Wisdom in Christ, believers might be led to salvation. Thus the intuition of God through creation no longer leads to salvation for the world; now only obeisance to the foolish message of the cross can accomplish this. The Apostle Paul uses here Creation and Wisdom tradition of early Judaism (*e.g.*, Wisd. 13:1-9) as an argument against a concept of wisdom which was establishing itself among Christians in Corinth. According to their conception, the wise could gain special access to God because of their own insight into the mystery of God's revelation. Insofar as he uses Jewish Wisdom and Creation tradition in a reproof, showing that the wisdom of the world was of no avail for salvation, Paul refutes his Corinthian opponents' conception of wisdom by proving the opposite. However, this critique does not imply that the Apostle repudiates Israel's Creation theology in light of the gospel and the knowledge of Christ! On the contrary, in 1 Cor. 1:26ff. Paul himself argues in terms of such tradition seen in the light of Christ, and, at the same time, appeals to the experience of the church in Corinth. The Corinthian church was composed mostly of people who had little or no importance in society. And, since a thriving church had developed out of a group of nobodies, the Corinthians could deduce that they had been called in Christ and elected to faith by the God who calls into being the things that are not (cf. v. 28, with Rom. 4:17). In and through Christ, God had (re-)created, justified, sanctified and redeemed the church. *Whereas the world has failed to recognize and acknowledge God through his works in creation, the church can and should appreciate existentially that through Christ the Creator God now performs his creative work in the church, and that he will bring his work to completion.*

We encounter a very similar argument in Paul's Epistle to the Romans. In Rom. 1:18ff., the eclectic logic of Paul's argument is even clearer than in 1 Cor. 1, but the basis of the argument in Old Testament and Jewish Wisdom tradition is the same. The heathen refused to give God the acknowledgment due him as Creator in view of his general revelation in the works of creation; therefore, God gave them over to the pernicious desires of their hearts and to a depraved mind (which could not discern the good) (v. 28). Since then, the Gentiles are in and of themselves too weak and incompetent to recognize and act upon that which is right (before God) (cf. also Rom. 2:14f.). But even in Romans, this argument does not lead to a complete repudiation of the theology of creation. For those versed in Jewish tradition, Paul implies in Rom. 3:24ff. that justification through faith in Christ restores - or imparts anew--the glory and righteousness lost in the Fall (cf. *Vit. Ad.* 20f.). In Rom. 4, the Apostle explicitly continues this point: the justification of the godless by faith alone means new creation. Characteristic of this new creation are the four mutually-interpretive predications of God in vv. 5, 17, and 24. Here God is seen as the God who "justifies the ungodly" (v. 5), "who makes alive the dead" (v. 17), "who calls into being that which does not exist" (v. 17), and "who raised Jesus our Lord from the dead" (v. 24). In and through Jesus Christ, God the Creator stands by his creation; he will not forsake it. *There can be no doubt that the reality of justification revealed to and taught by Paul contains a creation-theological moment; it is, in fact, the revelation of and belief in the one true Cod, who, as Creator and Redeemer, sent Jesus and raised him from the dead (thereby accomplishing the eschatological work of creation which proleptically incorporates the whole world.)* Believers can perceive in Jesus' resurrection who God is for them (and who he is for creation). The doctrine of justification proceeds from Jesus - his sending, his atoning death and his resurrection - to the Christian theology of creation.[12]

In keeping with what he says about justification, Paul does not stop with the gloomy picture in Rom. 1:18--3:20, that both Jew and Gentile stand guilty before God; that God has given mankind over to a depraved mind; and that Israel failed in regard to the word of God which was entrusted to them. For Paul, the New Creation begins already with justification, when sinners believe in Christ as reconciler and Lord (cf. 2 Cor. 5:17; Rom. 3:24ff.). Believers are simultaneously snatched from the *massa perditionis,* which is enslaved under the power of sin, and are placed in the service of God's saving righteousness (Rom. 6:18ff.). Since, as seen in the Old Testament, the righteousness of God is the power which brings about the harmony of the world (cf., *e.g.* Ps. 97:2, 5, 98:2, 7-9; 99:4, etc.), Paul's statement about "service to righteousness" is of great creation-theological interest. In that they serve the righteousness of God, baptized believers serve the future harmony of creation, *i.e.* its *shalom*-order. Rom. 12:1-2 develops this point in two respects. True service to God is service which corresponds to the Logos and devotes itself to God with body and soul. As seen in 1 Cor. 1:30; 8:6 and Rom. 8:2, the Logos is the new, saving order of creation which has appeared through Christ and is perceptible by faith.[13] Christians should no longer let themselves be conformed to the present age, but let themselves be transformed by God through the Spirit. And how does the Spirit effect this transformation? By the *anakainosis tou noos,* that is, by the renewing of the mind through orientation on Christ and on the Logos - the new, saving order of creation consisting in love and righteousness determined by Christ. Through this new orientation of their minds on Christ, believers are rescued from the depraved mind, which, given over by God, can neither recognize nor do what is good and right before God (Rom. 1:28). Now they regain the ability to know and act upon the good, pleasing and perfect will of God. According to Paul, none other than the Christians can and should be innovators of the good in the world, of that which pleases God. Applied to the theology of creation, this means that *with their new orientation to life by faith in Christ, Christians are now well able to recognize God in his work in creation again.* Since they have a world view based on Christ and stand within the new creative order revealed in Christ, believers are in a position to look at creation and perceive what in it corresponds to God's original and eschatological will. At the same time, they can see what still stands in the way of God's fully realizing his plan. According to the Apostle Paul, this tension, of seeing, on the one hand, a well-ordered world, and, on the other hand, a world which has gone totally awry, does not disturb the Christian; rather, it drives him to believe and hope in the completion of redemption (and of the New Creation), because the believer realizes that Christ was humiliated to the point of death on the cross before he was exalted to the right hand of God (Phil. 2:6-11).

12. Cf. Peter Stuhlmacher, *Reconciliation, Law, and Righteousness: Essays in Biblical Theology,* trans. Everett R. Kalin (Philadelphia: Fortress Press, 1986), pp. 30-93.

13. Cf. Wisd. 7:22--8:1; 9:1-3, 9-11, where "logos," "spirit of God," and "wisdom of God," are equated, and wisdom represents the creative order of the universe.

The four things which, according to the Apostle Paul, conflict with God's creative and redemptive will in the world are *sin, suffering, futility, and death.* In various ways, Christians experience these things in themselves and observe them in the world around them. As Rom. 8:18-25 shows, Paul shares the early Jewish view that, with the fall of Adam, "what had been made was judged. And so the entrances of this world were made narrow and sorrowful and toilsome; they are few and evil, full of dangers and involved in great hardships" (4 Ezra 7:llf.). Christians live in a world under condemnation as those who, by virtue of their special position, experience suffering with double intensity. On the one hand, they are despised and persecuted by unbelievers for their faith and witness; on the other hand, they are still burdened by tragedy and physical frailty common to all, despite the fact that they have been justified in baptism and have become a new creation. Paul knows this twofold suffering from his own personal experience (cf. the famous apostolic Tribulation Lists in 1 Cor. 4:9ff.; 2 Cor. 4:7ff.; 6:3ff.; also 2 Cor. 12:7ff.) and from that of his churches (cf. 1 Thess. 1:6; 2:14; Phil. 1:27-30). But, as the Apostle Paul first intimates in 2 Cor. 4:16-18 and then affirms in Rom. 5:3ff., the suffering and persecution experienced by Paul and other believers does not discourage them from believing in God's plan of creation and redemption; they actually strengthen their faith! In the face of suffering, Paul teaches believers to focus their eyes on the hope guaranteed in Christ, the hope of "the revelation of the sons of God" (Rom. 8:19), which is the "glorious freedom of the children of God" (v. 21). Moreover, the hope of believers is seen here as the hope of the whole creation. Paul alludes here to the eschatological revelation of the Son of Man and the saints in glory, described in Dan. 7:22; 12:3; 1 En. 45:3-6; 51:4f.; 62:2, 7-16. Jesus had promised this to the disciples (cf. Lk. 22:28-30); Paul takes up this idea in 1 Cor. 6:2ff. and brings it to bear in Rom. 8:19ff. The transformation into the glory of Christ which awaits the "saints" (Phil. 3:21) is a sign of promise for the whole creation (including subhuman nature). This is because God as Creator wants to exercise his right to save, that is, his righteousness. The creation as a whole will be redeemed through Christ from the power of death (1 Cor. 15:25f., 54f.). *Hence all creation derives hope for its own redemption from Christians - their faith, their hope in the midst of opposition and suffering, their new being - and, most of all, from Christ as the mediator of creation and redemption.* This redemption extends to the physical human body *(sōma)* and likewise to the rest of the physical universe (cf. Rom. 8:23).

In terms of the theology of creation, this means that Christians may not give up on creation, even though it still stands under judgment and has not yet been redeemed. Believers must live in the world and be a sign of hope that the expected New Creation has already begun. In terms of a creation ethic, this means that Christians have been called to a life of faith in which the world is not simply taken for granted and consumed as if there were no tomorrow (1 Cor. 7:31). On the contrary, they are called to use creation as a gift from God which is destined to be redeemed and glorified. It is true that "the form of this (earthly) world is passing away" (1 Cor. 7:31). But it is passing away in order to participate in the glory of Christ! Just as every human being is to be esteemed as one who was worthy of the sacrificial death of God's Son, as one bound for faith and the resurrection of the dead, and thus as one who is sanctified before God, so also the whole *ktisis* is to be cherished and preserved. *In other words, creation is to be used and protected as something which is permeated and determined by God's creative Wisdom in Christ, as something which will be freed from death and glorified.* If allusions to the messianic peace of Isa. 11:6-9 are found in the Marcan account of Jesus' temptation in the wilderness, this is all the more true in Rom. 8:18ff. and 1 Cor. 15:25ff., 53ff.

In his new interpretation which departed from that of his teacher Rudolf Bultmann, Ernst Käsemann indefatigably stressed that in Paul justification and the righteousness of God are to be understood as power and gift which have an apocalyptic, creation-theological dimension.[14] And, through Paul, the faith of the church stands in this same apocalyptic, creation-theological horizon. Käsemann's perspective has been adopted by J. Christiaan Beker.[15] Paul's earnest message is that the one true God, who created the world and elected Israel as a people for his own possession, has not relinquished his (saving) right over creation, but has reaffirmed it in Christ. Thus the process of justification as a process of new creation affects the *ktisis* as a whole, not just human beings or merely their "souls." The justification of the individual sinner anticipates the deliverance of the whole world from the clutches of death and the tyranny of Satan.

The first chapter of Hebrews and the prologue of John appropriate and develop Paul's theology of creation, which derives, as we have seen, from a harmonious blend of Jesus' teaching and the Old Testament. It cannot be doubted, therefore, that there are biblical traditions which can instruct and guide the formulation of a creation theology and a creation ethic to meet the challenge of the present ecological crisis. Theology has just begun to take up the challenge. I can only attempt, therefore, to suggest a few points which, in my opinion, are important for our conduct as Christians in the midst of the ecological crisis.

III. The Application of the Biblical Theology of Creation

In questions of what the gospel is and how we are to live in light of it, the witness of the Holy Scriptures is, and always will be, way ahead of us. Nevertheless, biblical texts should not be applied to our time thoughtlessly, but should be brought to bear on our situation only after careful consideration. The historical differences between biblical circumstances and our own are too great to be simply ignored. Since the time of the New Testament, there have been changes in eschatology which result now in more concern for the physical world; there have been historical and intellectual developments which are irreversible; and there has been a transformation in the human situation which is unprecedented. In the following, therefore, I am indebted both to Jürgen Moltmann's book, *God in Creation,*[16] and particularly to Oswald Bayer's volume, *Creation as Speech.*[17] Bayer develops his perspective from Luther and Johann Georg Hamann (1730-1788), while keeping the biblical creation traditions in

14. Cf. Ernst Käsemann, "God's Righteousness in Paul," *Journal for Theology and the Church* 1 (1965); pp. 100-110.

15. J. Christiaan Beker, *Paul the Apostle: The Triumph of God in Life and Thought*, 2nd ed. (Philadelphia: Fortress Press, 1982); *idem, Paul's Apocalyptic Gospel: The Coming Triumph of God* (Philadelphia: Fortress Press, 1982).

16. Cf. n. 1 above.

17. Oswald Bayer, *Schöpfung als Anrede. Zu einer Hermeneutik der Schöpfung* (Tübingen: J. C. B. Mohr [Paul Siebeck], 1986).

view throughout. Johann Georg Hamann was a highly-educated contemporary, friend and critic of the philosopher Immanuel Kant. The source of Hamann's critique of Kant and of the entire Enlightenment was his faith, which was awakened and sustained by the Holy Scriptures. Hamann believed that God had spoken so clearly in the Scriptures through his Spirit, that Christians should follow the Bible more than their own ideas about life and the world. However, Hamann was not lead by this conviction to a naive biblicism; for he tried to consider the irreplaceable truth of the Bible in light of the problems of his time. Two of Hamann's concepts appear to be especially important to our present discussion.

In the intellectual history of Europe, Johann Georg Hamann stands between the Enlightenment and burgeoning Romanticism. In regard to nature, he saw his contemporaries vacillating between two extremes. He writes: "Every creature becomes alternately your victim and your god."[18] On the one hand, nature is recklessly exploited and made into an object of human manipulation. On the other hand, nature is deified as an object of mystical speculation, and one becomes obsessed with living in harmony with Mother Earth. It is not at all difficult for us to see our own situation reflected in Hamann's critique. The ecological crisis in which we find ourselves today is clearly the result of ruthlessly exploiting nature. Having cracked the code of life itself, gene technology expands man's power over nature to new, terrifying dimensions. Now, even more than in Hamann's day, nature is a "victim." Yet the opposite tendency is also prevalent. For sometime now, old and young alike have been enchanted with a new romantic spirit which draws on old, Indian conceptions of the holiness and sanctity of nature. "Natural foods" and "natural medicine" are the new household words, and they cause industry to market as many products as possible with the seal, "all natural" or "biodegradable." The deification of nature is once again the going thing. It is not uncommon today for the two positions - nature as "victim" and as "god"--to cause a rift within families and between generations. In both cases, man has lost the standard for a proper relation with the world with which God has entrusted us.

It is, therefore, high time that we not only remind ourselves of the biblical tradition, as we have just done, but also think through another one of Hamann's concepts. According to Hamann, creation is "speech to the creature through the creature."[19] Bayer sees in this formulation "the essence of a Christian doctrine of creation."[20] When he refers to "speech to the creature through the creature," Hamann has in view the passages on creation through the word of God (Gen. 1; Ps. 33:9; 148:5), as well as Ps. 19 and the aforementioned texts on Christ as the mediator of creation. Creation is God's speech to us humans through his Son Jesus Christ, who became like us, yet without sin. In that he speaks to us through the creation in the person and words of Jesus, God declares his desire to be our Creator and to remain such. What does Hamann's creed, firmly rooted as it is in the Old and New Testaments, imply for us in the present ecological crisis?

18. "Jede Kreatur wird wechselweise euer Schlachtopfer und euer Götze" (Johann Georg Hamann, *Samtliche Werke. Historisch-kritische Ausgabe,* 6 vols., ed. Josef Nadler [Vienna: Herder (Thomas-Morus-Presse), 1949-1957], 2:206 pp. 25f.).

19. ". . . die [Schöpfung ist] eine Rede an die Kreatur durch die Kreatur" (*ibid.,* 2:198, p. 29).

20. Bayer, *Schöpfung,* p. 16.

As we live in the world, our dealings with nature must not drown out God's speech through creation. Or, to put it positively, we must preserve and protect nature, so that it remains a medium for God's communication. This implies that we as Christians must radically change our way of life. Not that we should stop ruling over creation and preserving it; for, according to Gen. 1:26ff.; 2:15, 19; and Ps. 8:6-8, that is the assignment given to human beings.[21] A Christian's dealings with nature ought to be characterized by an attitude of conservation which renounces the exploitation of nature whenever possible; an attitude which controls the use of food and energy and of water, land and air; an attitude which preserves both plant and animal. As believing Christians, we can no longer afford to continue living in relation to creation like everyone else. *In the midst of the ecological crisis, it is our task to prevent God's creation from being completely victimized by civilization or from being deified by the apostles of nature who are hostile to civilization.*

As Christians, we know that we need forgiveness of sins every day, because we are weak and prone to temptation. It is, therefore, important to keep in mind that God speaks to us through Christ our Savior and Lord. Through Christ, God reminds us that he is Creator. This has three consequences for us.

In our creaturely existence, we experience creation most intensely at those times when Christ comes closest to us and we to him. According to the universal experience of the church, this occurs in baptism, in the Lord's Supper, and in the worship services celebrated on the high feast days: Good Friday, Easter, Ascension, Pentecost, and Christmas. On all these days and occasions, we experience ourselves as those whom God accepts in Christ, as those whom he carries and leads through life. It is this experience which originally allowed us to be creatures of God and allows us to remain such. Let us then cultivate this experience and make it, according to Christian understanding, the criterion of creatureliness![22]

The first and most important expression of such creatureliness is to praise God with one's heart, mouth and hands. As long as we corporately and individually thank God for our lives and praise him, the world cannot be made totally into either a victim or a god. By praising God, we hinder the world from being victimized or deified and promote God's creative work.

There was never a time either for Christ or for his followers when they could have gone their way without opposition and suffering. In order to keep nature open today as a vehicle for God's communication, we need to oppose powerful interests and lobbies. This struggle cannot proceed without pain and suffering. Already the use of the word "renunciation" will leave a bitter taste in some mouths. But the real pain and suffering starts when Christians who are standing up for creation are branded as troublemakers, as reactionaries, or as religious fanatics. Let us not give up in this

21. Cf. Odil Hannes Steck, *Welt und Umwelt,* Kohlhammer Taschenbücher, Biblische Konfrontationen, 1006 (Stuttgart/ Berlin/ Cologne/ Mainz: Kohlhammer, 1978), pp. 78ff. The English translation of Steck's book was unavailable to me: *World and Environment,* trans. Margaret Kohl, Biblical Encounters Series (Nashville; Abingdon Press, 1980). Cf. also Phyllis A. Bird, "'Male and Female He Created Them': Gen. 1:27b in the Context of the Priestly Account of Creation," *Harvard Theological Review* 74 (1981); pp. 129-159 (here, pp. 137ff.).

22. Cf. Bayer, *Schöpfung*, pp. 29-32; Moltmann, *Creation*, pp. 69-71.

unavoidable struggle, but rather preserve, as we look to the crucified and resurrected Christ. Let us say with Paul, "I can do all things through Christ who strengthens me" (Phil. 4:13).

If creation is, according to Hamann's felicitous definition, "speech to the creature through the creature," then we as Christians absolutely cannot and should not deny that this speech can no longer be heard in many places. The destruction of nature, the resulting catastrophes, and the disruption of life through inhuman living conditions and diseases are processes which are so advanced, that, in some cases, God's creation can no longer be seen or experienced as the saving creative order which God affirmed in Christ. In all of these cases, there remain, according to the biblical creation traditions, only two ways open to us.

We must realize that this ruin of creation is largely the result of our own irresponsibility towards God's creative order. In this regard, it bears repeating that exploitation and misuse of creation go hand in hand with irresponsible militarization and with the economic strangle hold which Western industrial nations have on the so-called "underdeveloped" countries. The only proper response for us is repentance, which the Old Testament teaches us to utter in a penitential prayer of supplication or penitential lament. Christians should offer up such a prayer, even on behalf of those who are no longer able to do so. (Our prayers of supplication can be modeled on such texts as Ps. 38; 57; 102; 143; Neh. 9.) In view of the ecological crisis, we must try first to empathize with creation, consciously and repentantly groaning with it - to use the words of Paul - as it lies in travail (Rom. 8:22-23).

The second thing to be done in light of the ecological crisis goes beyond the first and is best described with a legend which is told about Luther. To the question what he would do if the Last Judgment were to begin tomorrow, Luther is reported to have answered, "I would still plant an apple tree today." We Christians are not promised that we can save creation by our own efforts, but it is our task to provide a sign of hope. In Christ, God has not revoked his affirmation of creation, but has reconfirmed it. And because we know this, we are called and authorized to testify to God's affirmation in any way we can.[23]

Amidst the ecological crisis in which we stand (largely because of our own failure and guilt), the biblical traditions show us how to lament penitently in our present distress; how to provide a sign of hope for creation; and how to lead a new life-style in deference to nature. In this way, we no longer selfishly misuse the creation which God has entrusted to us, but rather maintain it in its God-given order with "reverence for life" (Albert Schweitzer), preserving it for future generations.

23. Cf. Günter Altner, et al., *Manifest zur Versöhnung mit der Natur*, 2nd ed. (Neukirchen-Vluyn: Neukirchener Verlag, 1984).

Nature's Praise of God In The Psalms

Terence E. Fretheim

The theme of nature's praise of God has not often occupied the attention of Old Testament scholars.[1] In fact, according to theologian of nature Paul Santmire, it is "one of the least understood themes in the Old Testament."[2] I know of no scholarly article written on just this topic; in fact, consideration of a biblical theology of nature as distinct from creation is quite uncommon. There are a number of reasons for this, which we shall note. In any case, we have a lot of catching up to do.

My approach in this article will be to track some of the history of interpretation of such biblical material; move to considerations of genre, metaphor, and tradition, with some theological reflections along the way and in conclusion, we will give special attention to Psalm 148. Overall, the most basic questions will be: What kind of thinking about God and what kind of thinking about nature would have occasioned this kind of talk?

One fundamental problem relating to this issue has certainly been our preoccupation with the human as the center of the universe. In Psalm 148 one is no doubt pleased to be listed among the angels in the call to praise God and perhaps not so pleased to be included among creeping, crawling things and crabapple trees. One of the major difficulties with such a psalm is that it offends our anthropocentric sensibilities to be on a list with hills, horses, and hurricanes. Certainly human praise to God means more to God than the clatter of hail on tin roofs or the clapping of the musically inclined leaves of the aspen trees. Perhaps, but not as much as we would like to think.

This anthropocentrism is seen in biblical theological work in a salvation history that is focused on human beings, or an existentialism that sees all of reality from the perspective of human existence, or a political theology centered on the liberation of the human. Hence, nature has often come to be seen as having only an instrumental value, to be used for the enhancement of human life. Emil Brunner illustrates much thinking on this matter: "The cosmic element in the Bible is never anything more than the 'scenery' in which the history of mankind takes place."[3] Often concomitant with one or more of these perspectives is an understanding of God in terms of a radical transcendence, in almost a spatial sense, that has tended to remove God from too close a brush with the world.[4]

Often accompanying such perspectives has been an emphasis upon Israel's desacralization of creation, which in many formulations entails a secularization, indeed a profanation of nature. As a consequence, biblical-theological study has tended to abandon the study of nature to the sciences. (And in the process opened the

[1]Cf. J. Rogerson, "The OT View of Nature: Some Preliminary Questions," *OTS* 20 (1977) 67-84. In these reflections I use the word "nature" to refer to the nonhuman world.

[2]P. Santmire, *The Travail of Nature: The Ambiguous Ecological Promise of Christian Theology* (Philadelphia, 1985,) pp. 198-99.

[3]E. Brunner, *Revelation and Reason* (Philadelphia, 1946), p. 33n.

[4]Cf. the discussion of S. M. Daecke, "Profane and Sacramental Views of Nature," in *The Sciences and Theology in the Twentieth Century,"* ed. by A. R. Peacocke (London, 1981), pp. 127-40. Cf. K. Koch, "The Old Testament View of Nature," in *Humanity, Nature and God* (Geneva: WCC, 1979).

way for such views as creation science.) A distinction should be made between the desacralization of nature and the claim that no creature is divine or demonic. The language of desacralization is not helpful because it suggests that God is removed from the natural order, indeed suggests a separation of the spiritual and the material, which opens the way to a misuse of nature (the preservation of which must be grounded fundamentally not in a sense of stewardship but in the relation between God and nature).

What is needed is a unifying view of worldly reality which brings God, the human, and the natural order together in an interconnected whole. It is precisely this to which Genesis 1 and Psalm 104 and Psalm 148 testify.[5] There is no aspect of the natural order in which God is not intimately involved. God is to be distinguished from the world of nature, so that there is no identification, but not separated from it. God is a factor in every aspect of the natural world, albeit not all-determining. Such claims will be given flesh and blood from OT texts as we proceed.

In order properly to speak of Psalm 148 and related passages one has to be converted into a mode of perceiving reality that, at the least, is less anthropocentric and more inclusive of the value of the nonhuman for the world and for God. Such a conversion is easier now than it was less than a generation ago. For one thing, it is in tune with contemporary scientific perspectives, where the universe is understood to consist not of isolated elements but a complex set of interrelationships which fit together into a unified whole.[6] Moreover, we are living in a time when increasing numbers of people have an ecological consciousness, a new sense and experience of the oneness of all things, a recognition that there are continuities across the spectrum of all created things that calls for new images regarding creaturely relationships. Creation is a seamless web. And if this is so among the creatures, the more so in the relationship between Creator and creatures, for the oneness of creation and the oneness of the Creator are inextricably interconnected, or polytheism is very near at hand. To speak of desacralization can mean a return to Baalism in a different form; to remove God from intimate involvement with the world invites the introduction of other divine powers at the earthly level (Mother Nature?). Or, more drastically, the radical transcendence of God may lead to the death of God in the life of the world.

History of Interpretation

The history of interpretation of passages of this sort, however, does not often betray such a consciousness.[7] St. Francis of Assisi stands out because his sensitivities are comparatively rare; he belongs to a very thin tradition. In fact, his reflections find greater sympathies among interpreters today then during any other period since he claimed a creationwide family of creatures which included the human. One could perhaps cite certain aspects of the Elizabethan world view with its sense of the music

[5]Cf. O. H. Steck, *World and Environment* (Nashville, 1980).

[6]Cf. the comment of T. F. Torrance in *Transformation and Convergence in the Frame of Knowledge* (Grand Rapids, 1984), p. 253: In approaching the world of nature "We have to think in a dimension of ontological depth in which the surface of things is coordinated with a deep, invisible, intelligible structure . . . Really to know is to be in touch with a depth of reality which has the capacity for disclosure beyond what we can anticipate or imagine." Cf. also A. R. Peacocke, *Creation and the World of Science* (Oxford, 1979), pp. vii-viii and *passim*. N. Max Wildiers, *The Theologian and His Universe*, (New York, 1982), p. 170.

[7]For the history of Christian thought, cf. P. Santmire, *Travail of Nature*. Cf. also his "Toward a New Theology of Nature," *Dialog* 25 (1986),pp. 43-50; C. Y. Stewart., Jr., *Nature and Grace: A Study in the Theology of Nature* (Macon, 1983).

of the spheres and John Dryden's heavenly harmonies. There are certainly other examples. While not strictly an interpretation of these texts, but almost certainly informed by them in direct or indirect ways, the following reflections may be illustrative.

First, a passage from Hildegard of Bingen, a twelfth-century prophetess who speaks of the Holy Spirit in this way:

> *I am that living and fiery essence of the divine substance that flows in the beauty of the fields. I shine in the water; I burn in the sun and the moon and the stars. The mysterious force of the invisible world is mine. I sustain the breath of all living beings. I breathe in the grass and in the flowers; and when the waters flow like living things, it is I . . . I am the force that lies hidden in the winds; they take their source from me, as a man may move because he breathes; fire burns by my blast. All these live because I am in them and am their life. I am Wisdom. The blaring thunder of the Word by which all things were made is mine. I permeate all things that they may not die, I am life.*[8]

Second, from Martin Luther, sixteenth century:

> *God is substantially present everywhere, in and through all creatures, in all their parts and places, so that the world is full of God and he fills all, but without being encompassed and surrounded by it. He is at the same time outside and above all creatures. These are exceedingly incomprehensible matters; yet they are articles of faith and are attested clearly and mightily in Holy Writ . . . . For how can reason tolerate it that the Divine majesty is so small that it can be substantially present in a grain [of wheat], on a grain, over a grain, through a grain, within and without, and that, although it is a single majesty, it nevertheless is entirely in each grain separately, no matter how immeasurably numerous these grains may be? . . . His own divine essence can be in all creatures collectively and in each one individually more profoundly, more intimately, more present than the creature is in itself.*[9]

Third, from a twentieth-century prophet, Theodore Roszak:

> *Here and now, as we restore the orders of reality, we are in the stage of closing up all traditional dichotomies of Western culture, which have served as the bulwarks of the old Reality Principle. Spirit-flesh, reason-passion, mad-sane, objective-subjective, fact-value, natural-supernatural, intellect-intuition, human-nonhuman--all these familiar dualisms which have divided the spectrum of consciousness vanish as we create the higher sanity. The dichotomies are healing over like old wounds. Even science, in its awkward single visioned way, has been led to continuities that baffle traditional assumptions. It can no longer draw hard lines between matter and energy, organic and inorganic, man and lower animals, law and the indeterminate, mind and body. What is this but a final cold reflection of the visionary whole, the Tao, the One, at last appearing in the alienated mind as it reaches the end of its tether.*[10]

[8]Quoted in W. Lewis, *Witnesses to the Holy Spirit* (Valley Forge, 1978), pp. 156-57.
[9]Quoted in P. Santmire, *Travail of Nature*, pp. 129-30.
[10]T. Roszak, *Where the Wasteland Ends* (New York, 1972), p. 228.

Other directions in interpretation have more commonly been taken, however. Surprisingly, an allegorical interpretation of these passages has not been especially common. One occasionally finds such an approach among medieval commentators.[11] Some examples: The fruit trees are those who are zealous in good works, the cedars those who are lofty in contemplation, the wild beasts those who live a solitary life, the creeping things those who quietly and steadily busy themselves, the birds those who rise on high in heavenly meditation, and the hail are the great preachers who pour down stern and lashing rebukes on sinners! Occasionally, one finds a christological interpretation where the various natural elements are seen as "emblems of Christ."

One might also cite here a tendency toward a rationalistic interpretation of these verses, with not a little touch of arrogance in some formulations. Oesterley's views might be cited to illustrate how this lurks around the edges of many discussions: "However much there may be in the psalm which, in view of the advanced knowledge of later ages, cannot be accepted, such as the idea of the inanimate world and of animals praising God, we can appreciate the psalmist's conception, even though erroneous, of the instinct of worship as innate in the whole of created matter."[12]

Much more common among older as well as more recent commentators is an eschatological interpretation: such a responsiveness on the part of nature will be integral to the new heaven and earth, when all of nature takes on human characteristics (which in some formulations arrogantly seems finally to be a humanization of nature). The predominance of this motif in Second Isaiah and in the Enthronement Psalms, often interpreted eschatologically, has been one factor prompting this approach. The new role for the animal kingdom in other eschatological passages such as Isaiah 11 and 65 contributes to this interpretation. The occurrence of this theme in apocalyptic materials is also noted, such as the expanded version of Psalm 148 in the Song of the Three Young Men in the deuterocanonical portions of Daniel, or this striking passage from IV Ezra (5:5): In that day "the trees will drip blood and stones will speak" (Cf. II Baruch 73; I Enoch 69:16-24). Moreover, the only direct occurrences of this motif in the New Testament are in the book of Revelation (5:13; 12:12; 18:20); these are often cited by commentators, along with Rom 8:19-22.[13] All of this prompts one commentator to speak of Psalm 148 as "a song of liberty because all creation is loosed from bondage at last and is invited to sing forth."[14] But whatever the truth in an eschatological interpretation, especially in II Isaiah, it occurs often enough in noneschatological materials to warrant the claim that nature's praise is understood to be characteristic of present reality.

Another view on these texts is polemical.[15] What are gods elsewhere are here reduced to elements of the natural order in praise of Yahweh; these praise God, they are not themselves objects of worship. Aside from the fact that this gives a negative cast to a highly positive even celebrative text and context, one must be careful in overstressing the distinctions between Israel and other ancient Near Eastern religions on the relationship between nature and the divine. James Barr claims that already in

[11]E.g., Albertus Magnus and Hugh of St. Victor. Cf. J. M. Neale, *A Commentary on the Psalms*, IV. (London, 1883), p. 427.

[12]W. 0. E. Oesterley, *The Psalms*, (1939), p. 584.

[13]Cf. J. C. Beker, *Paul the Apostle* (Philadelphia, 1980), who considers this passage to be central in Paul's theology.

[14]Neale, *Psalms*, p. 427.

[15]Cf. P. Craigie, *Psalms 1-50* (Waco, 1983), p. 181.

Akkadian myths the gods have ceased to be aspects of nature.[16] One can certainly find ideas that "divinity was in nature or that nature was in harmony with the divine," but it is not so clear that there is always or often an explicit identification. One must distinguish between the animation of natural phenomena, a common idea, and their supernaturalization.

A more recent development is much more difficult to assess. It is suggested that in the Old Testament the natural order and the human are incorporated in a "psychic whole" in which all of nature is permeated by a diffused awareness. To use the language of Stadelmann, nature is understood to have a "psychic affinity" with the human, and natural elements such as stars (cf. Job 38:7) are understood as "beings provided with consciousness."[17] "The universe is thoroughly alive, and therefore, the more capable of sympathy with man and of response to the rule of its Creator . . . . Certainly we have here more than a mere poetical personification of the cosmos when it is invited to rejoice."[18] To assess this panpsychical interpretation along with the closely related vitalism is difficult because the sources and argumentation for this perspective are not carefully documented in OT studies.

One form of this perspective can be traced back at least to Gunkel, who states in his Psalms commentary: "Such exhortation of creatures to praise of God was not simply a 'poetic figure' in Israel; the concept of nature as animate still was lodged"[19] in human blood at that time.

One of the more influential studies in OT scholarship has been H. W. Robinson's *Inspiration and Revelation in the Old Testament.*[20] I am struck how often this work has been cited and uncritically so. He claims that "objects of nature were conceived as having a psychical life of their own." Natural objects have "a diffused consciousness with [their] own psychical . . . possibilities, and [their] own capacity to be indwelt or made instrumental by yet higher powers, and finally by the activity of Yahweh himself."[21] Another work that has popularized much of this kind of thinking about the natural order are the essays edited by H. and H. A. Frankfort.[22] The fundamental difference between ancient and modern thought regarding the surrounding world is that for moderns "the phenomenal world is primarily an 'It'; for ancient--and also for primitive--man it is a 'Thou.'"[23] But this does not mean that primitives personified the inanimate world; they simply did not know such a world.[24]

In the same volume, Jacobsen also states that the ancients did not regard the objects of the natural world as inanimate, but as possessing individual will and qualities.[25] "They are somehow alive; they have wills of their own; each is a definite

[16]J. Barr, "Man and Nature: The Ecological Controversy and the OT," *BJRL* 55 (1972) citing W. G. Lambert, *Babylonian Wisdom Literature* (Oxford, 1960), pp. 1-20.

[17]L. I. J. Stadelmann, *The Hebrew Conception of the World* (Rome, 1970), p. 94.

[18]*Ibid.*, p. 7.

[19]H. Gunkel, *Die Psalmen.* 5th ed. (Göttingen, 1968), p. 618. This is quoted with approval in D. Hillers of Psalm 148, p. 334 (cf. n. 37).

[20]H. W. Robinson, (Oxford, 1946). E. C. Rust, *Nature and Man in Biblical Thought* (London 1953), simply follows Robinson on these matters. Cf. also C. Bonifazi, "Biblical Roots of an Ecologic Conscience," in *This Little Planet,* ed. M. Hamilton (New York, 1970), pp. 203-33.

[21]Robinson, *ibid.*, pp. 12, 15-16, 47. It is probable that Robinson is somewhat dependent on J. Pedersen's *Israel: Its Life and Culture,* II (London, 1926); cf. p. 479, for some of these perspectives.

[22]H. and H. A. Frankfort, et al. *The Intellectual Adventure of Ancient Man* (Chicago, 1946).

[23]*Ibid.*, p. 4.

[24]*Ibid.*, p. 5. Cf. J. Rogerson, *Myth in OT Interpretation* (New York, 1974). p. 96.

[25]T. Jacobsen, "Mesopotamia," *Intellectual Adventure* pp. 130-134.

personality." "Any phenomena which the Mesopotamian met in the world around him was thus alive, had its own personality and will, its distinct self. But the self which revealed itself, e.g., a particular lump of flint, was not limited by that particular lump; it was in it and yet behind it; it permeated it and gave it character as it did all lumps of flint." "To understand nature was to understand the personalities in these phenomena, to know their character, the directions of their wills, and also the range of their powers. It was a task not different from that of understanding other" people.[26] G. E. Wright continues in the train of the Frankforts' perspective, noting that "Israel did not conceive of an inanimate nature any more than did polytheists . . . [but] continued to think of the elements of nature as possessing a psychic life of their own." He cites Isa.1:2 and Mic.6:2.[27]

In anticipation of our later discussion, it may be said here that the truth in this perspective is that natural phenomena must be of such a nature that God is able to sustain the close relationship with them that the biblical evidence implies. This relationship suggests that there is a certain inwardness or interiority such that more than external relationships are possible. To speak in this way does not necessarily lead to Panpsychism or vitalism, but it certainly suggests a greater continuity between the animate and the inanimate than we have commonly been willing to claim. At the least, the possibilities for an *internal* relationship between God and all created things must be left open. It also should be pointed out that the theological implications of an animate nature are rarely explored; it is usually left at the level of observation.

Genre and Metaphor

This praise of God on the part of nature seems never to occur in narrative material. It is found only in poetry, and there it is almost exclusively associated with hymnic literature, and that primarily in the hymns of the Psalter and in the transitional hymnic pieces in Second Isaiah. Being so genre-specific, this is of no little importance in interpretation, but its significance is uncertain. It gives no little credence to the oft-suggested notion (standing over against the animate creation idea, but never argued) that we have here to do with poetic license or poetic fancy or "highly poetic language." Or, the language of personification is used,[28] "a rhetorical figure by which an inanimate or abstract thing is represented as a person, or with personal characteristics." Allen speaks of "rhetorical calls to creation to praise its God" and metaphorical personifications.[29] Moreover, the fact that these texts have to do with Israel's worship life has suggested to interpreters that in the exuberance of the worship

[26]*Ibid.*, p. 134. J. Rogerson, *Myth*, p. 86, shows that the Frankforts are dependent upon the work of Ernst Cassirer and questions some of their methods. He notes particularly some of the differences between Jacobsen and the Frankforts, especially the former's distinction between the force in/behind the reality and the reality itself. Finally, though, Rogerson does not consider himself in a position to judge the validity of Jacobsen's material (cf. p. 94).

[27]G. E. Wright, *The OT Against its Environment* (London, 1950), p. 36; cf. p. 17; Eichrodt, *Theology of the Old Testament,* II (Philadelphia, 1958), p. 152. Israel did make some important distinctions among the elements of the natural order. There is no suggestion, e.g., that rocks and animals were considered equally imbued with energies. Yet, the use of *nephesh* for animals and human beings does not imply that nothing else in creation was considered alive. The land *('adamah)* is understood to be alive, with plants reproducing according to their kind and the waters bringing forth living creatures (cf. Genesis 1). The natural order is certainly not understood to be passive; it shares in God's creative activity.

[28]Cf. A. Weiser, *Psalms: A Commentary* (Philadelphia, 1962), p. 639; Eichrodt, II, p. 153.

[29]L. C. Allen, *Psalms 101-150* (Waco, 1983), p. 316.

of God a certain extravagance has taken control of the language. There is thus little if any correspondence of language and reality. The fact that so many commentators have taken one or more of these directions commonly means that very little theological attention is given to these materials.

How does one respond to such directions in interpretation? I am convinced they are quite inadequate, but it is difficult to demonstrate this directly. Certainly one avenue is to speak about the nature of language, particularly metaphoric language as well as the language of worship. Another approach is to set these materials alongside other Old Testament texts which relate God to the natural order and see whether this pushes us toward another interpretation; to this we will turn later in the paper.

First of all, the issue of language. To use the language of poetic license, literary figure or personification suggests that we are dealing with a fictive matter or a matter of some artificiality which does not in fact correspond with reality. "Such a classification of the sense of the text may domesticate it too quickly, assimilating it to a ready-made static catalogue of rhetorical figures drawn up from non-religious materials . . . . No one is more unimaginative than an interpreter who speaks so neatly and readily of the imagination."[30] That is to say, in this designation of the literary figure one has closed off a number of interpretive possibilities. The depth of the text, its expressive thickness, is not given its full range.

One important factor to be considered is the use of nature metaphors for God. For example, God is light, water, rock, fire, wind, as well as a few animals, such as the eagle. While language used to speak of God is drawn primarily from the human and human relationships, the use of nature metaphors opens up new avenues in considering Israel's way of thinking about God. If God is a rock or a mother eagle, for example, rocks and mother eagles are reflective in some sense of who God is. That is to say, there are continuities between rocks and eagles and the reality of God. It is in view of this that certain divine attributes are elucidated by reference to the natural order. For example, God's righteousness is like the mountains (Ps.36:6) or God's faithfulness is like the fixed orders of creation (Jer. 31:35-36).

As always with metaphor, there is an "is" and an "is not" in relating nature or human language for God and the reality of God; rock and mother eagle are descriptive of God in some ways, and in some ways they are not. Certain other qualifying metaphors need to be drawn into the discussion to discern where the continuities and discontinuities lie.[31] Nonetheless the point is still made: if rock and eagle and other natural metaphors for God are in some ways descriptive of God, then they reflect in their very existence, in their being what they are, the reality which is God. It is in view of this that nature's praise of God is to be understood and explicated.

To put it in other terms, it is basically in terms of their intrinsic rather than their instrumental value that they function as such metaphors. In themselves they are capable of showing forth the strength or the care or the glory or the faithfulness or the majesty of God. Such a use of natural metaphors serves to temper a certain anthropocentricity in our talk about God. In fact (and this is an ironic point, given the common understanding of the God/nature relationship), it could be said that God's transcendence is given a special boost by the use of such natural language, for among

[30]Kenneth Schmitz, "World and Word in Theophany," in *Faith and Philosophy* 1 (1984), p. 56.

[31]For a discussion of metaphor, see T. Fretheim, *The Suffering of God: An Old Testament Perspective* (Philadelphia, 1984), pp. 5-12.

other things it evokes wonder and awe in human beings; it is God's strength and majesty that are commonly lifted up. Generally, the use of natural metaphors for God opens up the entire created order as a resource for depth and variety in our God language.

We now take a closer look at some of the details of the hymnic genre in terms of Psalm 148. The structure of the psalm follows that of a typical hymn of praise, except that the call to praise is much more extensive. The calls begin in the heavenly sphere (vv. 1-4) and move to the earth (vv. 7-12), with heaven and earth brought together in v. 13c, with a final note on praise centered on Israel in v. 14. The calls to praise are followed by *ki* clauses in vv. 5b-6, 13. First of all, the calls to praise. These serve to express praise; they call attention to the range of God's creative work and hence God's praiseworthiness.[32] Also, the listing together of the creatures suggests both individuality and complementarity in praising. Each entity has its own distinctiveness in its praising according to its intrinsic capacity and fitness, with varying degrees of complexity. But each is also part of the one world of God contributing to the whole. The model of the symphony orchestra comes to mind. Ecological considerations are immediately present, for if one member of the orchestra is incapacitated or missing altogether, the scope, complexity and intensity of the praise will be less than what it might be. Ecological sensitivity is for the sake of the praise of God and the witness it entails, indeed for God's own possibilities in the world.

Moreover, the call to worship suggests that there may well be differing possibilities of response. Indeed, would it be possible to suggest that the call to praise implies the possibility of refusal? This is certainly true for the human beings, but for the other creatures? It could simply have reference to the fact that for some of the creatures, *e.g.* stormy wind and hail, praising is occasional not constant. Beyond that as we shall see, one should speak of the nonhuman creatures in terms of a kind of responsiveness such that they are drawn out or called forth by the divine work with and within them. In this interaction with God the creatures become more of what they are or have the potential of becoming. Without the call to praise some possibilities for praise might not be realized.

The reasons for praise are expressed in the two *ki* clauses of vv. 5b-6 and v. 13: In vv. 5b-6 the reason given is the fact of creation by God and being given a particular place within the created order for all time. It is thus praise for being what they are. This is echoed in v. 8b (cf. 107:25) with reference to the stormy wind fulfilling God's command. Praise occurs when the creature fulfills the task for which it was created.[33] In v. 13 the reason is expressed in terms of God's name being above all others. The concern is witness, making known the name of Yahweh among all those who do not honor Yahweh or who honor other gods. It is made clear that it is not just Israel which hears the witness of nature; all peoples hear this testimony (cf. Ps 97:6). In Isa. 42:10-12 nature and all peoples join together in a praise which is universal. It might be suggested that the call for all peoples/lands/nations/earth to praise God which is present in so many psalms (47:1; 96:1,9; 97:1; 98:4; 99:1; 100:1; 117:1; 49:1; 66:1) is made possible because of the witness of the natural order.

This witness element in the hymns of praise makes for decisive continuities with the songs of thanksgiving. In these psalms (and in the vow commonly spoken at the

[32]Cf. L. C. Allen, *Psalms 101-150* p. 316.

[33]Cf. A. A. Andersen, *The Book of Psalms,* II (London, 1972), p. 950.

end of the laments) gratitude is expressed not only to God, as important as that is; it is also to be expressed in the presence of others (see Ps.22:22; 109:30). Gratitude is giving testimony to others regarding what God has done (Ps.66:16; 34:11; 40:9-10). Indeed, the whole world is in view as the object of such witness (Ps.57:9; 18:49; 22:27).

Together then, the reasons for praise relate specifically to God for what God has done and then beyond God to God's relationship to those who do not honor Yahweh. These are the two central facets of praise--the honor of God and the witness to others (cf. Ps. 119:171-72). The one always entails the other. This is consonant with Miller's understanding of the songs of praise as both expressing praise and evoking praise, as language to God and about God.[34] These come together in a phrase such as "praise magnifies God,"[35] or to use Mowinckel's remarkably modern language, the song of praise "increases God's power and renown"; it "gives power" to God.[36] God himself is thus affected by praise, not simply those who (speak) praise or respond to it.

TRADITION

What fund of understandings in Israel about the relationship between God and nature contributes to the development of this theme? It is clear that nature's praise would not have sounded strange to Israel's ears. First, parallels in the ancient Near East should be noted. Delbert Hillers[37] effectively refutes von Rad's thesis[38] that the prehistory of this material is to be found in ancient Egyptian onomastica, encyclopedic lists that bear some similarity to the listings in Psalm 148 and Job 38. Hillers clearly demonstrates that the idea of nature's praise of God is to be traced back to pre-Israelite Mesopotamian and Egyptian hymns. Among his many examples, the following Egyptian hymn to the sun-god from the Ramesside period might be cited:

> *The gods jump up before you in praise,/ Mankind awakens, to adore your beauty;/ Beasts dance before you in the wilderness, . . ./ Earth [trembles] before the holiness of his name,/ Egypt gathers, the wilderness rises early,/ To behold his appearance in the morning.*[39]

Walter Beyerlin[40] notes another special parallel to Psalm 148, the Egyptian "Hymn of a 1000 strophes." He notes that this hymn to Amun from the post-Amarna period "depicts an obeisance in which all the world, along with nature, offers the praise of God'' (cf. II, 6-10):

> *"All trees rise before his countenance/ They turn toward his eye/and their leaves unfold./ The scaly creatures leap in the water/they come out from their pools for love of him./ The sheep and the cattle skip before his presence./ The birds dance with their wings./ They all observe that he is in his good time./ They live by seeing him as their daily need./ They are in his hand, sealed with his seal./ And no god can open them but his majesty.*

[34]Patrick Miller, *Interpreting the Psalms* (Philadelphia, 1986), pp. 64, 69.
[35]*Ibid*., p. 66.
[36]S. Mowinckel, *The Psalms in Israel's Worship*, I (New York, 1962), p. 88; cf. p. 81.
[37]D. Hillers, "Study of Psalm 148," *CBQ* 40 (1978), pp. 323-334.
[38]G. von Rad, "Job xxxviii and Ancient Egyptian Wisdom," in *The Problem of the Hexateuch and Other Essays* (New York, 1966), pp. 281-91.
[39]Hillers, *op.cit*., p. 333.
[40]W. Beyerlin, *Ancient Near Eastern Texts Relating to the Old Testament* (Philadelphia, 1978), p. 20.

It is to be noted that this final reference to "his majesty," *i.e.* the pharaoh, may well parallel the concluding reference to Israel in Ps. 148:14.

Moving to the Old Testament itself, there are a variety of materials which might be related to this theme, most notably the theophany. The language used to speak of God's appearances is not unlike that used for nature's praise. It is language which is bursting at the seams. Moreover, the theophany brings God and the natural order closely together; they act in concert with one another. The degree to which one should speak of literary convention or historical reality or liturgical simulation, or a combination thereof, is often raised in this connection. It is probably a combination, with one or another emphasized depending upon the theophany being studied. It does seem evident, however, that theophanies commonly involve more than internal sight, as do the praises of the elements of the natural order. There is an inarticulate yet visible praise. Moreover, the way in which nature is spoken of in these contexts suggests a certain perception regarding possibilities for nature in relationship to God.

One might cite the responses of nature to God's appearance in various Psalms. Look at what happens to nature in response to the presence of God! The earth quakes and the heavens rain down (68:8); the sea looks and flees and the mountains and hills skip like young animals (114:3-7); the cedars are broken and the oaks whirl (29:5-9); the mountains melt like wax (97:5); the waters are afraid and the deep trembles (77:16). While occasionally the language used is unusual, it is not unnatural; as in the praise passages there is often a certain correspondence with natural activity. The sea roars, the waters are troubled, and the hills skip. The storms are no more stormy than other storms and the earthquakes could have been measured on a Richter scale. There is no tell-tale trail of God-tracks in the response of nature which unambiguously reveals God. Yet, the intensity and magnitude of the language which is used to depict the experience are such that special attention is invited.

From another perspective, the God who appears is clothed in elements of the natural order. Smoke and fire emanate from him; darkness and clouds cover him; wings of the wind support him; lightnings surround him (Ps. 18:8-15). Light envelops him like a garment and the clouds are his chariots (104:2-4). What does it mean for natural phenomena to be considered the clothing or the companion of Yahweh? Certainly it means a fundamental compatibility between God and the natural order; they are not like oil and water in relationship to one another. The *finitum capax* could be cited here; the finite is capable of bearing the infinite.[41] As such, they are considered to be in the service of Yahweh (Ps. 104:2-4; 119:91); they serve God's purposes of revelation, salvation, judgment and instruction (cf. Amos 4:6-13; Exod. 14:21; Jonah 4). To see nature so closely bound to God indicates that God is internally rather than externally related to it; nature does bear Yahweh. *The fact that theophanies function as revelatory events means that the function of nature in theophany is only an intensification of what is true of nature otherwise.* There is ample material here to provide the basis for an understanding of God's relationship to nature such that nature's praise would be but another dimension of a widespread interresponsiveness between God and nature in the Old Testament.

This understanding can be extended by reference to other passages that speak of God's close relationship to elements of the natural order. The valuation of the

[41]Fundamental continuities with the Christian understanding of Incarnation and the Sacraments might be explored here.

nonhuman creation by God in Genesis 1 (and God saw that it was good) occurs independent of the creation and valuation of the human. In fact, both the human and the nonhuman are spoken of in the same language of valuation, yet without denying a hierarchy of valuation. All creatures were considered by God to have intrinsic value. It is striking that the valuation by God of the goodness of the creation is a valuation returned to God in praise: "O give thanks to the Lord, for he is good" (Ps.106:1; 107:1; 118:1; 136:1). In other words, the creatures reflect the goodness of their createdness back to God and as a witness to God toward the entire world.

Moreover, all of the creatures of the natural order are considered to be God's own possession. "All the animals in the forest are mine and the cattle on thousands of hills. All the wild beasts are mine and all living things in the fields" (Ps.50:10-11; cf. Ps. 24:1-2; 1 Chr. 29:11). God is not only a God of history; God is also a God of nature. Or, to put it in other terms, God is as active in the history of nature as God is in the history of humankind; from God's perspective we have to do with one history and one world.

Moreover, the relationship is such that God can draw the creatures out or call them forth, that they can be in some sense responsive to God's work with them or within them. God's call to the waters and the earth in Genesis 1 to participate in the creative activity suggests that a response is expected, that God and these natural elements are in a kind of relationship where there can be mutual interaction. And this is not uncommon elsewhere. God calls to the earth (Ps. 50:4; Hag. 1:11) and addresses natural entities (Isa. 45:8; Job 37:6). They in turn respond to God (Job 38:35; Ps. 145:10) and look or cry to God (Ps. 104:21; 145:15-16; Job 38:39-41; Joel 1:20) and even possess a kind of knowledge regarding God's activity (Job 12:7-9). God in turn responds with care and sustenance (Ps. 147:9; Deut. 10:12). God's closeness to creation is evident in that God calls them by name (Isa. 40:26; 147:4; cf. also God's naming of various nonhuman creatures in Genesis 1), and one has to recall the full significance of naming for Israel to capture the sense of this. Salvation language is used for the animal world as well as for humankind, from the story of the flood (cf. Gen. 6:19; 9:10) to everyday activity ("Humankind and beast thou savest, O Lord," Ps. 36:6) to the new heaven and earth (Isa. 11; 65). God is as concerned with the liberation of the animals as with human beings.[42] Moreover, God rejoices and delights in God's relationship with the nonhuman order of things (cf. Ps. 104:31; Job 38-39).[43]

Klaus Koch has an interesting if brief study of Hosea 2:21-22 in this connection.[44] In what might be called a "sociology of nature" he suggests that the Hebrew verb *'anah,* while having the basic meaning of "answer," may also have the sense of "to respond in a discussion," and it may in this context have reference to nonverbal reactions, to the providing of new impulses by one subject to another within a given relationship. Hosea appears to be "thinking of a coherent chain in which God is the initiator, but an initiator who acts in interdependence with earth, man, and nation . . . . nowhere does the Old Testament offer such a pregnant description of natural process as in this sentence of Hosea." The world of nature is a world of interrelated creatures, held together by divine interaction with the creatures.

[42]Cf. Paul Santmire, "The Liberation of Nature: Lynn White's Challenge Anew," *Christian Century* 102 (1985), pp. 530-33. Cf. George Landes, "Creation and Liberation," *USQR* 33 (1978), p. 80.

[43]Cf. Bruce Malchow, "Nature from God's Perspective: Job 38-39," *dialog* 21 (1982), pp. 130-33.

[44]K. Koch, "The Old Testament View of Nature," pp. 47-49.

If one says that God is truly present in, with, and under every aspect of the created order, what does it mean to speak of the presence of God? Is it only external, a presence *with* or a presence *to?* The texts suggest that God is able really to *relate to* every creature. There seems to be implied, as we have suggested, a certain inwardness characteristic of these creatures, or at least a nature which enables a relationship of consequence with God to exist. Given the relationships that human beings often have to animals and even trees and other natural elements[45] - and I think of our wonderfully curious calico cat - we dare not suggest that God is incapable of such relationships.[46] If a human being can speak this way about the natural order, given the alienation that exists, how much more should God be able so to speak.[47]

Koch goes on to speak of a dynamic interrelationship between Aelohim, Adamah, and Adam, a "triangle" in which there is movement every which way in the triangle, except from the earth to God. Why Koch stops short at this point is uncertain and seems unnecessary. But Koch's emphasis upon a nonverbal relationship between God and the nonhuman is important. Nonverbal praise or witness would simply be one aspect of such an understanding. Inarticulateness does not disqualify one from praise. At the human level one thinks of praise offered by those who dance or play musical instruments.

Finally, it might be asked what the historical function of this material was. The usage in II Isaiah seems to be reasonably clear.[48] Because the salvific deed God is about to accomplish is cosmic in its effects, the response of praise must be comparably cosmic. Because nature, too, participates in God's act of salvation, it too responds in praise. The interconnectedness of nature and history in God's redeeming activity is demonstrated in the response of both. Whenever this theme occurs, it seems to be in the service of kerygmatic or doxological claims regarding the cosmic dimensions of God's work, and hence may speak to narrower visions of God's work in the world current in Israel.[49]

Concluding Theological Reflections

Because nature is not fallen as human beings are,[50] though human sin has disrupted the natural order, it witnesses to the reality of God in ways more constant

[45]M. Buber, *I and Thou,* (Edinburgh, 1937), pp. 7-8.

[46]On the importance of a relational ontology, see D. J. Hall, *Imaging God* (Grand Rapids, 1986), p. 134 and *passim.* Cf. also J. Sittler, "Ecological Commitment as Theological Responsibility," *Zygon* 5 (1970), p. 174; J. Cobb, "Process Theology and Environmental Issues," *JR* 60 (1980), pp. 440-58.

[47]At the same time it is clear that Israel was not so ignorant of "scientific" causes that they attributed natural activity to God alone while we today would express the same in more "natural" terms. Cf. J. Rogerson, *OTS;* P. Addinall, "Walter Eichrodt and the Old Testament View of Nature," *ET* 92 (1981), pp. 174-78. Because of the infancy in Israel's understanding of the natural world, it is probable that it understood certain natural events *(e.g., eclipses)* as more God-related than we would. Yet, Genesis 1, Jer. 8:7, etc., indicate that Israel had considerable practical knowledge about the regularities of the life of nature (cf. Gen. 8:22).

[48]Cf. C. Westermann, *Isaiah 40-66: A Commentary* (Philadelphia, 1969), pp. 103, 144.

[49]It is uncertain whether one ought to include in this tradition the talking snake in paradise, Balaam's ass, Jotham's trees, Elijah's ravens, and Jonah's repentant animals.

[50]For the fullest discussion of this issue, see P. Santmire, *Brother Earth: Nature, God, and Ecology in a Time of Crisis* (New York, 1970). B. Malchow, "Contrasting Views of Nature in the Hebrew Bible," *dialog* 25

than human beings do. The heavens *do* proclaim the glory of God. The praise called for in Psalm 148 is the revelation spoken of in Psalm 19 and elsewhere. The fact that we do not recognize this as often as we should roots the problem of recognition in human beings rather than in the natural order. The problem is in our seeing and hearing, and perhaps most of all in our alienation from the nonhuman. It is this greater constancy that occasions some Old Testament comment on the nonhuman world as models for human behaviors. In Isa. 1:2 and Jer. 8:7 we find animals conforming to the will of God for their existence in ways not true of human beings. The nonhuman world may also be thought of as models of praise. To put it in the words of a contemporary hymn: "Stars and sun obediently shine . . . so we too should be voicing our love and rejoicing."[51] The integration of the human and nonhuman in Psalm 148 may well carry some of this understanding. Human beings should be praising as nonhuman entities do.

But more needs to be said about the relationship between the human condition and the natural orders. *No* human history is independent of the history of nature, and this for both good and ill. This suggests a symbiosis in praise; every element in all of God's creation is called to praise together, and the response of one affects the response of the other.

First, let us speak of this symbiosis from a positive angle. From the perspective of Genesis 1, the earth needs to be subdued and hence, as created, would not witness to God with pristine clarity; positively the human being is needed to bring at least the earthly orders to their fullest possible potential and that would entail their fullest possible potential for praise. There remains work to be done in nature by human beings in order for this to be realized.

Another way of speaking of the symbiosis of human and nonhuman in praise is to speak of their mutual support of one another in praising. That is to say, the natural order provides raw material for human praise. Without the natural order the praising metaphors at the disposal of the human would be fewer in number. Without the praise of nature, secondary human forms of praise would be much more meager, that is, we would be without much praise-full painting, music, and literature inspired by nature. In George Herbert's words, human beings have been made the secretaries of the praise of nature.[52] Without the praise of the nonhuman the witness of the human would not be what it ought to be. From the human side, human beings give voice to nonhuman praise; they make articulate what is inchoate in nonhuman praise. One could perhaps speak of the praise of the nonhuman in terms of the old Simon and Garfunkel song, "The Sounds of Silence." Human beings participate with the nonhuman in giving voice to silent praise. We live in a world highly charged with wonder and praise; it is up to human beings to give it clear voice.

(1986), pp. 40-43, believes that there are two contradictory views of nature in the Old Testament. One sees nature as "having been corrupted through human sin so that redemption is possible only in the eschaton. The other point of view sees nature as not having been decisively perverted by sin but as remaining good." It is not made clear wherein the "contradiction" lies, however. It seems to me that both perspectives have been integrated with one another into one understanding of nature as good and valuable and yet adversely affected by human sinfulness and in need of redemption.

[51]"Let All Things Now Living," *Lutheran Book of Worship*, no. 557. It is striking the extent to which nature's praise of God has been incorporated into the hymnody of the people of God. For a striking paraphrase of Psalm 148, see *Lutheran Book of Worship*, no. 558, "Earth and All Stars."

[52]See Daniel Hardy and David Ford, *Praising and Knowing God* (Philadelphia, 1985), p. 82.

On the other hand, from a negative perspective, what human beings do in their sinfulness affects adversely the possibilities for praise on the part of the natural entities. Human sinfulness can have an adverse effect on the ability of the natural orders truly to be themselves. To use a contemporary illustration, the heavens proclaim the glory of God with less clarity on a smoggy day in Los Angeles than on other days. Among the many biblical examples one might cite, cf. Hos. 4:1-3; Job 31:38; Isa. 24:4-7; Jer. 12:4; Joel 1:18; Zeph. 1:3. In Genesis 3, for example, the sin of humankind lessens the productive possibilities of the earth, and hence its praising possibilities.

The integration of heavenly, human, and nonhuman language in Psalm 148 may well recognize this interconnectedness of praise possibilities. That is, it is only as all creatures of God together join in the chorus of praise that the elements of the natural order or human beings witness to God as they ought. Hence, to call upon the elements of the natural order to praise God within a *human* worship context (Psalm 148 implies the call of a worship leader) contains an implicit call to human beings to relate to the natural orders in such a way that nature's praise might show forth with greater clarity. As we have seen, ecological activity is directly related to nature's praise possibilities. That is, by the way in which human beings relate to ecological matters they can enhance or inhibit nature's response to God's call.

This brings us back to the truth in the eschatological interpretation of these materials; in the new heaven and earth (and the totality of this language ought not be lost on us), nature's praise of God will have a clarity and a perfection unknown this side of the eschaton, when nature will no longer lament and groan but simply praise. To use the language of Isaiah 11 and 65: in the new heaven and earth the earth shall be full of the knowledge of the Lord as the waters cover the sea. In the present, *God* fills heaven and earth (Jer. 23:25), but not yet the knowledge of God. The steadfast love of God and God's faithfulness fills the universe (Ps. 33:5; 36:5; 57:10; 85:10-12; 119:64), but not yet the knowledge of that love and faithfulness.[53] The symbiosis of human and nonhuman in the praise of God is intended to fill the universe with the knowledge of God, with the knowledge of God's love and faithfulness.

To speak of this from God's perspective, God needs both the human and the nonhuman for the fullest possible witness to God in the world. Without praise, mission is muted. Moreover, if God is Lord of the universe and not just Lord of the earth or of human beings, then praise too must be universal. Without the witness of the nonhuman, mission is muted in vast stretches of the universe. God is enthroned not simply on the praises of Israel; God is enthroned on the praises of all his creatures. The realization of the kingship of God in the universe is dependent upon this creation-wide praise.

This may be the point of Ps.148:14, recognizing the difficulty of translation: God has made God's people strong, indeed has made them a praise in the earth, for the purposes of the universal praise of God. Whereas the prior mention of human praise (vv. 11-12) is generic, having reference to all people everywhere, in v. 14 there is an historical reference to Israel as the embodiment of praise. Just as the various other creatures show forth the praise of God by being what they are as God's creatures, so Israel having been made what it now is by God, shows forth God's praise by being

[53]This prominent theme should probably be related to nature's praise. All of God's creatures witness to God's love and faithfulness. See especially Psalm 136:5-9, 25; Job 38-41; Jer. 31:35-37; 33:19-26.

who they are, the redeemed people of God. The wonder of God and God's work can be seen in what has become of them, what they have been made by God.[54] If the verse also suggests that Israel shares in the praise that belongs to God, it would not be for its own self-glorification, but for the purpose of witness, just as the praise of God is not finally for God but for others. God's people in every age are called upon to continue showing forth the praise of God because of what they have been made by God. In this way they will join with that vast chorus of God's nonhuman creatures in honor of God and in witness to God.

These lines from "The Grandeur of God" by Gerard Manley Hopkins capture the essence of nature's praise of God:

> *The world is charged with the grandeur of God.*
> *It will flame out, like shining from shook foil;*
> *It gathers to a greatness, like the ooze of oil*
> *Crushed . . .*
> *There lives the dearest freshness deep down things . . .*
> *Because the Holy Ghost over the bent*
> *World broods with warm breast and with ah! bright wings.*[55]

[54]Cf. L. C. Allen, *Psalms 101-150*, pp. 312-13.

[55]For a discussion of Hopkins's earthy theology, see Nathan Scott, Jr., "The Poetry and Theology of Earth: Reflections on the Testimony of Gerard Manley Hopkins and Joseph Sittler," *Journal of Religion* 54 (1975), pp. 102-23.

Genesis I-III as a Source for a Contemporary Theology of Sexuality

Phyllis Bird

I should like to begin with a word of appreciation for the contribution of the Frederick Neumann symposium in fostering interdisciplinary dialogue in the theological interpretation of Scripture. As the Bible belongs to the whole church, occasions and means must be sought to engage the various theological disciplines in conversation about its meaning, conversation made more difficult, and more essential, by the increasing specialization and compartmentalization of our knowledge. For the impetus given by this symposium to the recovery of a more inclusive and theologically oriented discourse about the Bible I am grateful.

I am also grateful for the selection of a topic that I view as critically important in our time, namely creation, and for an approach to that topic that understands it as a Scripture-encompassing theme, not limited to the opening chapters of Genesis. While my own contribution is anchored in Genesis 1-3 (and confined to a single question within this corpus), my ultimate aim is to link these foundational texts with other canonical witnesses in a conversation shaped by contemporary questions, but attentive to ancient meanings. More specifically, I shall attempt to show how Genesis 1-3 may contribute to a constructive theological anthropology, with particular attention to human sexuality--and how it may not. I am concerned to show the limits as well as the contributions of these overexploited texts. While the topic of sexuality represents an exceedingly narrow focus within the universe-encompassing question of creation, it is given disproportionate attention in the primary Old Testament texts. By reason of this placement and prominence, the biblical interpreter is directed to consider the meaning and end of human sexuality in the context of theological reflection on creation.

A word about nomenclature: I have used the term "sexuality" as a term encompassing both the idea of gender differentiation (or gender dimorphism) and sexual endowment--in all its biological, psychological and social dimensions.[1] My intention in this usage is to employ a term that can comprehend the distinct interests and emphases of the two creation texts and at the same time allow formulation of questions based on contemporary understanding.

Genesis 1 and 2 are not the only Old Testament texts that speak of creation, but they are unique in that corpus in giving explicit attention to gender, or sexuality, as an essential and constitutive element of human creation.[2] Why does the author of Genesis 1 pause in his spare, cadenced account of the successive orders of creation to

[1] *Webster's Third New International Dictionarv of the Enqlish Lanquage* Philip Babcock Grove, ed. (Springfield, MA: G & C Merriam, 1961). Cf. James B. Nelson, *Embodiment: An Approach to Sexuality and Christian Theology* (Minneapolis: Augsburg, 1978) pp. 17-18.

[2] I use the designations "Genesis 1" and "Genesis 2" as shorthand references for the two accounts contained respectively in Gen 1:1-2:4a and Gen 2:4b-25.

mark this order of creatures as bisexual? And why does the author of Genesis 2-3 break into the story of *adam* and the *adamah* ("earthling" [human] and the earth) to recount the creation of another who is both derived from adam and stands over against him? What do these pointed expansions mean--for their ancient authors, and for modern theologians?

Traditional interpretation of Genesis 1-3 combined elements of two creation accounts (Gen 1:1-2:4a and 2:4b-3:24) to articulate a view of human origins, human nature, and the relationship of the sexes, which continues to exercise a powerful influence on contemporary theological thought.[3] However, the conflate reading on which this understanding was based ignored the distinct language, dynamics and intentions of the two passages. One of the contributions of modern biblical scholarship has been to re-expose, and sharpen, the long observed tension between the two accounts and to link each to a larger literary complex within the Pentateuch. By giving attention to stylistic and theological differences between the two accounts and identifying them with different historico-religious settings and purposes, modern critical scholarship has opened the way for a re-union of the texts in a reading that is attentive to their distinctive voices while honoring and preserving their peculiar contributions.[4]

I shall begin my treatment of the texts with a separate analysis of each literary unit, attempting to allow it to speak on its own terms. I shall then consider how the two may be heard together in a larger canonical and postcanonical context. Although my analysis of the primary texts must be abbreviated, I shall still give attention to the larger literary structure of each passage, which is critical to the interpretation of the key verses.

THE PRIESTLY (P) ACCOUNT (GEN 1:1-2:4A)

In the creation account of Genesis 1:1-2:4a (which I shall refer to by the conventional designation of "P" or "Priestly account") two distinct and unrelated statements about the creation, and therefore the nature, of humankind have been juxtaposed in 1:26-27. The first is concerned with the status and function of the human order in relation to the other orders of created life; it uses the language of divine image, or likeness, and of dominion, or rule, linked concepts in the tradition complex from which this language is drawn:

[3] The analysis presented in this paper is based on a recently completed article, "Sexual Differentiation and Divine Image in the Genesis Creation Texts" (to be published in *Imaqe of God and Gender Models*, ed. Kari E. Borresen [Oslo: Solum Forlag/Atlantic Heights, N.J.: Humanities Press, forthcoming]), and an earlier, detailed study of the Priestly account alone, "'Male and Female He Created Them': Gen 1:27b in the Context of the Priestly Account of Creation" (*HTR* 74 [1981], 129-159). The latter article should be consulted for full argumentation and documentation of the lexical and syntactic issues discussed in relation to Genesis 1.

[4] While the present state of Pentateuchal studies is characterized by wide scale erosion of the consensus that dominated critical scholarship for most of this century, I still find it necessary to employ a form of the traditional "documentary" analysis in my treatment of the two accounts united in Genesis 1-3. Cf. *HTR* 74 p. 135, n. 13. For a recent summary and assessment of modern Pentateuchal criticism see R.N. Whybray, *The Making of the Pentateuch: A Methodological Study*, *JSOT* Suppl. Ser. 53; (Sheffield: *JSOT*, 1987).

Let us make humankind **(adam)** *in our image,*
according to our likeness,
And let them have dominion over the fish of the
sea and the birds of the air,
and the cattle and all the earth
and everything that creeps upon the earth. (1:26)

This statement emphasizes human superiority over the other creatures, and responsibility for them, a superiority and a duty which it authorizes by the notion of divine likeness in the manner of an image (more specifically, a representation and representative of the Deity).[5]

The second statement is concerned with fertility or reproduction, an expression of a more general theme that runs throughout the chapter, namely concern for the sustainability of created life. That concern is addressed in the case of humankind by the blessing of fertility (shared with the other orders of living creatures, 1:22)[6] and by the specification of sexual constitution, which is its precondition:

Male and female he created them.
And God blessed them,
and God said to them:
"Be fruitful and multiply. . . ." (1:27b-28)

I cannot spell out here the full technical arguments for this simple and straightforward reading, which are laid out in an earlier article.[7] However, some further defense or explication of this interpretation may be called for in view of the popularity of Karl Barth's ingenious combination of Genesis 1 and 2 to find an "analogy of relationship" in the juxtaposed notions of image and sexual differentiation[8] and in view of Phyllis Trible's similar reading, based on a rhetorical analysis.[9] Two points require particular attention: (1) the meaning of the Hebrew expression, "male and female" *(zākār ûnĕqēbâ)*, and (2) the order of the statements within the account of human creation.

The Hebrew terms *zākār* ("male") and *ûnĕqēbâ* ("female") are biological, not sociological terms.[10] They are the same terms used elsewhere in the Primeval History by the same author to describe the pairs of animals Noah is instructed to bring into the ark:

5. *HTR* 74, pp 136-146.

6. Here sea creatures; on the omission of the blessing for the land creatures, see *ibid.*., p. 145.

7. *HTR* 74.

8. *Church Dogmatics* 3/1 (Edinburgh: T. & T. Clark, 1958) pp. 183-206, especially 194-195. Cf. *HTR* 74, pp. 131-132.

9. *God and the Rhetoric of Sexuality* (Philadelphia: Fortress, 1978) pp. 1-30. Trible's literary approach is distinguished from my own in that she is not interested in the intentionality of the author, while my concern is precisely to recover the author's intention, to whatever extent this is possible using literary-historical methods.

10. The clear distinction between the biological word pair *zākār* (male) and *nĕgēbâ* (female), used in Genesis 1, and the sociological terms *'îš* (man) and *'iššacircuâ* (woman), used in Genesis 2 , is obscured by harmonizing of the two accounts. Such harmonistic reading has affected German translations in particular, where the terms in Gen 1:27 are rendered "Mann und Frau" or "Mann und Weib" in several recent commentaries and Bible versions (cf. *HTR* 74,: pp. 50-51).

Of every living thing of all flesh, you shall
bring two of every sort into the ark,
to keep them alive with you; they shall be
male and female **(zākār ûnĕqēbâ)**.
(Gen 6:19; cf. 7:9)

Here the writer makes his intention clear by this added specification: the two of every sort must be a reproductive pair in order to assure the survival of the species. It is the same language used in Genesis 1, and it expresses the same concern. Here, as elsewhere, the Priestly writer exhibits a "scientific" bent in his interest in classification, order, and process and in his precision of language, which results in monotonous repetition of technical terms to give exactness to his description.

The Priestly account of creation in its present form is concerned not only with the sequence of the orders of creation but with the means by which the orders of life will fill the newly created world and perpetuate themselves in it. Whether one sees this interest as related only to the time of beginnings (and new beginnings after the deluge, Gen 8:17) or as a broader interest in the capacity of created life to sustain itself, it has left a significant mark on the present shape of the text.[11] Not only is there added to the report of the first and last acts of the creation of living creatures (vss. 20-21 and 26-27) a word of blessing in direct speech enjoining the species to propagate, there is also added to the description of each class of plant life an explicit word concerning its means of propagation:

And God said, "Let the earth put forth vegetation,
plants **yielding seed,** *and fruit trees bearing*
fruit **in which is their seed,** *each according*
to its kind (or "by species").(1:11)

This added specification, which is cumbersome in Hebrew as well as English and stands out in this otherwise streamlined account, is unnecessary to a simple classification of plant life, even one oriented toward consumption. It is dictated by concern for the perpetuation of the species, the same concern behind the blessings. But whereas reproduction by seeds appears to be automatic, requiring only the proper organs, sexual reproduction (at least as understood by ancient observation) requires a union of individuals in a "willed" act of cooperation. So the capacity given in design must be activated by a command, formulated as a blessing.

But why, one may ask, does the author fail to include the word of sexual differentiation in his description of the nonhuman orders of animal life that he applies to them in the flood story? The reason, I think, is that in the economy of description in Genesis 1 it is not necessary; it is assumed by the blessing. It is necessary in 6:19 and 7:9, however, where exemplars of the species are explicitly reduced to two and where there is no command to multiply (the word that activates the pairs is not given until they are sent forth from the ark in 8:17, where the command is formulated indirectly and without the word of blessing).

It is also necessary in the case of humankind in Genesis 1, but for a different reason. Sexuality cannot be assumed for humankind at the point where the blessing

11. Fuller discussion in *HTR* 74 pp. 146-147, 152.

must be spoken, because the single identifying mark of this order of creation that has been mentioned thus far is its resemblance to God, an identification introduced in the divine decree that initiates the act of creation ("Let us make humankind in our image, according to our likeness," vs. 26) and repeated in the report of the divine action ("And God created humankind in his image," vs. 27). For the Priestly writer the idea that God might possess any form of sexuality, or any differentiation analogous to it, must be viewed, I believe, as an alien and repugnant notion.[12] Something more had to be said about this creature before the blessing of fertility could be pronounced. That additional word is the word of sexual differentiation which expands the statement about the nature of humankind in preparation for the blessing. Unlike God, but like the other creatures, humanity is characterized by sexuality. This unique and exalted creature, whose special identity and vocation is determined by relationship to God, is still creature, by nature and design, including sexual constitution.[13]

Before I proceed to the Yahwist's narrative, a word is in order about P's use of the term *adam,* which I have variously rendered "humans" or "humankind." In Genesis 1, in keeping with P's normative usage elsewhere and with the general usage of the Hebrew Bible, *adam* is a collective term requiring the translation "humankind" or an equivalent expression.[14] Its collective nature is particularly clear in this chapter because of the marked parallelism in the construction of the account in which successive new forms of life are introduced. In Hebrew all of the terms used to describe these orders of life are singular collective nouns,[15] like *adam,* and all are translated in English by collectives or plurals: *deše'* "vegetation," *'ēśeb* "plants," *'ēs* "trees," *šeres* "swarms," *nepeš hayyâ* "living creatures," *'ôq* "birds," *běhēmâ* "beasts," etc. What is designated by each is a broad class or order of life, with its subdivisions into species indicated by the repeated expression "according to its kind" (*lěmînô,* more accurately rendered "by species").[16] Only *adam* has no subdivision; humankind for the Priestly writer is both species and order.

This collective understanding of *adam* in Genesis 1 needs to be kept clearly in mind when one moves to the story of the first couple in Genesis 2-3 or to P's personification of the species in Gen 5:1 in a genealogical construction. In Genesis 1 all statements relating to human creation pertain to the species as a whole. No basis is given in the parallelism of statements within the passage for associating sexual distinction with either status or function. The statement of sexual differentiation is structurally isolated in the verses devoted to human creation and is restricted in its intention to a biological concern. Precisely because P's terms of sexual distinction lack social definition or connection, however, the balanced symmetry of the language cannot be translated directly into a notion of sexual equality. Although Genesis 1 requires the inference of ontological equality of the sexes, it offers no help concerning the move from ontology to ethics, from the question of sexuality viewed in the context of nature to the question of sexuality viewed in the context of history and culture, a move that is essential to a full theological anthropology.[17] The Priestly account leaves

12. Cf. *HTR* 74, p. 148.

13. *Ibid.*, pp. 148-152.

14. *Hebräisches und Aramäisches Lexikon zum Alten Testament*, 3rd ed.; Walter Baumgartner, ed. (Leiden: E.J. Brill, 1967).

15. With the exception of the plural tannînîm "sea monsters" in 1:21; cf. *HTR* 74, p. 146, n. 45.

16. *HTR* 74, p. 146.

17. Cf. *HTR* 74, pp. 155-158.

the theologian with the problem of how to relate equality of created nature to sexually differentiated roles, responsibilities and values.

To summarize my analysis thus far: the meaning and function of the statement of sexual differentiation in the Priestly account of creation is considerably more limited than is commonly assumed. It says nothing about the image that relates humankind to God, nor about God as the referent of the image. Neither does it qualify the notion of human dominion over the creatures (or of subjugating the earth, vs. 28). It relates only to the blessing of fertility, making explicit its necessary presupposition. It is not concerned with sexual roles, the status or relationship of the sexes to one another, or marriage. It describes the biological pair, not the psycho-social pair; male and female, not man and woman or husband and wife. It does not presuppose an original androgyne (the progressive specification of attributes is logical, not temporal), but a bisexual (gender dimorphic) order of creatures as the crown of creation. And it is to this order that all statements of task and position refer.

One final word must be added to this statement concerning the meaning of sexuality in the Priestly account of creation. In my analysis thus far I have attempted to clarify the message of the text at the level of its grammar and to limit my interpretation to the intentionality inferred from that grammar. But I must note that there is another message in the text, which stands in tension to the message recorded at the grammatical level. While the author of Genesis 1 intends to speak about nature, not culture, and about order as a corollary of nature, the language he uses to describe the relationship of humankind to the other orders of creation employs social metaphors based on male experience and male roles ("ruling," vss. 26, 28; and "subjugating," vs. 28).[18] In this usage he exhibits the patriarchal assumptions attested elsewhere in his work (e.g. Gen 5:1-3; 9:1; and the male lineages that structure his history).[19] While the Priestly writer speaks of the species, he thinks of the male. He is, in short, no feminist, as some would have him be. But that does not mean that he cannot contribute to a feminist anthropology. The constraint of his language with respect to sexual distinction and the openness of his concept of image to new meanings invite theological speculation that moves beyond anything the Priestly writer intended or could conceive.

The Priestly author, I have argued, is concerned with the order of nature, not culture, and offers no theological reflection on the social consequences or correlates of human sexual differentiation. In contrast, the Yahwist focuses the attention of his two-part narrative on the tension between nature and culture, or the disparity between the created (intended) order and the historically experienced order--a tension exemplified in the relationship.of the sexes.

THE YAHWISTIC (J) ACCOUNT (2:4B-3:24)

The Yahwistic account of creation differs from the Priestly account to which it is joined, in language, structure, theology and temper. While it shows many signs of composite origin, its present literary form presents a two-part drama of interlocking

18. I am not arguing that these roles or actions are by definition or necessity male. I am simply arguing that in Israelite society, as in most comparable societies, such roles and activities were normally identified with males.

19. *HTR* 74, p. 151, especially n. 55.

episodes and ring construction that must be treated as a unit.[20] In the Yahwist's account, creation and "fall"[21] together tell the story of the conditions under which human life is lived. And although history begins outside the garden, the garden is the site of the estrangement that manifests itself in history. The seeds of destruction have already been sown when the journey of our ancestors begins.

This paper does not permit full consideration of the dynamics and intention of the Yahwist's account of origins, which is complex and shows signs of incorporating prior traditions. Nor does it permit an account of the place of Genesis 2-3 within the larger "historical" work. Consequently, I must limit my attention to those features of the composition that have particular significance for understanding the meaning of sexual differentiation in the account.

Of fundamental importance for an understanding of the author's statements about sexuality is the literary form and structure of the narrative. In the Yahwist's account, story and the storyteller's art replace the liturgical cadences and technical terminology of priestly declaration. Circular movement marks the narrative structure, in contrast to the linear progression of Genesis 1, and dramatic action is employed to describe states and relationships. Time has no meaning here and sequence of action no ontological significance. The first and final acts of creation together describe a single action; the creation of humankind is not complete until the woman stands beside the man, manifesting that essential aspect of humanity hidden or latent in the first exemplar. Only when the pair appear together on the stage does the divine-human interaction begin and the consequential action of the story. Similarly, in the account of the "fall," neither sequence of actions nor proferred motives is of consequence. The woman is not judged until the man has also eaten; and both are understood to have acted in full knowledge of the prohibition and its consequences.[22] Thus "order of creation" and "order of the fall" are notions foreign to the Yahwist's conception and composition.

How then does the Yahwist understand the relationship of the sexes and what is the meaning of his uniquely bifurcated account of human creation?[23] The essential

20. For fuller treatment and citation of literature see "Sexual Differentiation" (n. 3 above), sections of which are reproduced in the following exposition of the Yahwist's narrative.

21. The term "fall," as well as the concept, is alien to the text. I employ it only as a conventional designation. See "Sexual Differentiation," n. 26.

22. Although Trible's contrasting of the woman's reflective act with the man's "belly-oriented" acquiescence is an effective counter to traditional interpretations of the woman's role in the fall *(God and the Rhetoric of Sexuality,* p. 113), I doubt that the author intended to differentiate the responses so sharply, if at all. I would refer the narrative depiction of the man's and the woman's actions to customary male and female roles in food preparation and consumption, though a more specific mythic or aetiological tradition may underlie the representation. I take the woman's reasoning as describing the general human response with its attempt to justify disobedience. The storyteller allows the man and the woman in succession to represent thoughts and actions of the species: the man in naming the animals, the woman in rationalizing the desire for forbidden fruit.

23. While the separate creation of man and woman is known elsewhere (though not from the ancient Near East), the Yahwist's account is unique in its theme of the man's need for companionship (possibly an expression of the motif articulated elsewhere in the myth of the androgyne). It is also unique in encompassing the account of animal creation within the account of human creation, subordinating the animal orders to the human order by means of a circular structure comparable in effect to the linear structure of Genesis 1.

plot of the Yahwist's narrative may be summarized as follows. Yahweh God forms "the human" (*hā 'ādām*) as the first of the creatures, earth creature par excellence, by origin and vocation.[24] Presented as an individual *(hā 'ādam,* with the article, in contrast to P's collective *'ādām,* without the article[25] and envisioned as a male (specifically, a peasant farmer), the name by which he is designated betrays his true identity--and the problem of his singularity. For although he bears the appellation of the species, he does not fully represent it. The personification is defective in its limitation to the male alone. The remainder of the chapter describes in dramatic action the overcoming of that defect and the resolution of the tension latent in the initial presentation.[26]

The narrative is androcentric in form and perspective. It is told from the man's point of view and describes the man's need for a companion and helper. The resolution of the problem is accordingly signaled by the man's response, in his recognition that the one who confronts him is truly like him, not merely in appearance, but in substance--"of the same bone and flesh" (2:33). This climactic word of recognition, emphasizing the identity and equality of the two (now designated by the alliterative social terms, *'îš* "man" and *'iššâ* "woman"), gains significance and impact from the tension-heightening action that precedes it. There Yahweh forms from the earth all of the animal species in a trial-and-error attempt to produce a suitable companion for the man. It is only with the woman, however, that the man's need is finally met, for unlike the animals, the woman is not a separate order of creation, but shares fully the nature of *adam*. The dramatic requirement of creating two from one, which arises from the initial presentation of a single representative of the species, leads to the ingenious solution of extracting a rib from the human-presented-as-a-man and "building" a woman--a solution that recognizes the woman as one substance with the man, and hence one nature, yet unique.

The Yahwist's account gives special emphasis to the bisexual nature of the human species in order to stress the relationship between the sexes, here presented in psycho-social rather than biological terms. And although the help which the woman is meant to give to the man is undoubtedly help in procreation, the account in Genesis 2 subordinates function to passion. The attraction of the sexes is the author's primary interest, the sexual drive whose consummation is conceived as a re-union.

24. Formed from the earth *('adama)* to till the earth (2:5, 7; 3:23). Cf. Bruce D. Naidoff, "A Man to Work the Soil: A New Interpretation of Genesis 2-3," *JSOT* 5 (1978) pp. 2-14.

25. Cf. Ernest Lussier, "*ADAM* in Genesis 1, 1-4, 24," *CBQ* 18 (1956) pp. 137-139; and D. Barthelemy, "'Pour un homme,' 'Pour l'homme' ou 'Pour Adam'? (Gen 2, 20)" in *De la Tôrah au Messie: Melanges Henri Cazelles*. Maurice Carrez, Joseph Dore, and Pierre Grelot, eds (Paris: Desclee, 1981) pp. 47-53.

26. This summary traces one line through the narrative. However, the multilayered nature of the account requires a multileveled interpretation. At one level, the name and the characterization of the first human must be seen as determined by the tale of the man and the garden with its *'adam hā 'ădāmâ* (earthling/earth) aetiology, the tale that provides the framing *inclusio* for the two chapters. At another level, the name and the depiction of its bearer are to be understood in terms of the class designation *adam* and its incomplete realization or representation in the single specimen. Linked to an aetiology of sexual attraction, this understanding presents the species as essentially embodied in (a) man and (a) woman and views wholeness in terms of differentiation and union rather than identity or absorption. In the present form of the text, the latter interest dominates the chapter. However, I do not think one can eradicate the male image of *ha'adam* from this passage as Trible attempts to do in *God and the Rhetoric of Sexuality*, pp. 80 and 140, n. 8.

Genesis 2, like Genesis 1, contains no statement of dominance or subordination in the relationship of the sexes, but its narratively constructed emphasis on the equality of the two is the foundation and prelude to its negation in Genesis 3. There we encounter an explicit statement of the woman's subordination to the man--not, however, as representing the order of creation but rather as a sign of its sinful perversion. The Yahwist sees the disobedience of the man and woman to the divine command as the root sin that disturbs the original harmony of creation, and he sees the consequences of that sin in the painful and alienated existence which he knew to be the human lot. The estrangement introduced into the divine-human relationship works itself out in every other relationship.[27] Estrangement from God manifests itself for the man in estrangement from the earth, out of which he was created and on which he depends for his work, estrangement experienced as pain in his labor; and the estrangement from God manifests itself for the woman in estrangement from the man, from whom she was created and on whom she depends for her work, estrangement experienced in the pain of her labor, childbirth.[28]

But there is a further dimension of this pain of estrangement, which breaks the symmetry of suffering, and that is the destruction of companionship between the man and the woman. For the relationship of companionship, established in the creation and exhibited in the mutual drive of the sexes toward each other (*he* will leave father and mother, his own flesh and bone, to cleave to her [2:24], and *her* desire will be for him [3:16]), is broken by the added word of judgment: "he shall rule over her" (3:16). The companion of chapter 2 has become a master. The historical subordination of woman to man is inaugurated--and identified as the paradigm expression of sin and alienation in creation.[29]

REUNITING THE TEXTS: INTERPRETIVE CONCLUSIONS AND INFERENCES

The union of the Priestly and Yahwistic accounts of creation as successive episodes in a comprehensive statement of origins requires the canonical interpreter to observe both the order of the component accounts and the tension between them. It also requires attention to new meanings that move beyond the original terms and intentions of the individual accounts as they are brought within a new and larger context of interpretation. That interpretive context must finally include the canon as a whole, in interaction with the multiple and changing contexts of the interpreter. It requires, I believe, multivalent and multidimensional reading. What I shall offer is

27. Gerhard von Rad, *Genesis. A Commentary* (Philadelphia: Westminster, 1961) pp. 148-149.

28. Reading *'iṣṣĕbônēk wĕhērōnek* (3:16) as hendiadys with Westermann (1974:356) and most commentators. I cannot accept Carol Meyers' view that the verse speaks of multiplying the woman's work *and* pregnancies or Meyers' elimination of the sense of painful labor from the parallel clause, *bĕ'eṣeb tēlĕdî bānîm,* though her article makes a valuable contribution to the study of women's roles in ancient Israel; Carol L. Meyers, "Gender Roles and Genesis 3:16 Revisited" in *The Word of the Lord Shall Go Forth. Essays in Honor of David Noel Freedman.* Eds. Carol L. Meyers and M. O'Connor (Winona Lake, IN: Eisenbrauns, 1983) pp. 334-346. For recognition of the parallelism between the man's and the woman's punishment, cf. Patrick D. Miller, Jr. *Genesis 1-11: Studies in Structure and Theme, JSOT* Suppl. Ser. 8 (Sheffield: University of Sheffield, 1978), p. 48, n. 49.

29. The divine word spoken in judgment is neither a curse nor an eternal decree determining the fate of all future generations, but rather the dramatic representation of the consequences of sin as experienced in the generations known to the author. An aetiological tale of the painful conditions of life is joined by profound theological reflection on the root cause. That the examples chosen (field labor and childbirth) no longer represent the chief sources of pain in the lives of most Westerners today demonstrates their aetiological and historically conditioned character. They must not be absolutized but read as signs of an underlying disorder, whose clearest persisting sign is the continuing alienation of male and female perpetuated by patriarchy. See, *inter alia,* Claus Westermann, *Genesis* (BKAT; Neukirchen Vluyn: Neukirchen, 1974), pp. 355-363 and Trible, *God and the Rhetoric of Sexuality,* pp. 152-153 and 157.

one interpretation, or rather one set of interpretive comments and questions formulated in the context of reflection on the meaning of sexuality, informed by women's experience and feminist critique of patriarchy and its theological legacy.

Theological anthropology has been dominated by the concept of the divine image as determinative for an understanding of humanity in its created nature, and rightly so, since this stands as the lead and controlling statement of the combined creation accounts, giving to the human species a unique identity and dignity, grounded in a special relationship to God. It is therefore the foundational concept for all canonical reflection on the nature of humankind--and its place within the created order--for the relationship to God, according to the Priestly formulation, determines the relation to other orders of creation. Thus the concept of the divine image is essentially a statement about relationships in a "vertical" plane, relating humanity to orders "above" and "below."

In contrast to this lead statement which defines and locates humanity in creation and in relationship to the creator, the statement attributing sexuality to humankind is clearly a second order statement. But it is no less essential (or consequential) for an understanding of the species and its individual members. As articulated in the two-fold formulation of Priestly declaration and Yahwistic narrative, it is foundational for all relationships within the human order, social as well as biological. Thus it may be seen as the primary statement and root metaphor for relationships on the "horizontal" plane.

Traditional interpretation of Genesis 1-2 has commonly imposed the vertical concept of the image on the horizontal concept of sexual differentiation, transforming the hierarchy of orders into a hierarchy of the sexes. In the Priestly formulation, however, the two statements defining human creation are not connected, but presented as parallel and simultaneously valid declarations. How may they properly be related? Or can they be related at all? The silence of the text leaves to the interpreter the task of spelling out the implications of each of the juxtaposed statements for the other. However that is done, the integrity of each as an independent statement must be maintained.

My reflections and arguments in the remainder of this paper focus on these two primary statements of the Priestly writer, augmented or modified by the Yahwist, as I attempt to spell out their implications for a theology of sexuality. The attempt has made me painfully aware that I am stepping at this point into an area (or areas) of specialization for which I lack many of the essential tools. I grope with imprecise language and inadequate knowledge of the basic literature and categories of analysis (specifically in the fields of systematic theology and the study of human sexuality in its physical and psychological dimensions).[30] Often, I discover, I am unable to do more than identify a problem, and must rest my analysis with a question rather than a proposal.

1. The parallel statements about human nature in the Priestly creation account are alike in referring to the species as a whole, but they differ in two important ways: (a) while the divine likeness distinguishes the species from other orders of creation, sexuality does not; and (b) while the concept of the image admits of no differentiation

[30] The two books that I have found most helpful in treating sexuality in the context of Christian theology are James B. Nelson, *Embodiment: An Approach to Sexuality and Christian Theology* (Minneapolis: Augsburg, 1978), and Lisa Sowle Cahill, *Between the Sexes: Foundations for a Christian Ethics of Sexuality* (Philadelphia: Fortress, 1985), both discovered after I had completed the draft of this paper.

within the species, sexuality is expressed only in differentiation.

2. In P's initial and determinative usage, the divine image characterizes humanity as a whole. It must therefore characterize each individual of the species and cannot be limited to any subgroup. Whatever gender distinction means, it cannot involve denial or diminution of the God-like nature that characterizes the species. To be human is to be created in the image of God.

a. This understanding of the image as defining the species is not qualified by P's subsequent personification of the species in an individual named Adam, who perpetuates the essential created nature of the species by fathering offspring in his image. Adam is presented in Gen 5:la, 3 as an individual exemplifying the species. That the species *adam* is still understood as collective/plural and bisexual (i.e., sexually dimorphic) is evident in P's recapitulation of 1:27 in 5:2 and in his explicit referral of the name/common noun to the plural object: "Male and female he created them, and he blessed them and named *them adam* (5:2)." The Priestly writer's narrowed attention to the male line in history does not thereby limit humanity or the image to the male of the species, though it does betray the author's cultural presuppositions. The tension that remains in the text between adam as male and female and the male Adam who heads the Priestly genealogy is an essential clue to the canonical interpreter.

b. The Yahwist's individualizing of *adam* in his story of the first human pair also gives no support for collapsing the collective into a singular and claiming for the one in his gendered particularity what belongs to the species as a whole. A consistent grammatical distinction is maintained between the anarthrous noun of Genesis 1 (*adam* "humankind") and the noun with the article used in Genesis 2 (*ha adam* "the human one"). (Thus a similar tension appears in the sequential reading of Genesis 1 and 2 to that observed in the relationship of chapters 1 and 5.) And the Yahwist signals by narrative plot as well as grammar that "the human" and humankind are not fully coterminous in the first specimen of the species: There is something defective about the one standing alone.

c. The notion of the divine image in Genesis 1 does not describe a possession which can be quantified or lost. It is not variable in degree within the species either in relation to gender or to character. Therefore the notion of equality, or inequality, is inappropriate as a qualifier. And it is not lost or effaced by the disobedience of the pair or the consequent divine judgment.[31]

3. The concept of the divine image, though associated in the author's cultural milieu with the idea of ruling or governing, is essentially "empty" of content, describing a correspondence conceived in terms of form rather than substance: humankind is God's representation and representative within creation.[32] As an expression of a relationship to God employed to express a relationship to other creatures, the concept of the divine image invites ever new reflection on the content and character of both

[31] See *HTR* 7, p. 138, n. 22.

[32] *selem*, "image," as a metaphor for likeness is concrete, formal, holistic, and lacking in specific content--which makes it an ideal term for P, who employs it with changing connotations in changing contexts (cf. 5:1, 3 and 9:6). Cf. *HTR* 74, pp. 138-139. For its use as a royal motif in 1:26-28, see pp. 140-144.

of these relationships in changing times and circumstances.[33] And as an expression that describes and defines the species as a whole, its content must be drawn out of the experience of the species as a whole, female as well as male. Where the interpretive content has been derived exclusively or disproportionately from male models it must be considered defective. How might the relationship between human and nonhuman creation be conceived if it were understood in terms of female models of relationship rather than the male models of dominion and subjugation?[34]

4. Sexuality does not distinguish humankind from other orders of creatures, at least as P understands it; rather it is an aspect of human nature shared with other forms of life. Consequently, a biblically informed theology of sexuality must address itself both to the nature and function of the reproductive capacity and to the meaning of its transhuman character. I shall limit my comments to the first question, leaving the second for further reflection.

a. P's statement concerning human sexuality, contained in the words of sexual differentiation and of blessing, focuses solely on its biological nature. It declares that sex, as differentiation and union, is intended for procreation and is to be understood as a divinely given capacity and power governed by blessing and command.

b. The word that activates the endowment, however, addresses the species, not the individual, and is limited in its application by the setting in which it is spoken, a limitation made explicit in the qualifying amplification, "and fill the earth."[35] It is a word for beginnings as it appears in Genesis 1, not for all time; the "command" to "be fruitful and multiply" is neither absolute nor universal. It must be repeated and reinterpreted in changing historical/ecological situations.[36]

c. Thus sexuality as reproductive capacity is an endowment of the species as such, but its employment is goal oriented and historically conditioned. This conditioning of the capacity opens the way to ethical deliberation concerning the circumstances of its actualization.

5. Sexuality is expressed in differentiation--and union. It divides in order to unite. It creates both the need and the means to overcome the separation that it symbolizes. Sexuality is the primary means of self-transcendence on which all community depends. This dual aspect of sexuality as differentiation and union is masterfully portrayed by the Yahwist in his account of the oneness and otherness of the first representatives of the species.

a. J's account provides an essential complement to P by focusing on the psycho-social meaning of sexuality and its historical manifestations. Companionship, the sharing of work, mutual attraction and commitment in a bond superceding all

33. *selem*, which is employed in Genesis 1 only in an adverbial expression modifying the verb of creation, does not describe a relationship in the sense of a means or mode of relating (*HTR* 74, p. 139). I use "relationship" here as a formal term.

34. Patrick Miller has suggested (in the discussion following the presentation) that the concept of nurture might provide a more adequate metaphor for the content of the relationship. A wealth of possibilities are suggested by roles of the mother as manager of the household, provider, trainer, teacher, mourner, etc.

35. See *HTR* 74, p. 152.

36. It is repeated in P in the following passages: (underlined citations are imperative [blessing form], others indicative): *9:1, 7 (Noah);* 17:6 (causative with God as subject; Isaac as object); 17:20 (causative; Ishmael); 28:3 (causative; Isaac); *35:11* (Jacob); 47:27 (Jacob); 48:4 (causative; Jacob); Exod 1:7 (descendants of Israel). Dependent on P: Exod 23:30 (Israelites in Canaan); Lev 26:9 (Israel). In extra-P usage the root *PRH* ("to be fruitful") as a term for human and animal increase, is typically related to possession of land and/or security against foes (usually in reference to a future or restored Israel). In all usage, the word of blessing, whether direct or indirect, future or past, has a particular end or goal related to a particular situation of need. Cf. *HTR* 74, p. 152 especially ns. 60, 61.

other human bonds and attractions--these are the ends for which adam was created male and female and these are the signs of intended partnership. For J, sexual differentiation is the ground and precondition of community, which requires the individual to reach beyond the self for fulfillment of basic needs.

b. But the requirement of an "other" to satisfy the individual's needs opens the way to exploitation, whose tragic consequences J so clearly depicts in the historical relationship of (the) man to (the) woman.

c. The Yahwist's attention to the social and historical dimensions of sexuality requires the canonical interpreter to consider the socio-historical conditions under which the relationship of the sexes takes place. And the ethical judgment implicit in his account requires corresponding ethical reflection and judgment by the contemporary theologian. Biblical anthropology, as exemplified in the combined P-J creation account, joins to the question of nature or ontology the question of history and ethics. The movement from ontological speculation to ethical reflection and judgment, exhibited in the present order of the combined texts, thrusts the interpreter forward into the full canon of Scripture as the arena in which the meaning of human existence as male and female must finally be understood--and prepares the reader to discover that meaning in negative as well as positive experience. The creation texts alone cannot adequately instruct us on what it means to be human and to be male and female.

6. Sexual differentiation as a mark of the species means that no individual--and no class composed of a single gender--can fully represent the species, an understanding reflected in the J narrative and the well-known German saying, "ein Mensch ist kein Mensch." Does this mean that the couple must be understood as the primary unit of the species, rather than the individual? And does this not imply that the divine image is not fully present in the individual, thereby qualifying my earlier statement that it applies to every individual of the species without qualification or quantification? My tentative answers to these questions are as follows:

a. While male and female together describe the species, which cannot be fully known without both, and while sexual union is the primary purpose of gender differentiation, the human couple cannot be viewed as the basic unit of the species, since it is neither a universal nor a naturally occurring phenomenon. It is rather a bio-social construction, a highly variable and achieved union of sexually mature individuals chosen from a range of possible partners. The multiple variables of age, physical capacity, inclination, number and duration of partners, etc., all militate against construing the socially and/or sexually united couple as the basic human unit. Consequently we must maintain that the individual, which is to say every individual, in his or her sexually defined particularity is "the" representative human being, fully human and in no way defective as a representative.

(1) This means that the definition of the species and the definition of the individual are not fully coterminous, since the species has a communal nature which rests on individual differentiation. While the species is defined as male-and-female, the individual of the species is defined as male-or-female. The species is then both an aggregate, defined by its members (male and female), and an identity-giving entity (whether understood in terms of an abstraction or of shared "substance"), defining its members (divine image).

7. Do these observations mean anything more than that the species is made up of all of its members, young and old, black and white, left-handed and right-handed, etc., and that in terms of species identification, all such variables are incidental? And may not the same be said of other species? More pointedly we may ask whether gender is a theologically significant variable in a way in which size, pigmentation or cranial proportions are not? Is the isolation of sexuality as the single significant attribute of differentiation in the biblical creation accounts perhaps to be understood as the reflection of a set of economic and cultural needs or interests that no longer exist or no longer warrant the priority given to them by these accounts? Is it appropriate for contemporary theology to give so prominent a place to sexuality as a defining attribute of humankind? And to what extent must the biblical view of sexuality be modified by modern understanding of sexuality as a far more complex phenomenon than previously assumed? Again I venture tentative answers.

a. With respect to the prominence and isolation of sexuality from other observed variables of human constitution, I would argue that it deserves primary attention and theological reflection not simply because of its place in biblical tradition, which must be assessed and reappropriated, but also because it is essential to the survival of the species (biblically interpreted as the divinely ordained means of assuring the continuity of a "good" creation) and is universally recognized and universally invested with cultural (including religious) meaning. Perhaps one may say that it is of all attributes of the species the most extensively invested with symbolic meanings. It is an essential component of individual self-definition and of social location and assessment. For these reasons, I would argue, it must have a prominent place in any theological anthropology.

b. A final word concerning individual variation and the question of "arbitrary" definition: Gender as a dimorphic classification is based on observed genital differentiation (now known to be genetically determined), but sexuality as its expression is exhibited in a wide range of physical and psychological forms and an even wider range of behavioral and attitudinal variables. What is the significance of this variability for an understanding of gender? Does variation in sexual performance, size of physical organs, etc., mean that the individual is more or less male, or female? Here I think the answer must be the same as in the case of the question concerning the divine image. Gender is not quantifiable, nor is it properly subject to qualitative analysis. It is a given, a defining attribute of each individual. But as an attribute that is essentially social in its expression, it can and must be evaluated and regulated. It is the Yahwist's contribution to remind us that the good gift of sexuality may become the means and the sign of alienation within the species, that what was intended for fulfillment and self-transcendence may become the occasion and instrument of deprivation and oppression.

Creation and the Human Predicament in Job

J. Gerald Janzen

The depth of the human predicament is not suffering as such. Suffering that is intelligible may be intensely unpleasant, even terrible. We may instinctively recoil from it. Yet our sense of reality, our loyalty to truth, however weak or obscure, helps us to endure such suffering as a part, however dark, of the scheme of things.

What throws us into the depth of the human predicament is suffering that is at odds with our understanding of the scheme of things. In such a case we are left to endure it nakedly, without the support of our understanding. Then the suspicion arises that our understanding of the scheme of things is itself at odds with the real scheme of things, or, worse yet, that there may be no final scheme of things. Our meaningless suffering may be the clue that the whole thing is meaningless, or it may be a call to us to revise our understanding of the whole thing. Such, in the most general terms, is the human predicament.

Frank Moore Cross takes us into the Joban version of this predicament, with these words in his magisterial study of Canaanite myth and Hebrew epic.[1]

> *The argument of Job attacked the central theme of Israel's religion. It repudiated the God of history whose realm is politics, law, and justice, whose delight is to lift up the poor and to free the slave. The God who called Israel out of Egypt, who spoke by prophet, the covenant god of Deuteronomy, did not reveal himself to Job . . . . He was revealed in the defeat of the dragon of chaos, in the myths of creation . . . . The Lord of history failed to act. 'El or Ba'l, the transcendent creature spoke. Only he lived. Job saw him and bowed his knee.*

I believe Cross correctly frames the issue in terms of alternative ancient theologies, alternative understandings of the scheme of things. The issue is their comparative adequacy for enabling Job to deal with his sort of suffering in such a way that life's worth is neither cheaply forfeited nor too dearly purchased. But when Cross sees Job repudiating the Israelite tradition of "the God of history whose realm is politics, law, and justice" in favor of Canaanite El or Baal as transcendent Creator "revealed in the defeat of the dragon of chaos, in the myths of creation," I do not follow him. The issues here are crucial to the interpretation of Job, and call for us to review briefly the relevant ancient Near Eastern myths of creation before we examine Job.

In Canaan, Richard Clifford has argued,[2] the myth of creation through defeat of the dragon of chaos is the founding myth of monarchical city-state society. Clifford's analysis dovetails with work by H.H. Schmid[3] who has argued that the Hebrew word

[1]Frank Moore Cross, *Canaanite Myth and Hebrew Epic* (Cambridge: Harvard University Press, 1973), pp. 343-44.

[2]Richard J. Clifford, "Cosmogonies in the Ugaritic Texts and in the Bible," *Orientalia* 53 (1984), pp. 183-201.

[3]Hans Heinrich Schmid, *Gerechtigkeit als Weltordnung* Tübingen: J.C.B. Mohr [Paul Siebeck], 1968).

sedaqah, "righteousness" - a central category of Israelite politics, law and justice - has its original use in the context of Canaanite royal society and its supporting cosmology. In the latter context, *sedaqah* is the powerful and wise acting of the king, divine or human, manifested in the secure and fruitful ordering of the world, cosmic or social. "Righteousness," then, is the action of "world-ordering." In Israel the use of this word continues to presuppose as an ultimate frame of reference the creation and ordering of the world. In a subsequent programmatic article, "Schöpfung, Gerechtigkeit und Heil,"[4] Schmidt argues that in the ancient Near East generally, including Israel, all interpretation of existence moves within the comprehensive horizon of creation and world-ordering, characteristically modelled on the creation and ordering of the monarchical state.

Similarly in Mesopotamia, when the watery goddess Tiamat threatens the society of the younger gods, Marduk defeats her in battle, sets up the two halves of her split body like a sea-wall to hold back the waters of chaos, and within this safe zone creates the cosmos. For this he is acclaimed king by the gods, who build Babylon as his capitol city. Thorkild Jacobsen[5] shows how this myth mirrors and founds city-state monarchy in Mesopotamia. Indeed, the threat of Tiamat to the younger gods may mirror the threat to Babylon after Hammurapi by the people of the Sealand (the "Land of Tiamat"), while Marduk's victory over Tiamat may mirror Ulamburiash's victory over the Sealand and his consolidation of Babylon's empire in security and prosperity. The cosmogonic victory and continuing rule of Marduk manifest his power, wisdom and justice, and ground the rule of the Babylonian king "on earth as it is in heaven."[6]

How is suffering to be interpreted within such a theology of creation? Logically, such a cosmology provides an intelligible account of the prosperity of the upright and the suffering of the wicked. The upright, who live by the laws of the cosmic realm, participate in the security and abundance ensured by the orders of nature and society established and maintained through the divine king's power and wisdom. Those who rebel against social and cosmic order must incur divine judgement. If they are allowed to go unpunished, the order of things will deteriorate into chaos through their lawlessness and the lawlessness their unrequited actions encourage.

[4]Hans Heinrich Schmid, "Schöpfung. Gerechtigkeit und Heil. 'Schöpfungstheologie' als Gesamthorizont biblischer Theologie." *Zeitschrift für Theologie und Kirche* 70 (1973), pp. 1-19. An English translation (unfortunately omitting an important section relating to the New Testament) appears as "Creation, Righteousness, and Salvation: 'Creation Theology' as the Broad Horizon of Biblical Theology," in Bernhard W. Anderson, ed., *Creation in the Old Testament* (Philadelphia; Fortress Press, 1984), pp. 102-117.

[5]Thorkild Jacobsen, *The Treasures of Darkness* (New Haven: Yale University Press, 1976), pp. 188-191.

[6]In *From a Broken Web: Separation, Sexism, and Self* (Boston: Beacon Press, 1986), Catherine Keller presents a powerful feminist reading of the *Enuma Elish* in which Tiamat symbolizes feminine energies which Marduk the young male here slays in order to establish patriarchal monarchical society. For all its suggestiveness, such a reading overlooks the fact that in the ancient Near East, inside and outside the Bible, the waters of the sea often represent the onrush and attack of armies (who are of course the instrument of royal international strategy). This common usage may, as Jacobsen suggests, underlie or derive from the battles between Babylon and the people of Tiamat, i.e., the Sealand (who were not a matriarchy). I find myself in frequent agreement with Keller's general analysis of the nature of true (or creative) versus false (or destructive) wisdom and power; but I do not find helpful her rigid differentiation of these alternatives along gender lines. The attempt to characterize feminine investment in war as merely the result of women's co-optation into a primarily male military consciousness, is an ideological *tour de force.*

Sooner or later, however, the question arises: What is to be made of suffering that falls upon a loyal servant of Marduk? This question is in fact addressed in the late second millenium, in the text known as *Ludlul bel nemeqi*, "let me praise the Lord of Wisdom."[7] Significantly, *Enuma Elish* itself sheds no light on the situation other than the implication that Marduk opposes the enemy and the sinner on behalf of the loyal community. For the sufferer observes in bewilderment that "What seems good to oneself / is a crime before god. / What to one's heart seems bad / is good before one's god," and concludes that the minds and the ways of the gods are unfathomable and incomprehensible. All one can do is hope that the wrath of Marduk will give way to mercy. That Marduk has done so in the case of this sufferer is cause for praise, but the praise remains blind and uncomprehending.[8]

How is it with Job? What is his understanding of the cosmos and of its Creator, such that his innocent sufferings become inexplicable and threaten all sense of meaning? Then, when God finally addresses him with a portrayal of the origins and character of the cosmos, what kind of cosmos does Yahweh offer to Job? How does it compare with the cosmos he had presupposed? and how may the cosmos that Yahweh offers be supposed to bear on his predicament?

First, then, what cosmology does Job bring to his predicament? Or, more broadly, what cosmology is implied as the Book of Job opens? Let us assume, for the moment, that it is some form of the cosmological understanding current in Israel at the time the book was written. Israel's accounts of cosmic and social ordering stood in varying proportions of continuity and discontinuity to the ancient cosmogonies described above. It is increasingly recognized that in some measure Israelite Yahwism shared what has been called the "common theology" of the ancient Near East. Thus, portrayals of Yahweh as divine king and warrior in part resemble royal portraits of other gods. Also, to some degree the divine covenant with Israel resembles ancient vassal treaties with their sanctions of blessing for loyalty and curse for disloyalty. To that degree, the logic of Yahweh's wise and strong rule as it bears on the interpretation of human suffering is a logic Israel shares with the ancient world: By the terms of the covenant, the loyal will be blessed and the rebellious cursed. This state-treaty or covenantal logic, H.H. Schmid argues, has its roots in creation theology. Again, at a number of points the Hebrew Bible portrays Yahweh as slaying the dragon of chaos, either in cosmic creation or in historical redemption consonant with such creation. In principle, therefore, there need be no contradiction, such as Cross supposes, between Yahweh the divine king and warrior who delivers Israel from Egypt and who calls for covenant obedience, and the Creator god who defeats the dragon of chaos. Deutero-Isaiah, for example, explicitly draws this correlation (Isa. 51:9-11), while already the

[7]W.G. Lambert, *Babylonian Wisdom Literature* (Oxford: Clarendon Press, 1960), pp. 21-62. Subsequently discovered material completing the opening hymn to Marduk is published in D.J. Wiseman, "A New Text of the Babylonian Poem of the Righteous Sufferer," *Anatolian Studies* 30 (1980), pp. 102-07, and discussed further in William L. Moran, *Journal of the American Oriental Society* 103 (1983), pp. 255-260.

[8]Moran, *op. cit.*, p. 256, quotes *Enuma Elish* Tablet VI, line 137, where Marduk as 'Mir-Ša-kuš-u is "angry but judicious, wroth but forgiving," and shows how these two sides of Marduk underlie the symbolism of night and day, darkness and light, that runs through *Ludlul.* Thus Marduk is "a god of darkness and wrath, but a god too, of light and a sudden and matching mercy" (p. 258). In spite of this thematic connection between *Ludlul* and the *Enuma Elish,* the cosmogonic narrative as such sheds no light on the sufferer's plight, but in fact provides the cosmological setting within which that plight is incomprehensible.

old hymn in Exodus 15 shows how Israel adapted the imagery of creation battle to celebrate its own origins in the defeat of Pharaoh at the Sea.

Yet in the end Israel gave a different account of cosmic origins. As Frank Cross observes, "there is in the Genesis creation story no element of cosmogonic conflict."[9] To be sure, what precedes the rise of cosmic order looks suspiciously like the chaos which Marduk slew: "The earth was formless and void, and darkness was upon the face of the deep [the tehom]." This chaos, however, gives way to cosmic order not through conflict but through the divine word which calls all things into existence. Perhaps the clearest vestige or "eggshell" of the cosmogonic portrayal in *Enuma Elish* is the firmament of the second day, erected to hold back the waters and provide a space within which a habitable and fruitful earth may emerge. Similarly, in Deutero-Isaiah, where creation themes are very prominent, the cosmogonic battle motif appears clearly only once, in 51:9-11, on the lips, we may note, of the exiles who cry out for the arm of Yahweh to vindicate them against their enemies. When that arm, a recurrent motif in Deutero-Isaiah, is finally "bared," or revealed, in Isaiah 53, it is portrayed as winning its spoils by an astounding and incomprehensible inversion of the old cosmogonic battle. All this is to say that the author of Job had a choice of cosmogonic conceptions to bring to bear on Job's predicament.

With this brief reference to Israel's creation traditions we may turn to the Book of Job, and begin with 1:9-10:

> *Does Job fear God for nought?*
> *Have you not put a hedge about him and his house and all that he has, on every side?*
> *You have blessed the work of his hands, and his possessions have increased in the land.*
> *But put forth your hand now, and touch all that he has, and he will curse you to your face.*

We may notice here two aspects of the Satan's words: the image he uses, and the logic he connects with that image. First, the image of the encompassing and protective hedge recalls the hedge or wall with which Yahweh surrounded Israel (Psalm 80, Isaiah 5); it recalls the firmament of Genesis 1; and ultimately it recalls the sea-wall Marduk made out of Tiamat's body to hold back the floodwaters. It is within such an enclosed space provided by God that Job enjoys safety and abundance. Secondly, the logic of the Satan is the logic that goes with common understandings of monarchical ordering and rule: The loyal are favored, and the disloyal are punished; conversely, the benefits of royal favor motivate the subject to loyalty, while unrewarded loyalty eventually produces demoralization, disaffection and even rebellion. Like the gods

[9]Frank Moore Cross, "The 'Olden Gods' and Ancient Near Eastern Creation Myths," in Frank Moore Cross, Werner E. Lemke, and Patrick D. Miller, Jr., eds., *Magnalia Dei: The Might Acts of God* (G.E. Wright Volume) (Doubleday: Garden City, NY, 1976), p. 335. Catherine Keller reads Genesis 1 as a "a monotheistic polemic against creation by either procreation or combat . . . . The Word takes the place both of warrior's weapons and woman's womb." (*From A Broken Web*, p. 81). This Word she takes to be the unilateral and unimpeded expression of transcedent will. For a positive reading of Genesis 1 responsive to feminist concerns (and congenial to the general thesis of the present paper), see Jürgen Moltmann. *The Trinity and the Kingdom: The Doctrine of God* (San Francisco: Harper & Row, 1981), pp. 108-111; and *God in Creation: A New Theology of Creation and the Spirit of God* (San Francisco: Harper & Row, 1985), *passim*.

who acknowledge Marduk's kingship for his acts of chaos-slaying and cosmos building, Job (in the Satan's view) serves God in gratitude for a life that is securely hedged and abundantly provided. Presumably such loyal service will bring him God's continuing favor and blessing. (As the friends will argue, it is only those who step outside this safe zone by stepping outside the law who have anything to fear.) However, the Satan asserts, if the hedge is removed and Job suffers loss, he will no longer serve God loyally, but will cast off allegiance with a curse. The Satan's image is appropriate to the cosmology of the *Enuma Elish,* its Canaanite counterparts, and aspects of Israelite tradition in continuity with its neighbors; and the Satan's logic is appropriate to the understanding of ordering power and the logic or "wisdom" of government implicit in that cosmology.

We move now to the dialogues. It has been observed that Job's cursing of the day of his birth (chapter 3) at a number of points draws on creation language reminiscent of Genesis 1. Already here, however, Job also introduces images from the cosmogonic battle, as he says of the night of his conception, "Let those curse it who curse Sea, / who are skilled to rouse Leviathan."[10] (We shall meet these two figures again in the speeches from the whirlwind.) In his second speech (chapter 7) Job cries out to God, "Am I the Sea, or a sea monster,/ that you set a guard over me?" Am I the embodiment of cosmic evil and chaos? Accompanying this cosmogonic image, Job here and increasingly elsewhere characterizes God as a warrior attacking him with armies and weapons against which he has no defence except his conscience. Eliphaz in his first speech asserts God's retributive justice in both cosmic and social events: the same God who gives rain upon the earth and sends water upon the fields delivers the lowly and frustrates the devices of the crafty (5:8-16). In his third speech Job rebuts Eliphaz's theme: The events of nature and society no longer display divine justice, but only crafty strength: "He alone stretched out the heavens, / and trampled the waves of the sea . . . ./ Beneath him bowed the helpers of Rahab. / How then can I answer him?" Such a cosmogony now signals for Job not a god of justice, but only a god of naked imposed will.

The cosmogonic battle imagery occurs on Job's lips as late as chapter 26: "By his power he stilled the sea; / and by his understanding he smote Rahab. / By his wind he bagged the sea; / and his hand pierced the fleeting serpent." In the old days such imagery would have encouraged Job, explaining his own well-being and the misery of the wicked. In his present condition the cosmic battle only terrifies him with its ruthless power, irrestible in its acts and inscrutable in its aims.

We come now to the divine speeches, with their portrayal of the origins and the character of the cosmos - what Marvin Pope refers to as their "seemingly magnificent irrelevance" to Job's problem.[11] By now, however, it should be clear that cosmological discourse as such is supremely relevant to Job's predicament, for cosmology is the frame within which his predicament arises. What is profoundly suggestive is that Yahweh does not attempt to answer Job's questions within the cosmology in which they arise. Within that frame, Job and the friends have already canvassed the options:

[10]This way of reading Job 3:8 reflects the translation of Marvin H. Pope, *The Anchor Bible: Job* (1973), p LXXXI.

[11]Marvin H. Pope, *The Anchor Bible: Job* (1973), p. LXXXI.

Either Job is a sinner, whether high-handed or inadvertent; or the God who has slain the dragon is, after all, interested only in power and not in justice. What Yahweh does by way of answer to Job is to redescribe creation, in such a way that the cosmic context for his unmerited suffering is changed, and therefore, by implication, his suffering itself is open to new significance. This redescription of the cosmos Yahweh achieves by a variety of rhetorical strategies, only a few of which there is space to examine here.[12]

The upshot of this redescription is that God's creation is indeed ordered - ordered for life. But it is ordered according to an unconventional wisdom which enjoys the wild freedom of life as much as its orderliness. Thus, for example, God celebrates the wild ass, to which Job earlier had likened himself (6:5), and which Zophar had then taken as an epitome of stupidity (11:12). Indeed, God has loosed the bonds of the swift ass to inhabit the steppe and the salt land, whose inhospitable regions humans naturally shun. There the wild ass may scorn the tumult of the city (sic!) and not hear the shout of the driver, free to range the mountains for pasture. Similarly God celebrates the wild ox, who does not find its food in a human crib, nor is bound to the furrow with ropes. The implication seems to be that God's ordering wisdom (and with it the theological significance of human suffering) is not adequately analogized in terms of the tightly domesticating orderliness of human economics or city-state politics.

The ostrich in its relation to its young (39:13-17) is peculiarly instructive of God's unconventional wisdom.

The wings of the ostrich wave proudly,
but are they the pinions and plumage of love?
For she leaves her eggs to the earth,
and lets them be warmed on the ground,
forgetting that a foot may crush them,
and that the wild beast may trample them.
She deals cruelly with her young,
as if they were not hers;
though her labour be in vain, yet she has no fear;
because God has made her forget wisdom,
and given her no share in understanding.
When she rouses herself to flee,
she laughs at the horse and his rider.

In the Bible, birds are frequently celebrated for building nests in the safety of high trees and rocks. This is their birdly wisdom; and when it becomes a figure for similar human efforts. Yet such wisdom, become obsessive, can betray a lack of trust in God's protection, a self-reliance curved in upon itself of which defensive city-walls are both literal means and architectural metaphor. In turn this incurved self-reliance can lead to all manner of injustice, as Habakkuk in his time says of Babylon: "Woe to him who gets evil gain for his house, to set his nest on high, to be safe from the reach of harm"

[12]See more fully the analysis in my commentary on Job, in the series *Interpretation: A Bible Commentary for Teaching and Preaching* (Atlanta: John Knox, 1985), pp. 225-247.

(Hab. 2:9). Over against such characteristic attempts to order and secure oneself and one's own in a dangerous world, the ostrich that lays its eggs on the unguarded ground constitutes Yahweh's redescription of birdly wisdom, a wisdom that appears as folly[13] to the mentality of the *Enuma Elish,* the Baal myths, and indeed, aspects of the royal Jerusalem theology at least as popularly understood and acted on.

The bold point God makes through the ostrich comes again at the beginning and the end of the divine speeches. At the end (40:15-41:26; EVV 40:15-41:34) God celebrates two gigantic creatures, Behemoth and Leviathan, figures that achieve mythic significance in the ancient Near East. For example, the legendary king Gilgamesh demonstrates his royal prowess as a hunter by slaying Huwawa the gigantic beast of the forest." In Canaanite myths Leviathan is the sea-dragon, generically similar to Tiamat. Here in Job, Behemoth and Leviathan are God's pets, terrifyingly powerful and unrestrainable, yet a part of creation.

These two figures are matched at the beginning by Yahweh's presentation of Yam or Sea, another Canaanite analog to Babylonian Tiamat. In Canaanite mythology, as we have seen, Baal defeats Sea, thereby establishing his cosmic kingship, and constructs a royal palace. How differently Yahweh deals with Sea! (38:8-11).

> *Who shut in Sea with doors,*
> *when it burst forth from the womb;*
> *when I made clouds its garment,*
> *and thick darkness its swaddling band,*
> *and prescribed bounds* **(huqqi)** *for it,*
> *and set bars and doors,*
> *and said, "Thus far shall you come, and no farther,*
> *and here shall your proud waves be stayed'?*

In this redescription of creation the cosmos does not arise by the defeat of Sea, but includes the birth of sea - a portrayal that according to Marvin Pope[14] is without parallel in ancient mythology. When Sea is born Yahweh does something that can be portrayed only by two different images. First Yahweh is described as shutting in or hedging Sea, setting bars and doors, and saying "Thus far, and no further." This is reminiscent of the walls of Babylon, the firmament of Genesis 1 and the hedge we heard about in the prologue. But this image is then balanced by another from the realm of child care: garment and swaddling band. Yahweh does indeed set bounds to the free and formless energy of Sea; but Yahweh will not reduce that formless energy to rigid control, let alone to rigor mortis. Yahweh rules sea with swaddling bands and with words of command, the way a parent raises and trains a child - not with coercive force, but with discipline and persuasion. It is to be noted that the divine address to Sea is called a *ḥoq* - one of the standard Hebrew words for law or ordinance. But by its association with the imagery of birth and of swaddling bands, the term itself *(ḥoq)* is resituated within the social setting of the family, where the logic, or wisdom, of

[13]The divine irony runs through the whole passage, especially in the questioning play on "love" in v. 13, the "forgetting" in v. 15, the "cruelty" in v. 16, and especially the reference to God's withholding wisdom and understanding. This irony is a fitting response to Job's ironic portrayal of God's "wisdom and might, counsel and understanding" in 12:13-25.

[14]Marvin H. Pope, *The Anchor Bible: Job* (1973), p. 293: "The present allusion presents an otherwise unknown motif, the birth of the sea-god and the use of swaddling bands to restrain the violent infant."

"ordering for life" is different in tenor from that of royal wisdom and law as conventionally practiced.

What of Job? Where does he fit into the picture? Why are humans not included among the creatures in this redescription of the cosmos? I suggest that Job is given no human figure with which to identify *in* the cosmos because he is being summoned to relate himself vocationally *to* the cosmos. As Job and God stand side by side looking *at* the cosmos, God asks Job a series of questions: Who are you? Where were you? Are you able? These questions all sound like put-downs, rhetorical questions whose answer is obvious. Yet from chapter 1 on, if we read carefully, we discover that again and again, supposedly rhetorical questions in fact turn out to function ironically, initially masking and then disclosing genuine questions, so that we have to reverse the obvious answer before we can make sense out of them. That, I think, is what is going on here. God is asking Job a whole series of questions, at least some of which at a deeper level should be answered positively if Job is to continue to retain his integrity and make sense of his vocation. A few examples must suffice:

First, under the question "are you able?" God throws the whole wild animal world at Job, concluding with the figures of Behemoth and Leviathan, and asks Job if he is equal to handling them. On the surface the proper answer is No. Yet in Psalm 8, as in Genesis 1, humankind is called to have dominion over all this realm; and in Psalm 8 this realm culminates in the same two figures: Behemoth, and the unnamed "whatever passes through the paths of the seas." In Genesis 1, the human dominion over the animals does not involve violence, insofar as humankind there is presented as vegetarian (compare also Isa. 11:6-9). When God re-presents the wild animals to Job, I take it God is re-presenting the royal vocation of *'adam* to peacable dominion and stewardship of what is free and wild. There is this difference: In Genesis 1 the vocation is given through a word of command. Here God re-presents the human vocation, not in a word of command, but in a question, "are you able?" which may be heard as calling for a "No" or a "Yes." An ear trained in one sort of wisdom - the wisdom of the friends and of the Satan, and of conventional royal cosmologies - will hear God's call for a self-abasing answer. The wisdom God wishes to convey to Job invites him to say "yes, I am able," and thereby enter into his vocation in all its terrible glory. For true royal wisdom may consist not in slaying what is free and wild, but in learning to live as steward of a world in which such free wildness has its own place.

What should lure Job to say "yes"? The integrity of his own experience. At one point, under the rubric "where were you?" God asks him (38:16-18).

Have you entered into the springs of the sea,
or walked in the recesses of the deep?
Have the gates of death been revealed to you,
or have you seen the gates of deep darkness?
Have you comprehended the expanse of the earth?
Declare, if you know all this.

The careful reader will have noted that Job again and again has used the language of deep darkness to describe his own experience. The place God describes is precisely where Job has been since chapter 1: If Job is honest to his experience, he will say, "Yes, God, I have been there."

But what does it mean to say that Job has walked in utter darkness (like the Servant of Yahweh in Isaiah 50:10), and has not lost his integrity nor his loyalty to God? It means, I suggest, that Job has moved from day six of creation, where he is simply a creature, a product of divine creativity, to the precreation darkness before day one, where God stood to say, "let there be light." To stand there is to enter into the depths of what it means, biblically, to image God, to share in world-ordering. But the world-ordering God would share with Job does not impose so rigid a law as to stamp out all freedom, all accident, all chance. So rigid an ordering - obsessively fearful of chaos and freedom, so controllingly predictive of the future - would benefit a Marduk and the societies Marduk legitimates, but not Yahweh or the people of Yahweh. At once with freedom and fidelity, justice and generosity, Yahweh makes a world whose dependable orders breathe with flexibility, willing for freedom to exist as the condition for worth to arise. In the world Yahweh has created, it is possible for a righteous, innocent person such as Job to suffer terribly. Likewise, in Yahweh's world it is possible for religiously zealous but mistaken people like Job's friends to wrong the innocent sufferer terribly through their false accusations, and yet not utterly forfeit their own place in creation. So badly do they misrepresent Yahweh's world that, true to their own theology, they merit Yahweh's wrath (47:2). Yet for Yahweh to deal with them as they deserve would be folly (42:8 reads, in Hebrew; "I will accept his prayer for you not to deal foolishly with you"). If they will ask Job to pray for them, and if Job will pray for them, Yahweh will forgive them as Job has. None of these actions are logically necessary; but their enactment arises under the aegis of a logic of creative felicity. That they are possible is part of the freedom and contingency of Yahweh's world, in which human actions co-operate with the divine actions toward re-establishing living order. Such a God, willing to entertain and even to suffer the uncertainties of such a world, appears already in the Prologue, where Yahweh staked the divine reputation, and the vindication of the divine image in humankind, upon how Job would answer the Satan's accusation.

To participate with God in a world whose life arises from generosity and issues in ordered freedom, leaves one open to undeserved suffering. That suffering arises as part of the price of participating in a world ordered by the power of persuasive address. That is what it means to be dust royally imaging Yahweh. The ancients were not wrong to conceive deity in royal terms. But they were wrong in supposing that royalty manifests itself in absolute invulnerability (or impassibility), and through overwhelming coercive power and aggressive control by means of a tight system, an airtight logic, of reward and punishment. The mystery of God's royalty is imaged in dust-and-ashes Job, suffering inexplicably, unshakably loyal to a God whom he does not as yet understand, and invited finally to share with God in the celebration and ordering of a world where the accepted risk of freedom is the creative ground of cosmic fellowship. It is not far from this to the astounding portrayal of Yahweh's "arm" in Isaiah 53 - the servant whose spoils of victory are won, not at the expense of enemy peoples, but on their behalf through unmerited suffering. If that portrayal in turn is later associated with the figure of Jesus, nevertheless, I believe, the turning point comes in Job. After him we can no longer think of creative power or creative wisdom in quite the same way. Nor, therefore, the human predicament.

ISAIAH'S CREATION THEOLOGY

BEN C. OLLENBURGER

Nowhere in the Bible does creation assume greater theological significance than in the book of Isaiah. The importance of creation in Isaiah 44-66 is evident, but it will be my contention that, while most chapters of Isaiah do not speak explicitly of creation, and thus do not provide evidence for an Isaianic theology *of* creation, an understanding of creation is important to what Isaiah *does* say about a variety of things. This essay will attempt to show something of the character of Isaiah's creation theology and along the way to suggest how this theology may bear on the way we think of creation, insofar as our thinking means to be biblical.[1]

I

The creation texts in the Hebrew Bible are concerned primarily with questions of order, with the nature of that order, its preservation and its quality, including its moral quality.[2] The Bible's way of articulating this concern is typically that of cosmogony, a description of the imposition of order frequently narrated in terms of God's mastery over the hostile forces of chaos. These forces are usually not destroyed but are disarmed and confined within limits that make life possible and make the world a dependable realm *for* life.[3] The world's dependability and its order, the order of creation, are interwoven in such a way that the latter precedes the former; life on the earth is dependable when the order of creation is maintained. Conversely, life becomes precarious and security is vulnerable when the order of creation comes under threat or is violated.[4] Thus, Psalm 33 describes creation in vv. 6-7 - God made the heavens and their host, bringing together the sea and putting the deeps in storehouses - in order to say in v. 18 that God will deliver the people from death and keep them alive in famine. On the other hand, Psalm 74 describes creation in vv. 12-17 - you shattered[5] the sea by your strength, you smashed the heads of the dragons, crushed the heads of Leviathan, and so forth - in order to complain in vv. 1-11 that creation has fallen into disorder, life and security have been compromised, and chaos now prevails.

[1]I will not argue about the dates of specific Isaianic texts. In this essay, I Isaiah will refer to Isaiah 1-39 and II Isaiah will refer to Isaiah 40-55. These are literary designations, not historical ones. The redactional history of Isaiah is, to say the least, up in the air. Within II Isaiah, attention will be given only to Isa. 40-45, and I will leave III Isaiah completely out of consideration (cf. 64:7; 65:17-18; 66:22).

[2]Bernhard W. Anderson, "Mythopoeic and Theological Dimensions of Biblical Creation Faith," *Creation in the Old Testament*, ed. B.W. Anderson; Issues in Religion and Theology, 6; (Philadelphia: Fortress, 1984), pp 1-24, esp. pp. 7-11, "Creation and Order."

[3]Rolf Knierim, "Cosmos and History in Israel's Theology," *HBT* 3 (1981), pp. 59-124, especially his section on "Creation as structured by cosmic space," pp. 74-80.

[4]On cosmogony in Israel and among its neighbors see F.M. Cross, *Canaanite Myth and Hebrew Epic* (Cambridge, MA: Harvard University Press, 1973); Lynn Claphan, "Mythopoeic Antecedents of the Biblical World-View and Their Transformation in Early Israelite Thought," *Magnalia Dei*, Wright *Festschrift*, ed. F.M. Cross, W.E. Lemke, P.D. Miller, Jr. (Garden City: Doubleday, 1976), pp. 108-19.

[5]Translating *pôrarta* as "you shattered." See Mitchell Dahood, *Psalms II:50-100,* Anchor Bible; (Garden City: Doubleday, 1968), p. 205.

Significantly, in Psalm 74 chaos prevails because God's enemies have ruined the sanctuary, they have roared in the midst of God's assembly (vv. 3-4), and God is urged, "Redeem . . . Mt. Zion where you have dwelled" (v. 2b).[6] This is significant for our purposes because it is in relation to Mt. Zion that Isaiah thinks of creation, because Zion is the dwelling place of the Lord of hosts (*yhwh seba'ôt,* Isa. 8:18). There is no description of the world's origins in I Isaiah, nor is there any report of a cosmogonic battle between God and the sea or Leviathan that issued in an ordered world. It is not creation as origin that interests Isaiah, but the *world as creation* - the world that is established and ordered by the God who is identified in Isaiah's inaugural vision as the King, the Lord of hosts, seen enthroned in the temple on Zion.[7] And it is on the basis of the world so ordered that Isaiah inveighs against the injustice practiced against the poor, the foolishness and arrogance of the wicked, and the faithlessness of Jerusalem's Kings, all of which seems for Isaiah to be emblematic of pervasive and culpable pride.

The relation between creation, so understood, and Isaiah's "ethics" has been treated recently by John Barton, who proposes that this relation can best be understood in terms of "natural law." Barton argues that Isaiah of Jerusalem "begins with a hierarchically ordered universe whose moral pattern ought to be apparent to all . . . whose reason is not hopelessly clouded, and derives all particular moral offenses from the one great sin, a disregard for natural law."[8] But what evidence is there that Isaiah assumed a hierarchically ordered universe with an obvious moral pattern? The only hierarchy Isaiah assumes is the one constantly proclaimed; namely, that Yhwh is exalted, and that Yhwh's exaltation entails the subordination of all and everyone else (Isa. 2:6-22).[9] There would seem to be nothing unnatural, or contrary to natural law (or the law of nations), in the measures taken by Ahaz and Hezekiah in defense against the impending threats of a Syro-Ephraimite coalition or an Assyrian aggressor, nor is it obvious why even someone whose reason is not hopelessly clouded should

[6]Martin Metzger, "Eigentumsdeklaration und Schöpfungsaussage," *"Wenn nicht jetzt, wann dann?"* Kraus, *Festschrift* ed.H.-G. Geyer, J.M. Schmidt, W. Schneider, M. Weinrich; (Neukirchen: Neukirchener Verlag, 1983), pp. 37-51. According to Metzger, Yhwh's ownership of the world expresses that Yhwh secured the existence and security of the world and defends it from sea floods that threaten it (p. 50). On Psalm 74, and other issues discussed in these paragraphs, see Trygve Mettinger, *The Dethronement of Sabaoth, ConBOT,* 18 (Lund: CWK Gleerup, 1982), pp. 67-72, esp. p. 70.

[7]"I saw the Lord seated on a high and exalted throne" (6:1); ". . . my eyes have seen the king, Yhwh of hosts" (6:5). On the epithet "Yhwh of hosts," see my *Zion, the City of the Great King, JSOTSS,* 41 (Sheffield: *JSOT,* 1987), pp. 37-38, and the literature cited there.

[8]John Barton, "Ethics in Isaiah of Jerusalem," *JTS* 32 (1981), p. 13. Barton draws on H.H. Schmid, but while Schmid does speak of the "order of the world" and "the order of creation" ("Creation, Righteousness, and Salvation: 'Creation Theology' as the Broad Horizon of Biblical Theology," *Creation in the Old Testament,* ed. B.W. Anderson; Issues in Religion and Theology 6; (Philadelphia: Fortress, 1984), p. 111, he does not equate this with something like a natural law transparent to all reasonable people, except perhaps with respect to wisdom literature. Rather, Schmid describes (as an example) the new basis for ethics created in Israel after "the traditional foundation of ethics in the world's immanent order had lost its binding force" ("Justice and Righteousness in the Ancient Near East and the Old Testament," unpublished paper given at Princeton Theological Seminary, 1983, p. 6). See further Schmid's comments on the "Nichtidentifizierbarkeit von heiler Welt und faktisher Wirklichkeit" in the Bible ("Altorientalische Welt in der alttestamentlichen Theologie," *Altorientalische Welt in der alttestamentlichen Theologie* (Zürich: Theologischer Verlag,1974), p. 163-64.

[9]See *Zion, the City of the Great King,* pp. 110-12. Isaiah also puts this "heirarchy" in terms of the contrasts between *'ēl* and *'ādām, rûah* and *bāśār* (31:3).

think it apparent from the natural order of things that Jerusalem's best defense against military aggression is to exercise faith in Yhwh by giving rest to the weary and engaging in quietness and trust (28:12; 30:15).[10] Isaiah's judgment against Jerusalem is grounded in the refusal of its leaders to hear the *tôrat yhwh*, the instruction of the Lord (30:9), and it is by repudiating this instruction that they incur guilt, and not by being dense to a morally ordered natural hierarchy.[11]

The order of creation which Isaiah assumes and shares with the Jerusalem cult tradition is the order established and maintained by the one who is sovereign over creation and exercises that sovereignty on, and on behalf of, Mt. Zion. Jonathan Paige Sisson has recently summarized this set of notions. He speaks of:

> *the formation of a cultic tradition that perceived YHWH in Zion-Jerusalem as the sole author and guarantor of the order of creation. He was the giver and sustainer of life, whose residence on Zion, the omphalic mountain, ensured the continuing fertility of nature. He was, at the same time, the lord of heaven and earth, the divine warrior, whose claim to dominion extended beyond the community in Jerusalem to the ends of the earth. Indeed, the universal dimension of his Kingship was grounded in the act of creation, which was understood as a single event in which the deity had subdued the forces of chaos and instituted a set world order, encompassing the natural, social, and political spheres of life.*[12]

This theological premise is stated with clarity in Isaiah 37:16 which, although most likely not from 8th Century Isaiah, is a precise interpretation of Isaiah's theology: "Yhwh of hosts, God of Israel, enthroned on the cherubim, you alone are God over all the kingdoms of the earth; you made the heavens and the earth."[13] Creation here serves to ground God's sovereignty over the nations which are subject to God's purposes. Hence, God can say to Sennacherib:

> *"Have you not heard? From long ago I have fashioned it (made it,* **'ôtô 'aśîtî** *from days of old I have formed it; now, I have brought it to pass . . . . Because you have raged against me, and your roaring has come to my ears, I will put my hook in your nose, my bit in your lips, and will turn you back on the way by which you came" (37:26, 29).*[14]

[10]J.J.M. Roberts, "Yahweh's Foundation in Zion (Isa. 28:16)," *JBL* 106 (1987), pp. 27-45.

[11]Anthony Battaglia shows that the premise of all natural law theories is "That human moral reason is trustworthy because it is in touch with reality," and he goes on to cite as one of natural law's basic assertions that "in the long run, some choices 'work' and others do not;" *(Toward a Reformulation of Natural Law* New York: Seabury, 1981, pp. 15, 16). Isaiah subscribed to the assertion, but not to the premise. For a criticism of the terms "natural law" and "orders of creation" in ralation to the Bible, see H.-J. Kraus, *Systematische Theologie im Kontext biblischer Geschichte und Eschatologie* (Neukirchen: Neukirchener Verlag, 1983), pp. 220-21.

[12]Jonathan Paige Sisson, "Jeremiah and the Jerusalem Conception of Peace," *JBL* 105 (1986), p. 430. As Sisson describes those whom Jeremiah opposed, those who held to the "Jerusalem Conception of Peace," Isaiah would have opposed them as vigorously as did Jeremiah.

[13]H. Wildberger, *Jesaja 28-39, BKAT* 10/3; (Neukirchen: Neukirchener Verlag, 1982), pp 1425-26. On the relation between Isaiah 36-39 and 2 Kings 18:30-20:19m see *ibid.*. 1368-74, with comprehensive bibliography.

[14]Reading *šā'ôn* (roar) for *ša'anan* (secure) in 37:29. *šā'ôn* accords better with the preceding *hitraggaz* and with the following *'ālāh bĕ'ōznāy*. For the textual discussion, see Wildberger, *Jesaja 28-29*, p. 1419.

The claim about creation in this text is a claim about sovereignty, and it is specifically a claim about the subject of that sovereignty, namely, the God enthroned on the cherubim, Yhwh of hosts. The work which God does in the exercise of this sovereignty is the work of the creator, whether the object of that work is the formation of the heavens and the earth, or the western campaign of Sennacherib. In either case, it is *creatio ex nihilo* in exactly the way Otto Weber summarizes the meaning of the term: "God bears the ground and the presuppositions of this creative activity in himself."[15] Because the God enthroned on Zion *is* the maker of the heavens and the earth, it is the ground and presuppositions of God's activity, and not those of either Hezekiah or Sennacherib, that determine Jerusalem's fate.

A similar claim is made in Isaiah 22. There, the measures taken to secure Jerusalem against a siege, while apparently quite sensible - the fortification of Jerusalem's wall and the construction of a water supply (22:8b-11) - are said to be in vain, because "You did not look to the one who fashioned it (made it, *'ôśēyhâ)*, nor did you consider the one who formed it *(yôṣērāh)* long ago.[16] Terms at home in the context of creation (*'āśâ* and *yāṣar*) are employed to make clear that Jerusalem's destiny, its security or its destruction, is determined by the "Lord God of hosts" of whom verses 12 and 14 go on to speak, rather than by the adequacy of Jerusalem's preparations or the strength of its enemy.

In 17:12-14, Isaiah also uses the vocabulary of creation in expressing confidence that the nations cannot finally succeed in destroying Zion.

> *Ah! the tumult of many peoples, they roar like the roaring of the seas. And the roaring of the peoples, they roar like the roaring of mighty waters. (The nations roar like the roaring of many waters.) But, (Yhwh) bellows at it, and it flees away, pursued like chaff on the mountain before the wind, or tumbleweeds before the storm. At evening there is terror; before morning it is no more. Such is the fate of those who rob us, the lot of those who plunder us.*[17]

Isaiah here speaks of the defense of Zion in exactly the same way that Psalm 104 speaks of creation, the founding *(ysd)* of the earth, with the waters fleeing when Yhwh bellows and his voice thunders (v. 7). Similarly, the mighty voice of Yhwh over the many waters in Psalm 29 concludes with Yhwh enthroned over the flood as king

[15]Otto Weber, *Foundations of Dogmatics*, ed. Darell L. Guder; (Grand Rapids: Eerdmans, 1981), Vol. 1, p. 501. H.-J. Kraus suggests that a better term would be "creatio *contra* nihilum," *Systematische Theologie,* p. 209, note 7.

[16]Wildberger, *Jesaja 13-27 (BKAT* 10/2, Neukirchen: Neukirchener Verlag, 1978), pp. 825-26 suggests that a spatial meaning for *mrhwq*, "from afar," citing Jer. 23:23 as evidence. That translation is possible, but in light of 37:26, where he translates *mrhwq* as "Von lange her," the temporal meaning suggests itself as more likely. The force of the term here and in 37:26, where it is joined with *mymy qdm,* seems to be that the present events do not mark a departure in God's purposes for Zion, and that they should not constitute a crisis of faith.

[17]17:13a, bracketed in the translation, may be an explanatory gloss on 12b, or it may preserve a variant reading of the line, in either case attesting the more typical *mayim rabbîm* in place of *mayim kabbîrîm.* The verb *g'r*, traditionaly translated "rebuke," is closer to "roar," as shown most recently by James M. Kennedy, "The Root G'R in the Light of Semantic Analysis," *JBL* 106 (1987), pp 47-64. I have translated it "bellow" in order to differentiate *g'r* from *s'h*.

forever. This language is no different from that of Psalm 46, in which the tumult of the threatening nations is repelled by Yhwh's voice, Zion remains a secure refuge, and the elimination of war is coincident with Yhwh's exaltation among the nations[18] - or from that of Psalm 76, in which the God whose abode is in Zion bellows and thereby disarms the warriors. The same view is expressed, finally, in Psalm 65, which begins by declaring that praise is owed to God in Zion, and continues by describing the God who "pacifies" the ends of the earth and the distant sea (v. 6),[19] who establishes the mountains by his strength, who silences the roaring of the seas, the roaring of their waves, *and* the tumult of the peoples (vv. 7-8). This description of God's action issues in reflection on the order of nature (vv. 10-14), which is also ascribed to the action of God, but the order of nature is secondary to the order God established in silencing the roaring seas, and that action is strictly parallel to silencing the tumult of the nations.

In all of these texts, including those from Isaiah, God acts as creator - *ex nihilo* - to repel the forces of chaos and thereby to establish order on the earth, an order centered on Mt. Zion, where God reigns as king and thereby acts as creator and defender.[20] The order which God creates and defends as king can be considered cosmically, naturally, or politically.[21] Isaiah's consideration is primarily political, focused on the order of the community gathered around Zion, and Zion as the central symbol of that order. Yhwh founded *(ysd)* Zion, and this is to be understood on the basis of near eastern analogies, as an act of creation. Patrick Miller points to an example in the Harab myth concerning the Mesopotamian city of Dunnu. He shows that:

> *the building of Dunnu . . . is a primordial act. It is not only that a city is built, but that it is an act of the creation. It takes place "in the beginning" (I. 1). The god and the goddess Harab and Ersetu build the city as a part of their creative activity. Indeed it is the second (or third) and concluding creation (ll. 1-6).*[22]

"Yhwh founded Zion, and in it the poor of his people find refuge" (Isa. 14:32). That promise, a fitting motto to the book of Isaiah, is the guarantee of Zion's security defended against every chaotic threat, whether in the form of international aggression,

[18]The combination of breaking weapons and putting an end to war, on the one hand, and God as ruler of the world, on the other, is apparently unique to the Bible, though each is attested independently elsewhere. See Nahum M. Waldman, "The Breaking of the Bow," *JQR* 69 (1978), pp. 82-88. On the relation of Isa. 17:12-14 to Ps. 46:4 and similar texts, see Wildberger, *Jesaja 13-27,* p. 673.

[19]I follow Dahood in treating *mbth* as a hiphil participle of *bth* (Dahood, *Psalms II:50-100*, p. 112). This would seem to fit the series of participles in vv. 7 and 8, and would better accord with the content of v. 8.

[20]O.H. Steck, *Friedensvorstellungen im alten Jerusalem* (Zürich: Theologischer Verlag, 1972), pp. 13-20, 31-32.

[21]See George S. Hendry's distinctions among cosmological, political and psychological parameters of theology, *Theology of Nature* (Philadelphia: Westminster, 1980), p. 22. This is a useful set of distinctions, although it tends to identify cosmic order too quickly with nature, thereby obscuring the close connection in the biblical texts between cosmic and political order.

[22]Patrick D. Miller, Jr., "Eridu, Dunnu, and Babel: A Study in Comparative Mythology," *Hebrew Annual Review* 9 (1985), p. 238. For other examples of the deity "founding" the temple/city, see Moshe Weinfeld, "Zion and Jerusalem as Religious and Political Capital: Ideology and Utopia," *The Poet and the Historian*, ed. R.E. Friedman (Chico: Scholars Press, 1983), pp. 75-115, esp. pp. 105-106.

domestic injustice, or royal efforts at military defense. All of these are, according to Isaiah, manifestations of pride - the opposite of faith or trust - and self-exaltation in the face of the Lord's own and exclusive exaltation.[23] Trust in the Lord is the only social or political strategy that Isaiah countenances in "the faithful city" (1:21), and it is the only realistic strategy for those who invoke the God who dwells on Zion and has founded it. As J.H.M. Roberts has put it, "The 'poor of his people' in 14:32 corresponds to the one who trusts' in 28:16 . . . ," in the face of an imminent threat.[24] The object of trust is, of course, the subject of creation.

II

It is appropriate at this point to ask whether, or the extent to which, our texts really speak of creation. The question is appropriate because some have denied that creation is really the subject matter of those cosmogonic texts that are, as I have claimed, the theological and linguistic environment of Isaiah. For example, Dennis McCarthy concluded from an investigation of the *Chaoskampf* motif in Israel's ancient poetry that:

> *Israel seems to have done something quite new in applying these 'creation' words to the description of its position as a saved and chosen people among peoples, all under God's guidance. What is 'created' is a social or political order. In Exodus 15 Israel is constituted a nation at Egypt's expense. In Deuteronomy 32 all nations have their place and their guides assigned to them; a whole social order is brought into being. We can and do call this sort of thing creative, but it is scarcely creation in any technical sense since it does not touch at all upon absolute beginnings of a whole world.*[25]

He concludes that "there is little or no effort to use all these ideas and images as consistent, independent wholes. Rather they are merely sources for means to describe what is important, and this is once again the proper ordering of the world of men."[26]

In the main, McCarthy is right. TheBible makes no effort to form independent wholes of these ideas and images of the *Chaoskampf* and its atendant motifs, or to organize them into a self-contained doctrine of creation which has no function and no importance beyond itself. McCarthy's statement requires correction only insofar as he limits creation's ordering to "the proper ordering of the world of men." The world of women is also ordered, of course, and the world of God's creation is not just a world

[23]I have treated these matters in chapter 4 of *Zion, the City of the Great King*.

[24]"Yahweh's Foundation in Zion," p. 39.

[25]"'Creation' Motifs in Ancient Hebrew Poetry," *Creation in the Old Testament*, p. 79. Arvid Kapelrud states it succinctly: "Creation is when something new which was not there before is produced," "Creation in the Ras Shamra Texts," *ST* 34 (1980), p. 3.

[26]"'Creation' motifs," p. 85. Cf. Carroll Stuhlmueller, *Creative Redemption in Deutero-Isaiah*, Analecta Biblica, 43; (Rome: Biblical Institute, 1970), pp 86-90; Otto Kaiser, *Die mythische Bedeutung des Meeres in Aegypten, Ugarit und Israel*, *BZAW*, 78; (Berlin: de Gruyter, 1959). Mettinger has argued to the contrary in *Dethronement of Sabaoth*, pp. 67-72.

of men and women.[27] But given that correction, we can agree with McCarthy's observations.

We must disagree, however, with the conclusion McCarthy draws from these observations. That is, we should not take the absence from the Bible of an independent and systematic cosmogony or *Chaoskampf,* or even the absence of creation in what he calls a technical sense, to determine the proper use of the term creation. It is easy to be misled here by attending narrowly to the history of discrete motifs or units of tradition and to literary or religious parallels, and then defining the content of a text on the basis of what can be isolated and compared and thus classified. Such practice is entirely legitimate and is to be respected in historical scholarship, but the useful isolation, comparison,and classification of traditions can obscure the character of some feature of a text within its own framework.[28] To demand of "creation" that it refer only to absolute beginnings, and to deny its appropriateness when creation language is used "in function of something else," is virtually to deny the possibility of speaking of creation with respect to the Bible.[29] A decision has to be made, in other words, how the definition and content of creation will be determined.

This issue bears directly on the theological interpretation of scripture, the overarching concern of this symposium. Without question, in the context of the theological interpretation of scripture priority in the definition and content of creation must be assigned to the biblical texts themselves and to the way in which they speak of creation.[30] Here it cannot be a matter of proposing to limit our definition to some prior convention, according to which creation may only refer to an absolute beginning, but of inquiring how and to what end the Bible actually speaks of creation, and more precisely, how and to what end the Bible speaks of God the creator. McCarthy's observation that in the Bible creation language is always used "in function of something else" is not, in that case, a prohibition against speaking of creation, but is a clue that to speak biblically of creation is also to speak of this something else. McCarthy is also correct in noting that creation language in the Bible - though he would not agree that it *is* creation language - is concerned preeminently with the claim that "Yahweh is king over all,"[31] and with the moral, political, and natural order that this

[27]Claus Westermann, *Genesis 1-11: A commentary* (Minneapolis: Augsburg, 1984), p. 176; James M. Gustafson, *Ethics From a Theocentric Perspective, Volume One: Theology and Ethics,* (Chicago: U. of Chicago, 1981), pp. 180-85.

[28]Compare H.-J. Kraus's criticisms of Westermann's Genesis commentary in this regard: "In his commentary on the first two chapters of Genesis, Westermann delved so deeply into isolated features of the text that he was unable to see and evaluate the internal and external relationships between creation and history;" *Theology of the Psalms* (Minneapolis: Augsburg, 1986), p. 64.

[29]The quote is from McCarthy, "
'Creation' motifs," p. 75. Of Genesis 2 - 11, he says that "from the special point of view we are adopting here, it is extremely difficult to speak of creation as being there in a meaningful sense" (p. 76). He implies similar difficulties with Genesis I (p. 75), because P's interest is in the proper cult (p. 75). Since his "special point of view" makes it difficult to speak biblically of creation "in a meaningful sense," the point of view requires modification.

[30]This point seems obvious; it is stressed by Karl Eberlein in his most useful work, *Gott der Schöpfer - Israels Gott,* Beiträge zur Erforschung des alten Testaments und des antiken Judentums, 5; (Frankfurt: Peter Lang, 1986), p. 94.

[31]"'Creation' Motifs," p. 83. Note also David Gunn's comment that creation "as it came to be understood in Israel" was in terms of "the great imposition of order by Yahweh;" "Deutero-Isaiah and the Flood," *JBL* 94 (1975), p. 496, note 13.

king brings about and governs. If that is the case, and I agree that it is, then to speak biblically of creation and thus of God the creator is necessarily to speak of God's dominion and of its order and purpose.

While priority in theological interpretation is given to the biblical texts themselves, they do not alone determine the definition and content of, in our case, creation. Theological interpretation is also situated within theology, and thus within a particular history of interpretation. Christian dogmatic theology is not the only available or appropriate secondary context within which to inquire of creation. Not all interpretation is theologically interested, and not all theology is Christian. But insofar as - in my case - theological interpretation of scripture wants to contribute critically and constructively to the church's talk of creation, as that talk is explicated and guarded in dogmatics, then this context, too, must be taken into account in determining the definition and content of creation. And in this context, creation cannot be limited to talk of origins, but must include the entire, diverse biblical witness to God the creator.[32]

This is not the place to review dogmatic exposition of the doctrine of creation, as if I could do so, but some brief comments are in order. First of all, I believe that Schleiermacher spoke with genuine insight in remarking that the differentiation and juxtaposition of creation and preservation - or creation and providence - is somewhat artificial and derivative. While we may not be persuaded by his argument for their unity in the feeling of absolute dependence, we can agree with his historical observation that the expansion of the creed to include *poiētēn ouranou kai gēs* prepared the way in the fourth century for just such singular concentration on creation in a technical sense, which treats the absolute beginnings of a whole world, that McCarthy now observes to be lacking in the Bible. In the earliest Christian creeds, *poiētēn ouranou kai gēs* is historically and theologically an expansion and specification of the basic confession of faith *eis theon patera pantokratora.*[33] The confession that God is creator here interprets and grounds the confession of God's universl dominion in a way that is not dissimilar from the relation between kingship and creation, or God's creation and God's ownership of the earth in the Bible.[34] It seems to me that this relation, as it is

[32]Weber, *Foundations of Dogmatics,* pp. 464-66; Karl Barth, *Church Dogmatics,* 3/1; (Edinburgh: T. & T. Clark, 1958), pp. 11-22.

[33]This expansion on the earlier form of the creed is accorded dogmatic importance by Schleiermacher, *The Christian Faith* (Edinburgh: T. & T. Clark, 1928), pp. 153-44. His comment that the intention of this expansion is that "nothing, no point of space and no point of time should be exempted from the Divine All-Sovereignty" seems to be theologically on target, even if historically simplistic. See also Hendry, *Theology of Nature,* p. 117. The growth of the creed can be seen in Philip Schaff, *The Creeds of Christendom,* Vol. 2, (New York: Harper & Brothers, 1877), pp. 47-51. The addition of a creator clause was meant to combat gnostic views and is for that and other reasons entirely legitimate, not least because it requires Christians to rely almost totally on the Hebrew Bible for the basis of what they say about the creator, and hence about creation - a requirement that would have troubled Schleiermacher, who suggested that we "utterly discard Old Testament proofs for specifically Christian doctrines . . ." (*Christian Faith,* p. 610, #132).

[34]On the relation between kingship and creation see my *Zion, the City of the Great King,* ch. 3. On creation and ownership of the earth see Metzger, "Eigentumsdeklaration und Schöpfungsaussage." Much recent theology, particularly that assigned the label "neo-orthodox," has insisted on the priority of the creed's second article to its first. I agree with Gustaf Wingren's criticisms of the rationale for this insistence: *Gospel and Law* (Edinburgh: Oliver and Boyd, 1961), pp. 11-12. The same criticisms would apply, logically, to an insistence on the priority of history (the "second article") over creation (the "first article") in the Bible. On this matter see especially Knierim, "Cosmos and History."

expressed in the creed, is particularly well preserved in the earlier Reformed dogmatics, which placed creation and providence in the closest possible relation, sometimes referring to providence, as did others, under the term *creatio continua.*[35] As Johannes Braun put it in the seventeenth century, "In respect of God the same action is creation *and* providence; God works all things by a single, most unified will, that they exist, remain in existence and work.'[36] And it is perhaps instructive that Calvin quotes Psalm 33, which narrates God's creation of the world, at the beginning of his treatment of providence, commenting that unless we speak also of providence, "we do not yet properly grasp what it means to say: 'God is creator.'[37] The reformed dogmaticians did not entirely escape the temptation to subsume providence under alien categories, but their fundamental understanding of providence as the action of God the creator, and ultimately both creation and providence "in function of" the glory of God, is true both to the confession of God's creation as the ground of God's dominion and to the function of creation language in the Bible, and especially in Isaiah.[38]

[35]Heinrich Heppe, *Reformed Dogmatics* (Grand Rapids: Baker, 1978), p. 251. Here, in quoting Ursin, the term is actually *creatio continuata,* which has a different connotation. The same term was used in Lutheran orthodoxy; Heinrich Schmid, *The Doctrinal Theology of the Evangelical Lutheran Church* (Philadelphia, United Lutheran Publication House, 1899). On *creatio continua* see Barth, *Church Dogmatics* 3/3m p. 60; Emil Brunner, *The Christian Doctrine of Creation and Redemption,* Dogmatics, vol. 2: (Philadelphia: Westminster, 1952), pp 149-50. The objections of Kraus *(Systematische Theologie,* p. 216) and Weber *(Foundations of Dogmatics,* pp. 503-505) to the notion of *creatio continua* are significant; however, if the term is used to appropriate the action of providence to God the creator, rather than referring to a perpetual creating which ignores the completion and goodness of creation from which God rested, I believe the objections can be met. Westermann also objects to *creatio continua* and commends in its place the notion of "blessing," which he equates with "the power of fertility," *Genesis 1 - 11,* p. 175. "Blessing" has the advantage of being a biblical term, but hardly comprehends what is at stake in the earlier discussions. Brevard Childs grasps the issues very well, without invoking the older vocabulary, *Old Testament Theology in a Canonical Context* (Philadelphia: Fortress, 1986), pp. 30-34. Jürgen Moltmann retrieves the earlier discussions, but in such a way that *creatio continua* follows on "God's evolutive immanence in the world," *God in Creation* (San Francisco: Harper & Row, 1985), p. 206.

[36]Quoted in Hepe, *Reformed Dogmatics,* p. 251. Hendry notes that the Bible does not marvel that things have been created, but "expresses wonder at the continuance of created things . . .; it marvels at God's providential sustenance of his creatures, but not at his creation of them (Ps. 75:3; Job 34:34)" (*Theology of Nature,* p. 185).

[37]*Institutes of the Christian Religion,* LCC, 20; ed. John T. McNeill; (Philadelphia: Westminster, 1960), 1.16.1, p. 197. Moltmann says with respect to "Creation in history," "God does not create anything new, but creates unremittingly what he once created by sustaining and preserving it". (*God in Creation*, p. 209). This *creatio continua* he distinguishes from *creatio nova,* citing Isa. 43:18-19, and he rightly notes that traditional talk of preservation was influenced by ancient cosmologies (pp. 208-209). However, by grounding *creatio nova* in the Bible, and *creatio continua* in "the knowledge of nature made accessible to us by evolutionary theories" (p. 206), he creates the bifurcation that he must overcome by substituting one cosmology for another.

[38]G.S. Hendry objects both to the Reformed tendency to collapse creation into providence, as in the Heidelberg Catechism, and to Luther's reduction of creation to "God created me" (*Theology of Nature,* p. 17). The Answer to Question 26 of the Heidelberg Catechism interprets belief in God the creator as the belief "Dass der ewige Vater unsers Herrn Jesu Christi . . . um seines Sohnes Christi willen mein Gott und Vater sei . . . ." (Philip Schaff, *The Creeds of Christendom* [vol. 3; New York: Harper & Brothers, 1877] p. 315. The problem is less a reduction of creation to providence than a Christological and existential reduction of creation. The Reformed tendency to move from creation to providence is, so long as it does not amount to a total collapse, commensurate with the Bible's own tendency, as Hendry admits (p. 185) and as McCarthy has argued from a completely different angle. Cf. also Weber, *Foundations of Dogmatics,* p. 468. The Mennonite Dortrecht Confession of 1632, treats creation and providence in a paragraph separate from and prior to a paragraph on the creation of humankind, thereby avoiding Luther's

These considerations do not determine whether the *Chaoskampf* at Ugarit was a cosmogony, or whether the cosmogonic texts in the Bible are about the origin of the world. They do suggest, however, that in the context of theological interpretation of scripture we may speak of creation in a broader sense, and even that we must do so. In his *Dogmatik,* Regin Prenter claims at the outset of his exposition of "The God of Creation" that "The biblical witness understands creation . . . as God's battle against all destructive powers . . . ."[39] I believe that his claim is correct.

III

I have argued that, although rarely explicit, creation is theologically implicit in I Isaiah. The allusions to creation are clearest in those texts whose central concern is the security of Zion and, of course, in 37:16, where it is brought into the foreground. Isaiah's words against the injustice rampant in Jerusalem, or the faithlessness of Judah's kings, assume God's relation to Judah and Jerusalem whose actions are in defiance of God's sovereign presence. It is already the logic of these texts, however, that not only Israel but the other nations as well are subject to God's disposition, because these nations, specifically Assyria (10:5-19), are to be the instruments of God's judgment against Jerusalem. This logic virtually compels Isaiah in the direction of creation (as in 10:15, "Will the axe vaunt itself over the one who cuts with it . . .?") because it is the language of creation that is best suited to express the universality and irresistibility of God's dominion. Of course, the language of creation was already available to Isaiah, as I am assuming, from the Zion tradition itself, whose principal texts - Psalms 46, 48, 76 - use that language to speak of God's defense of Zion and, hence, the order which Zion symbolizes. It is not surprising, then, that Isaiah comes closest to explicit talk of creation when speaking of the security of Zion against the threats of all the nations and peoples, and then speaks explicitly of creation in the mouth of Hezekiah, who prays for the defense of Jerusalem against Sennacherib, who has done God's work with greater enthusiasm than God intended.[40]

The same logic that brings I Isaiah into theological proximity with creation drives II Isaiah to sustained use of it, but the theological issues involved are different in the two cases. I Isaiah had to hold together the royal administration of Judah and Jerusalem, on the one hand, and the kingship of Yhwh on Zion, on the other. That is to say, Isaiah had to deal theologically with the relation between Judah's Kings, whose responsibility it was to order and defend the political community gathered

existential reduction, and places creation of the world and providence in separate clauses under the principal confession that "God is the Creator of all things," thereby giving providence its proper relation to creation without collapsing the two. The text is in Thielman J. van Braght, *Martyrs Mirror* (Scottdale, PA: Herald, 1985) 39. Schaff does not include Dortrecht among christendom's creeds, which mention the Anabaptists only to place them under a *Damnatus*.

[39] *Schöpfung und Erlösung: Dogmatik* (Göttingen: Vandenhoeck & Ruprecht, 1960), p. 180.

[40] This should not be understood as if Isaiah was driven to creation out of some psychological need, or as if the notion of creation dawned on Isaiah or on Israel as a result of some experience. Repeated claims along the lines of "Belief in God as the creator of all things in the beginning was . . . derived from experience of him in the history of the people" (Norman Young, *Creator, Creation and Faith*, [Philadelphia: Westminster, 1976] p. 35). are both historically and theologically dubious.

around Zion, and Yhwh the king enthroned on Zion. The difficulty posed by that theological problem is evident in the varied evaluations of Isaiah's solution, which range from those who consider him a perceptive political realist to those who call him a theological pacifist and even group him with the *Schwärmer*.[41] II Isaiah, on the other hand, had the problem of holding together the reality that imperial rule was in the hands of foreigners and the confession that Israel's God was still king. His doctrine of creation, if you will permit the term, served to hold these things together by encompassing both the international conquests of Cyrus and the restoration of Israel to Zion.[42] It is likely, in fact, that only a rigorous and thoroughly consistent thinking of *God as creator* was capable of holding together these otherwise incompatible beliefs. We will follow that thinking in Isaiah 40-45.

The premises and goals of II Isaiah are set immediately in Isa. 40:12-31. The argument of this text moves in three major stages, beginning with a series of rhetorical questions about the creator (40:12-17) and concluding with an exhortation to faithful waiting (40:27-31) that assumes the undeniable truth of what has gone before. The first stage focuses on a set of inferences (40:15-17) derived from the threefold claim, implicit in the rhetorical questions, that the world has been ordered by no one but Yhwh, that no one has the measure of Yhwh's spirit or gives Yhwh counsel in creation,[43] and that no one instructed Yhwh in justice, knowledge, or understanding. The inferences immediately drawn (40:15-16) are that the nations are a drop in the bucket and dust on the scales, the isles are like powder, and even Lebanon is insufficient for fuel and its animals for sacrifice. Summarizing the first stage of the argument is the concluding inference (40:17) that all the nations are nothing in relation to the creator. They are considered less than nothing; indeed, they are *tohû*.

The first stage of the argument, then, establishes that the creator acts to order the world without need or benefit of counsel and has disposition over the nations, who are themselves too insubstantial to resist the creator's purposes. The claims about the creator, and the inferences derived from those claims, are designed not only to attribute creation to God, though they certainly do that, but especially to render the nations insignificant in relation to the justice, knowledge, and understanding of the creator, whose own counsel determines the order of creation. No one could have thought that the nations were responsible for creation; the point is rather that the nations themselves, as (so to speak) uncreated *tohû*, are subject to the ordering power of the creator.

The second and third stages of the argument follow a parallel structure. Both are introduced with a question about comparability: "To whom, then, will you compare

[41]Cf. C.A. Keller, "Das quietistische Element in der Botschaft des Jesajas," *TZ* 11 (1955), p. 89.

[42]Gerhard von Rad says something similar about II Isaiah: "The reason for this sudden incorporation of the creation tradition into the prophet's preaching is to be found in the new situation in which Israel was placed. Abruptly confronted with the Babylonians and with the power of so great an empire, appeals to Jahweh and his power need to range more widely . . . ." (*Old Testament Theology* [vol. 2: Edinburgh: Oliver & Boyd, 1965], p. 241). I would not see this incorporation as sudden.

[43]R.P. Merendino argues that in v. 13, the subject of *ywdy'* is Yhwh and the object suffix has *'yš 'stw* as its antecedent; he translates "ja (wer ist) der Mann, dem er seinen Ratschuss Kundgäbe?" (*Der Erste und Der Letzte* [SVT, 31; Leiden: E.J. Brill, 1981], pp. 74, 76). That requires a change in subjects between v. 13b and v. 14. It seems more consistent to take *'yš 'stw* as the subject of the verb in v. 13b, with Yhwh as the antecedent of the object suffix.

God *('ēl)?*" (40:18), and "To whom, then, will you compare me?" (40:25); and both draw conclusions from these introductory, rhetorical questions. The second stage (40:18-24), which assumes and expands upon the first, begins by answering the question of comparability in a purely negative way: an idol cannot be compared to God because it is merely the product of laborious human artifice (40:20).[44] Following this summary dismissal of idols, 40:21-23 resumes the rhetorical questions, conveying the implicit claim that Israel has heard and has known, because it has been told from the beginning, and should thus understand the foundations of the earth (40:21).[45] The content of this knowledge and understanding is then spelled out in a series of participles whose subject is the creator, "enthroned above the vault of the earth . . .,"[46] and stretching out the heavens (40:22). This sequence of participles is continued and concluded in striking fashion with the claim that the creator reduces princes to nothing and has made the rulers of the earth *tohû* (40:23), a claim that is then elaborated in language very similar to that of 40:6-7; the rulers of the earth are like the withering grass to which II Isaiah's audience is compared at the outset (40:24).

In both the first and second stages of the argument, then, the language of creation is used to make a negative claim about the nations and their rulers: both are *tohû,* chaos, of no consequence or substance in the face of the creator. The idol passage in 40:18-20 intervenes in almost transitional fashion, but it says that even an idol is established *(hakîn);* it will not quaver *(lo' yamût).* If an idol is not comparable to God, how much less so the nations and their rulers?

The second stage of the argument thus reaches an intermediate, negative conclusion; the conclusion is made definite and positive in the third stage (40:25-31), which also makes explicit for the first time in the entire chapter that the creator is Yhwh.[47] Here the question of comparability (40:25), posed in the first person, issues in the claim that the one who created the heavens is the one who commands heaven's host through great power and might (40:26). This can be compared with the structural parallel in 40:19-20: whereas an idol is created through human skill and effort but is itself powerless, the creator is the one who commands heaven's host in power.[48] The

[44]The translation of 40:19b-20 poses serious difficulties to which no satisfactory solution has been proposed. See Merendino, *Der Erste und der Letzte,* pp. 87-88; C.R. North, *The Second Isaiah* (Oxford: Clarendon, 1964), pp. 82-83.

[45]"Foundations" *(môsědôt)* is usually emended to something like "from the foundation of" *(mîsudat, BHS)*, but there is no support for the reading and it is not clear what it might mean that Israel "has understood from the foundation of the earth." It is perhaps best to leave the text as it is; Israel should have understood the foundations of the earth on the basis of what has been declared to it from the beginning; for example, that God owns the earth by virtue of having founded it (Ps. 24:1-2). The foundations of the earth are mentioned in connection with knowledge and understanding in Ps. 82:5.

[46]So translated by Richard J. Clifford, *Fair Spoken and Persuading: An Interpretation of Second Isaiah*, (New York: Paulist, 1984), p. 78.

[47]The only prior mention of Yhwh is in the construct *rûah yhwh* of 40:13. The same expression, with a different meaning, occurs in 40:7. Other than these expressions, Yhwh is mentioned prior to 40;28 only in 40:5, in the phrase, "for the mouth of Yahweh has spoken," which is typical in Isaiah (cf. 1:20: 9:1: 24:3; and elsewhere).

[48]40:18-20, or some portion of it, is often considered an interpolation. For the evidence and a partial bibliographic survey, see Merendino, *Der Erste und Der Letzte,* pp. 90-92. Its fit within the structure of the passage tells in its favor, however, either as original to the text or as part of a structurally sensitive redaction. The point of this and other idol passages in II Isaiah is not simply to polemicize against idol worship; it is to contrast the power active on behalf of Israel and Zion with the powerlessness of those nations, rulers, and gods whom Israel fears (41:5-10).

third stage also parallels the second in following the question of comparability with another: "Do you not know? Have you not heard?" (40:21, 28a). The question in 40:28a is preceded by a quotation that is the occasion for the entire argument: Israel's complaint that it is beyond the scope of Yhwh's vision; its case eludes God (40:27). Having thereby centered the argument directly on Israel, the third stage does not pose the further rhetorical question of 40:21, "Has it not been declared to you?" Rather, it offers the content of that declaration: "The everlasting God is Yhwh, the creator of the ends of the earth" (40:28b). In this way it is made clear at the climactic stage of the argument that II Isaiah's emphasis on God the creator is meant to counter a specific objection, which is quoted in 40:27. Furthermore, while both the first and second stages of the argument moved from rhetorical questions to the conclusion that the instruments of international political order, the nations and rulers respectively, are insubstantial and even chaos, the third stage of the argument concludes with a promise to Israel (40:28c-31). The creator who commands the heavenly host in extreme power does not faint or grow weary, and those who wait on the God who is creator will not faint or grow weary, but will renew their power. By inference, then - and it is an inference that II Isaiah would want us to draw - the weary people who receive this message are stronger than the nations and kings whose gods are idols, because the creator of heaven and earth is Israel's God.

The argument in 40:12-31 sets out the theological basis on which II Isaiah will make the controversial claim that Cyrus, the Persian conqueror of Babylon, was acting on God's initiative as God's agent.[49] That claim is not stated baldly until the end of ch. 44, but is alluded to in 41:2-4, 25-29. These allusions occur within the context of a theme that is adumbrated in 40:18-20 and then dominates chs. 41 - 44: the inability of the gods and their images to declare or to make known or to announce beforehand what is to take place, from which it is concluded that these gods are not the power behind the unexpected event of Cyrus, nor are their patron nations and rulers. That power belongs alone to the creator, and because the creator is Israel's God, Israel need not fear as the nations do whose only security is their idol (41:1-4, 5-7, 8-16).[50] Within this framework it is also made clear that Israel is Yhwh's servant (41:9) - that both Cyrus and Israel are and remain, in quite different respects, the agents of Yhwh[51] - and that the international event under discussion is precisely on behalf of Israel. This is to be demonstrated through a transformation of nature (41:17-20), which will provide further and irrefutable evidence that this event is by the hand of Yhwh, and that Yhwh has "created it" *(bĕrāʾāh,* 41:20).

This discussion is continued through 44:8, which concludes once again that Israel need not fear, because the only God has been and continues to be the subject

[49]This is not an argument from creation, of course; it depends upon what has been declared to Israel from the beginning (40:21). This and other features of II Isaiah's talk of creation raise a question about the sources of that talk, and particularly about whether II Isaiah was drawing on "official" theological sources, on elements of exilic popular religion or "subreligion," or fashioning a radically new conception of creation. These points are debated by Eberlein (*Gott der Schöpfer,* pp. 83-93, with bibliography) but cannot be taken up here.

[50]On these verses see E.W. Conrad, *Fear Not Warrior* BJS, 75; (Chico, CA: Scholars Press, 1985), pp. 82-85.

[51]I am indebted to the work of my colleague, Millard C. Lind, "Monotheism, Power, and Justice: A Study in Isaiah 40-55," *CBQ* 46 (1984), pp. 432-46.

of declarations that ground the present in the actions of Israel's king and creator (43:15). The intervening material in chs. 42 and 43 introduces yet another derivative theme: since it has been declared to Israel that its God is the creator (40:28) and that the Cyrus event is the action of the creator, Israel is God's witness. Israel's commission as Yhwh's servant in 42:1-4 is grounded ultimately in God as creator of the world (42:5), and it is to the servant that the "new things" of which II Isaiah speaks at such length have been declared (42:9). Ironically, the servant is itself deaf and blind (42:19), and is in that respect like the fabricated idols.[52] But while the idols are formed by artisans to whom they owe their existence and their stability, Israel is formed by the creator (43:1). Israel's past (42:23-25) and its future (43:5-7) are united in the domination of the creator for whom it was formed (43:15, 21). Exile is not testimony to any other domination, nor are the events transpiring within exile; on the basis of what has been declared to it, Israel is to bear witness to the continuity of its past and its future in the action and word of God the creator, whose dominion is universal.[53] International politics is not excluded from that dominion, nor is nature, and neither is Israel. All three of these are together in terms of creation (41:20; 43:19).

Idols are finally reduced to an absurdity in 44:9-20, and the contrast is once again drawn between idols crafted by artisans and Israel formed by God, in 44:21-22. These verses introduce a lengthy unit that concludes in 45:22-25, and draws together the implications of what was first set out in 40:12-31. First, 44:24-28, which consists of a series of participles describing God's action, draws from the premise that God alone is the creator the conclusion that diviners and sages are confuted (just as nations and rulers are *tohû,* 40:17, 23); however, it takes a new turn by linking creation to God's intention to rebuild Jerusalem and Judah's cities to lay the foundation of the temple (44:26, 28b). Further, the instrument of these actions will be Cyrus, now named explicitly, and God's address to Cyrus is set in strict parallelism with God's address to the deep (*ṣûlâ*) and to the rivers (44:27, 28a). The restoration of Jerusalem, the site of God's dwelling, is an act of creation,[54] performed on behalf of *(lĕma'an)* Israel (45:4) in order that *(lĕma'an)* the knowledge that only Yhwh is God may be universal (45:6). Second, 45:9-13 counters the understandable objection to the appointment of a foreign king to be God's anointed shepherd and Jerusalem's temple builder by appealing once more to God the creator of heaven and earth and Israel's maker, in language reminiscent of 10:15.[55]

[52]Cf. 41:1, 21-24, and 43:8-10. Those texts which invite either the gods or Israel to debate, or which charge Israel with failing to bear witness, are framed by God's promises to transform nature on Israel's behalf (41:17-20; 42:14-17; 43:19-20; 44:3-5), and ultimately to God's own glory (41:20; 43:21). In 55:12-13, the transformation of nature follows on a contrast between the thoughts and ways of God and Israel, introduced by an appeal to convert (55:6-11).

[53]The continuity of Israel is stressed especially by Lind, "Monotheism, Power, and Justice."

[54]Cf. also Ps. 74:15, where God dries up the rivers in creation.

[55]Each of these sections is introduced by a hymn (44:23; 45:8), the first one praising what Yhwh has done, the second what Yhwh has created. On the hymns in II Isaiah see T.N.D. Mettinger, *A Farewell to the Servant Songs* (Lund: CWK Gleerup, 1983), pp. 23-28; Andrew Wilson, *The Nations in Deutero-Isaiah,* Ancient Near Eastern Texts and Studies, 1; (Lewiston, NY: Edwin Mellen, 1986), pp. 60-61. Clifford has drawn appropriate attention both to the importance of I Isaiah for understanding II Isaiah, and to the connections between Isaiah 10 and 45 (*Fair Spoken and Persuading,* esp. pp. 117-18). Regarding 45:9 and 10:15, he comments on the "narrow-minded arrogance of Israel" in refusing "to let Yahweh be the God who does something new" (p. 121). It seems excessive to characterize as "narrow-minded arrogance"

This coordinated focus on both cosmic creation and the restoration of Jerusalem is continued and expanded in 45:14-19, where restoration becomes exaltation. In 45:14 Zion/Jerusalem is addressed in language typical of the sovereignty rhetoric of the ancient near east and told that the nations will come to her in forced pilgrimage bearing tribute.[56] Significantly, the exaltation of Zion is tied to the universal recognition of Yhwh's own sovereignty (45:14b, 22-25), and both are grounded in the purposes of the creator (45:18-19). Stated negatively, God neither created the earth *tohû*, nor instructed Israel, "seek me in *tohû*." Rather, God formed the earth to be habitable *(lěšebet)* and speaks with justice and equity. The present chaos is overcome and the order of creation restored with the exaltation of Zion, where Yhwh is to be sought and where the nations come in pilgrimage to bow their knee to Yhwh who alone has declared it and alone has created it.

IV

The remaining chapters of II Isaiah continue the emphasis on Zion's exaltation introduced in ch. 45, though the references to creation are fewer.[57] In these chapters the exaltation of Zion and of Yhwh is coupled to the humiliation of Babylon and its gods (chs. 46, 47), and this drama of humiliation and exaltation is personified in the servant (49:4, 7; 50:6, 8; 52:13; 53:3).[58]

It is particularly in speaking of Zion that II Isaiah continues the tradition of I Isaiah, not only to the extent that Zion is prominent in both portions of the book, but particularly in the way that God's sovereignty is exercised in relation to Zion. In I Isaiah, God is at the same time the guarantor of Zion's security and the agent of Jerusalem's judgment, in each case on behalf of the order appropriate to God's dwelling place. As Bernhard Anderson has put it, "In Isaiah's message the conflict between the cosmic order and the mundane sphere, which evokes the judgment of God, is basically the clash between the righteousness that belongs to the cosmic realm and the gross injustice that prevails in human society."[59] In II Isaiah's terms, the restoration of cosmic order is referred explicitly and consistently to God the creator, and the restoration of cosmic order entails the restoration of Zion/Jerusalem.

Israel's assumed protest against the declaration that a Persian monarch, and not a son of David or even an Israelite, should be the instrument of their restoration and the builder of God's temple. It is one thing to say that an Assyrian is the instrument of God's judgment, and quite another to say that a Persian is Yhwh's *mašîaḥ*. This is a genuine stumbling block; it confutes wisdom.

[56]This language is typically addressed to kings, as in Psalm 72. See Pierre Grelot, "Un parallele Babylonien d'Isaie 60 et du Psaume 72," *VT* 7 (1957), pp. 319-21. The Babylonian parallel Grelot cites is published in C.J. Gadd, "Inscribed Barrel Cylinder of Marduk-Apla-Iddina 11," *Iraq* 15 (1953), pp. 123-34. The theme in II Isaiah is treated by Andrew Wilson, *The nations in Deutero-Isaiah*, pp. 232-44. The pilgrimage to Zion is described more elaborately in 49:22-23, and especially in 60:4-7. Not everyone has agreed that Zion is being addressed in 45:14, despite the feminine singular pronouns. For the range of opinions see H.-J. Hermisson, *Deuterojesaja* BKAT 117; (Neukirchen: Neukirchener Verlag, 1987), pp. 33-34. D.D.W. Watts assumes without comment that Cyrus is addressed, ignoring the feminine context (*Isaiah 34-66,* Word Biblical Commentary; [Waco, TX: Word, 1987], pp. 158-63).

[57]References to creation are in 48:7 (new events are created; cf. 41:20); 48:13; 51:9-11, 13, 16. See also 46:11 (analogous to 22:11b; 37:26); 49:5 (the servant was formed in the womb); 54:5 (Zion's maker is its husband [or builder]).

[58]I take the servant to personify or symbolize Israel; Zion can symbolize the community as well (51:16b).

[59]"The Holy One of Israel," forthcoming in the *Festschrift*, pp. 11-12. I am grateful to Professor Anderson for a copy of his paper.

In Christian theology, the doctrine of creation has been used especially as a way of mediating the particularity of Israel's or the church's faith and a consideration of the world on and in its own terms. It has provided theological grounds for the formulation of natural law, or for the justification of natural law previously formulated;[60] it has furnished the warrant for a mediation between theology and science and, when creation has been understood primarily as nature, furnished the warrant for natural theology;[61] it has been the theological justification of institutions, particularly the state, and of the norms by which they are guided.[62] The wisdom literature offers biblical precedent for such mediation, as well as for its limits. However, Isaiah's creation theology is radically different.

According to Isaiah, the order of creation is precisely counter to that which Israel is able to discern apart from God's declaration. It is an order of which Isaiah's various audiences must be persuaded against everything that their own wisdom and experience can discern. II Isaiah does not appeal to creation because there is in the world of nature or its history some basis for hope and understanding, but because God the creator is, by virtue of being the creator, able reliably to declare that the unprecedented events of Israel's experience are God's own acts, and thus God's own creation. II Isaiah takes considerable care in saying that Israel did not know and could not have known beforehand, on any basis whatever, that these events are on its behalf. This knowledge is strictly dependent upon God's own declartion (48:6-8; 55:6-11). Nature is not in these texts the context and source of knowledge; rather, it points to the creator who declares what is to be known, and it does so in being transformed by the creator (41:17-20).

Above, I endorsed the suggestion that creation and providence be considered together, following an earlier dogmatic tradition. They are certainly held together in Isaiah, and especially in II Isaiah, but in a way that modifies traditional protestant views. In the dogmatic tradition, creation and providence can be considered in the abstract, and even though the dogmaticians could speak of special as well as of general providence, and of extraordinary as well as ordinary providence, the discussion remains abstract in its typography and ontology of divine acts.[63] In Isaiah, creation and providence are made concrete in relation to Israel, and it is quite impossible for Isaiah to speak of God's plan or God's defeat of chaos or God's preservation and restoration of cosmic order without speaking of Zion and of Israel. In this respect, Isaiah knows of no special providence alongside a general one, and no extraordinary providence alongside an ordinary one; rather, the providential action of God the creator is on behalf of and with respect to Israel and Zion in the presence of the startled nations and witnessed by nature. Isaiah is bound to speak in this way because the God of whom Isaiah speaks as creator is never other than Israel's God, Yhwh. But at the same time, the creator's action in redeeming Israel and restoring Zion is genuinely the restoration and the recreation of cosmic order in which the nations share as well. The

[60]Charles E.Curran, "Paul Ramsey and Traditional Roman Catholic Natural Law Theory," *Love and Society: Essays in the Ethics of Paul Ramsey,* JRE Studies, 1; ed. J.T. Johnson, D.H. Smith (Missoula: Scholars Press, 1974), [[/ 47-65.

[61]Most recently, John C. Polkinghorne, "Creation and the Structure of the Physical World," *Theology Today* 44 (1987), pp. 53-68.

[62]Emil Brunner, *The Divine Imperative* (Philadelphia: Westminster, 1947).

[63]Schmidt, *Doctrinal Theology,* pp. 190-93.

earth is genuinely ordered and pacified in this action of the creator on behalf of Israel, but this ordering does not occur apart from the witness of the servant - or apart from the Torah that proceeds from Zion, where God adjudicates international disputes (Isa. 2:2-4). Even the preservation of heaven and earth is subordinate to God's action toward Israel, to God's covenant of peace with Zion (51:16; 54:10).[64] But in that covenant of peace with Zion, heaven and earth are genuinely preserved. Creation and providence form a unity, but not a unity that excludes or exists apart from covenant.[65]

Isaiah's creation theology comports ill with a theology of creation from which are derived "orders of creation," embodied in institutions of power and domination.[66] Somewhat surprisingly, perhaps, it was Rudolf Bultmann who saw with special clarity, and stated with boldness in the 1930's, that creation theology is first of all *critical,* and precisely of those institutions that claim authority from the orders of creation.[67] In I Isaiah, even Judah's kings and princes are instruments of chaos, overcome by the king enthroned on Zion. As the instrument of God the creator, Cyrus the king is an instrument in service of the world's reordering, but this service is performed on behalf of Jerusalem and the temple, and thus on behalf of God; apart from the purposes of God the creator, nations and rulers are mere chaos. And II Isaiah makes clear that history within the order of creation is borne by the servant, not by Cyrus. This, too, is astonishing, and in that respect bears more certain and more articulate witness to God the creator than does all the glorious harmony of nature.

An appropriation of Isaiah's creation theology is difficult in these days, and in any day after the holocaust. Any doctrine of creation tied so thoroughly to God's sovereignty as is Isaiah's, and as is the dogmatic tradition's, will and must provoke serious questions. One of those questions is raised by Moltmann, who says that such a doctrine of creation has led the human being to confront the world as its ruler:

> *For it was only through his rule over the earth that he could correspond to his God, the Lord of the world. God is the creator, Lord and owner of the world; and in the same way the human being had to endeavour to become the lord and owner of the earth.*[68]

No understanding of God the creator, Lord, and owner of the world, could be more diametrically opposed to Isaiah's than one in which humankind sought to "correspond" to God in such a fashion.

[64]On the "covenant of peace," see the illuminating essay by Bernard F. Batto, "The Covenant of Peace: A Neglected Ancient Near Eastern Motif," *CBQ* 49 (1987), pp. 187-211.

[65]The Reformed linked creation and providence to covenant by speaking first of God's *operationes internae,* the eternal decree, and then of the *operationes externae,* of which creation and providence are the *opus naturae* and covenant is the *opus gratiae* (Heppe, *Reformed Dogmatics,* p. 190). There is much to be said in favor of this, though its distinction between nature and grace poses many of the same problems as Gerhard von Rad's talk of II Isaiah's creation theology as a "'soteriological' conception of creation" (*Old Testament Theology,* vol. 2, p. 240).

[66]See the comments of Paul Hanson, *The People Called* (San Francisco: Harper & Row, 1986), pp. 117-20.

[67]"The Task of Theology in the Present," and "Faith in God the Creator," *Existence and Faith,* ed. Schubert M. Ogden; (Cleveland: World Publishing, 1960), pp. 158-65, 171-82.

[68]*God in Creation,* p. 1.

In 1934, Bultmann said that we must accept faith in God the creator "as the critical principle for dealing with the concrete questions of our time."[69] And that was a time in which there was no lack of attention to nature as a source for the knowledge of God, or to the history of nature reaching its climax and glory in a king and his kingdom. As a critical principle, creation is a dangerous memory for kings and rulers, and so for us. For the oppressed of the earth (Ps. 76:13; Isa. 14:32), it is a basis for hope.

69"Faith in God the Creator," pp. 172-73. Actually, Bultmann speaks here of "faith in creation," but I take the title of the article to reflect more accurately his intention.

PAUL'S USE OF CREATION THEMES: A TEST OF ROMANS 1-8

STEVE KRAFTCHICK

I. INTRODUCTION

There is a correct impulse in asking if Paul can provide some help for dealing with our present sense that human life and the world of nature are on the brink of catastrophe. There is no need to pretend profundity about assessing the present times. One need look no further than the local elementary schools to discern today's prophets for here are children who realize that the world may end before they return home. Children who ask their elders what will happen if we keep ignoring the stress placed on the environment. They are cognizant of utter destruction and they are frightened. The fear does not recede with age - it grows deeper. The fear deepens and our only relief is the eventual numbness it brings.

Now, the realization that we may have gone too far, that technology may not save us, that the combination of pollution, gluttonous use of resources, and nuclear proliferation, presents a scenario more real than imagined. And, like all who have preceded us, we turn to those people and texts which have provided guidance in the past when chaos threatened. Thus, it is entirely appropriate to look to Paul for help here, to hope for an authoritative word, to ask for understanding which can reveal the next course to take.

It is appropriate, but it is not clear that it will be forthcoming. Not that Paul does not want to talk; he does, but, he may be unable to. Before we can ask for Paul's word we must attend to more primary questions. Does Paul actually speak about the creation, that is, our world as a palpable and real environment? And if he does, can Paul speak for creation in the face of a crisis like ours? The two questions are of course interrelated,but they are not identical, for the first is primarily historical and the second interpretive. Paul may have been concerned with his world and so addressed the issue of living in it, but it is not clear that what he had to say is meaningful or appropriate for us or for our world.

The first question is easily answered--to some extent--Paul does speak about the creation. But he does so sparingly and for the most part indirectly. A quick scan of his letters suggests that, if creation played a role at all, it was only a minor one. The term *ktisis/ktizo* itself is only used eleven times in the accepted authentic letters. Romans uses the verb once (1:25) and the noun seven times, with the majority of these falling in chapter 8. The verb is used once more in I Cor. 11:9 and the noun twice more, once in II Cor.5:17 and again in Gal.6:15. The last two instances refer to the *kainē ktisis* and while this term is clearly dependent on the idea of creation, the remarks Paul makes about it are derived by analogy rather than directly stated. Further, both comments are used in polemic texts suggesting that one cannot begin with these statements but must end with them. Before we can understand what Paul meant about the "new creation" we must first understand the situations he was addressing and his understanding of the "old creation."

Paul employs the term "creation" in a number of ways. There is a doctrinal use, that is, Paul believes in God as the Creator of the cosmos. He also uses it as a reference to the stories of Genesis which were authoritative for him and it is used to refer to the spheres of existence in which he finds himself. In this last sense he understands it to include society (including Jews and Gentiles as part of his mission efforts), environment, and those realms which he cannot see but knows to be real.

Paul also refers to the creation when the term itself is absent, using it to support his ethical and theological arguments. For example, the concept of created order is used thematically in I Cor. 11:9 where he adduces Gen. 1:27 as an illustration to make his point about head coverings for woman, but his major thrust is not to discuss the idea that God has created the male and female so much as it is to argue that there is a proper order for Christian community. Here his argument is grounded in the idea that church order must be commensurate with the created order, for as the representative of the new creation it must reflect the nature of God. A similar argument is found in I Cor.10:26 where the question of what one may eat is discussed. Once more the argument is based on a quotation from the Psalms which refers to God as the Creator. All forms of food are acceptable because all things proceed from God. Once more the thrust of the argument is about ethical behavior based on an understanding of God as Creator. Hence, even though it reflects a position towards the creation it must be admitted that Paul's focus is on church relationships rather than protology.[1]

Paul also uses creation motifs and doctrine to ground his theological arguments. For example, even though Paul may have inherited them from Hellenistic Judaism, the references to the First and Second Adam have as their ultimate source the Genesis account. In the same way creation forms a context for his understanding of the resurrection (I Cor. 15)[2] and his understanding of redemption (Romans 8). Thus as Nils Dahl noted:

> *The Christian correlation of salvation and creation is not merely derived from the eschatological idea that the end shall be like the beginning; it has also antecedents in the applications of the creation-pattern to historic and actual experiences of God's dealing with man. What we find in the New Testament is due to the coincidence of eschatological doctrine and actual experience, where eschatology is "realized", and "reality" as given in Christ, is eschatologically interpreted. As in Judaism, both the actual facts of central religious significance and the last things*

[1]So also the use of quotations in I Cor. 8:6. The quotation has been attributed to Hellenistic moralists who used classical Stoic texts but the reason such a text appeals to Paul is its idea of one creator. Cf. John G. Gibbs, *Creation and Redemption: A Study in Pauline Theology* (Leiden: E.J. Brill, 1971), pp. 68-69.

[2]The resurrection becomes an instance of God's creative power. In this regard one should consider Paul's use of analogy in Rom. 4:17. The one who calls into existence that which is not, gives life. Hence the resurrection is an act of this creating God. One should also consider Paul's statements about the connection of this life to the general resurrection and his remarks about dying and living with Christ, baptism, and perhaps the indwelling of the Spirit in this context. Consider here the remarks of Gerd Theissen in his book *The Shadow of the Galilean* (Philadelphia: Fortress, 1987) where he suggests that resurrection belief can be understood in terms of *creatio ex nihilo.* (p. 173).

> *are put in relation to creation, or thought to be predestined or pre-existent; but in the New Testament these two lines of thought fall together, as that which is already given in Christ is thought to be part of the last things.*[3]

We should also note that there are some positions which Paul does not take. For instance he rarely uses *phusis* as a norm for measuring the character and behavior of humans as the Stoics did. Instances of this occur (I Cor. 11:14 and Romans 1:18-32), but they are infrequent and it is clear that Paul does not share a similar sense of equality between the human and nature which the Stoics have. For him creation and humans are connected as for the Stoics but his belief in God as Creator separates him from a common Hellenistic motif which incorporates God, human and creation. God interacts with and sustains creation, but God is not completely identified with it.

If it is the case that Paul will not accept a complete identification of God with nature it is also the case that he steadfastly refuses to argue that created matter is intrinsically evil. It is not the matter which will inherit the kingdom of God, but as the previous citation from I Cor. 8:6 demonstrates it is not to be denigrated, because it proceeds from God. Further, while he admits that the resurrection body differs from the physical body Christians now possess, Paul does not argue for the immortality of the soul which has shed its outer shell of flesh. Once more his belief in God as Creator will not allow for this gnostic option of denigration. Whatever else one may conclude about I Cor. 15, it is clear that Paul wants to argue some form of connection between the present form of existence and that which is to come.

It should be clear that when one begins to consider the terms specifically referring to creation, along with his use of the doctrine as a belief and as a motif, the semantic field increases rapidly. Simply beginning with the terms in Rom. 8 we note that he ties the creation to sin, redemption, the spirit, and the fidelity of God, and with this we see that Paul's understanding of creation is tied to his major themes of redemption, resurrection, the righteousness of God, and God's relationship with humanity and the world. Sometimes these links are obvious, sometimes they are more indirect, but, as we follow the string farther, we eventually realize that Paul's understanding of God's justice, anthropology, and christology are tied in some manner to his belief in God as the one who has produced the creation.[4]

However, as felicitous as the discovery of these connections is, such a realization also sounds a warning note. We cannot simply pick and choose among Paul's statements about the creation until we find some that seem to fit our needs, because he has linked them in a manner which we would betray if we were to do so. This sophisticated form of proof texting may be prevalent, indeed attractive, but it is invalid. The links between Paul's remarks make it imperative that we understand his statements in their theological and historical frameworks and that we understand them in relationship to each other rather than as individual statements about the doctrine of creation or redemption. What may appear to be only an aspect of Paul's thought, and a minor one at that, could turn out to be at the heart of his theological system. Initially one may think that he or she is only examining a few pieces of stray thread, but pulling

3. Nils Dahl, "Christ, Creation, and the Church," *The Background of the New Testament and Its Eschatolgy*, ed. W.D. Davies and D. Daube, (New York: Cambridge University Press, 1964), p. 432.

4. See beside the study of Gibbs also John Reumann, *Creation and Redemption*, (Minneapolis: Augsburg, 1973).

on them will result in the unraveling of Paul's garment. One will be left with a lap full of wool or perhaps dacron - and a naked Paul. Perhaps we will cause him to move to the present, if only in search of garb, but it is doubtful that the clothes he will receive will fit properly or as well as his old garment.

If then, we cannot peruse Paul and choose those isolated statements which seem to fit our present use and must recognize that he has connected them, the obvious question becomes: How do we discover the relations among these statements which dictate how they should be read? Our task is not the collection of statements but a search for the manner in which Paul connects the various themes. We must ask if he gives them equal weight, so that one statement is as important as another, or if he has placed them in some form of hierarchy so that one statement should be read as prior to another.

Paul's use of the terms suggests that he does have a hierarchy in place. As we have noted, sometimes creation is only a peripheral term used as an illustration while at others it is the base upon which his arguments are constructed. This shift in perspective occurs in both ethical and theoretical/theological argumentation, but realizing this only moves us to the more difficult question: What is Paul's organizing principle, if indeed, principle is the proper term, and how do we discover it? Or in another formulation: Is there a level at which we can see the interconnectedness of Paul's various statements and at which we may begin to find a coherent structure for them? And with this we have arrived at the center of the debate in Pauline studies, the manner and constituted mode of his thought.[5]

II. The Problem of Coherency and Interpretation

As with most of the significant debates about the New Testament this one begins with the arguments Bultmann and Käsemann had over the ultimate thrust and meaning of Paul's cosmological and anthropological statements. Bultmann argued that Paul's cosmological statements had as their primary referent the nature of the human, *i.e.* they were statements of anthropology.[6] Käsemann, to the contrary, argued that Paul's anthropological statements served the purpose of Paul's cosmology.[7] The debate has continued in various forms but the most recent, and perhaps best articulated, participant has been J. C. Beker, and it is his position which I will use to express the problem before us.[8]

5. The discussion dominating Pauline studies in recent years has been the search for the coherent center of Paul's thought. As we will see, the reliance on one theme for explicating Paul has achieved minimal success and proves as frustrating as the attempts to find the single unifying principle of the New or Old Testaments. The principle either becomes too specific causing us to neglect part of the material, or too general, making its use of little help for interpreting Paul's particular expressions. Cf. on this matter the recent paper by Hendrikus Boers at the 1986 annual meeting of the SBL, in which he assesses the current work of Daniel Patte and J.C. Beker alongside that of E.C. Käsemann. "The Foundations of Paul's Thought: A Methodological Investigation." (unpublished)

6. So Bultmann, *The Theology of the New Testament*, trans. Kendrick Grobel (New York: Charles Scribner's Sons, 1955), p. 191.

7. E. Käsemann, "On Paul's Anthropology," *Perspectives on Paul* (Philadelphia: Fortress, 1971), pp. 1-31.

8. J.C. Beker, *Paul the Apostle: The Triumph of God in Life and Thought* (Philadelphia: Fortress, 1980). Beker also criticizes Käsemann for narrowing Paul's thought to one single theme which disallows Käsemann to distinguish the variety of symbols that Paul used. Thus, Beker charges Käsemann with mistaking the theme of righteousness as the theme of Paul's theology instead of recognizing it as one theme among many, which expresses a deeper more primary structure (the apocalyptic Christ event). (See p. 17).

Neither Beker nor Käsemann find Bultmann entirely wrong. In fact, both want to credit his interpretation for its insistence on the centrality of address to the listener. Nevertheless, Beker faults Bultmann's analysis of Paul's thought because Bultmann's existential hermeneutic strips Paul of his primary expressions.[9] By insisting that the core of Paul's thought is found in the centrality of the cross Bultmann "short-circuits" Paul's gospel in four ways:

First, emphasis on the cross obscures the future element in Paul's thought, with the result that "the larger context in which the cross functions is overlooked [and] the relation between the cross and resurrection is distorted."[10]

Second, such a distortion obscures Paul's understanding of the resurrection of Christ as the first fruits of the general resurrection. As a result, Bultmann's view draws the resurrection into the cross and so obviates the forward movement of the resurrection.

Third, Bultmann's understanding of death and resurrection as dialectically related do not do justice to Paul's equal insistence on their consecutive relationship.[11]

Finally, when the centrality of the cross is not understood in its apocalyptic context, "it not only promotes an individualism that disregards the cosmic solidarity of Paul's anthropology but also leads to such an exclusive emphasis on Christology that it collapses future apocalyptic into the Christ-event."[12]

The final result is that such a course of interpretation encourages an individual distortion of Paul's gospel "so it can chart our future as human beings only in terms of our individual obedience to the cross and a cruciform life. It has nothing to say about the future of the world or our future communal solidarity in the kingdom of God."[13]

It is hard not to side with Beker in this debate. The points he makes bear directly on our desire to allow Paul to speak about our situation in creation and about creation as something more than a backdrop for humanity. Moreover, his position is attractive because it argues that the essential Paul is concerned about the same things which concern us. When we couple this with the realization that existentialist philosophy is no longer sufficient for our age, it is clear that Bultmann's program neglects a major facet of Paul's thought. The radical reorientation of the time elements in Paul's expressions which allowed him to redefine the idea "future" minimalize Paul's cosmic orientation and temporal framework. Further, such a position appears to violate Paul's insistence of solidarity between the human and creation. The result, as Käsemann noted, is that Bultmann's position brings one particularly close to a gnostic idealism.[14]

Beker cautions that, if we want to listen to the essential Paul then we must also recognize that apocalyptic thought is at the center, not the periphery, of his conception of the universe. If one wants to find the "essential Paul" it is necessary to recognize the pervasive and formative nature of apocalyptic conceptions for his expressions. But just here is the rub, for while Paul speaks about the very things which concern us, he conceives and speaks of them in a language which is almost unintelligible to us.

9. *Paul the Apostle,* pp. 35-36.

10. J. C. Beker, *Paul's Apocalyptic Gospel* (Philadelphia: Fortress, 1982) p. 72.

11. *Ibid.,* p. 73.

12. *Ibid.,* p. 73.

13. *Ibid.,* pp. 73-74.

14. Käsemann, "Paul's Anthropology," pp. 13-14.

Beker himself is aware that it is problematic to bring Paul into our situation. In his initial book *Paul the Apostle,* Beker established that apocalyptic orientation and conceptualization were crucial for understanding Paul. But, in his second book *Paul's Apocalyptic Gospel,* he wonders whether such a Paul is understandable in a modern world. He concludes, "A direct transfer of Paul's formulation of the gospel to our situation cannot succeed."[15] And this dilemma occurs precisely because of the apocalyptic nature of Paul's gospel.[16] He correctly asks: "But even if we grant the necessity of, and the existential need for, an apocalyptic gospel, has it not become untenable for us in the face of the sheer continuation of time? . . . How long can the urgency of *kairos,* the sense of a coming fulfillment of time, withstand its frustration by *chronos* the persistent continuity of clock time?"[17]

Beker answers that this stumbling block can only be avoided by making three adjustments in our course. First, we must realize that Paul's hope in the imminent coming glory of God cannot be duplicated in the twentieth century. Second, people who have focused on chronological time have distorted the core of the gospel. And third, we cannot follow II Peter by reinterpreting "imminent."[18] "In other words, the 'literal' intent of Paul's apocalyptic thought needs to be interpreted for us on two levels. It should refer primarily to the coming actualization of God's triumph and only secondarily to its 'imminent' arrival."[19]

Actually, Beker's three adjustments become one, since the first is simply a restating of the problem before us, the second is a warning against misusing apocalyptic conceptions, not a reason to keep them, and the third is a more precise statement of the first. Instead of a literalistic reading of Paul, Beker calls for a catalytic reading which "treads the path between a rigid biblicism and an exclusive existentialist interpretation of apocalyptic."[20] With such a reading Beker is suggesting that revision is necessary, but he does not suggest the actual route we should take.

Here Beker comes close to Bultmann in advocating a process of demythologizing. He differs however in not accepting the philosophy which Bultmann applied since Paul's gospel is unnecessarily restricted by the existentialist framework. Clearly Beker wants to maintain Paul's hope in a concrete occurrence of God's final incursion into history.[21] Yet, at the same time, he must readjust Paul's temporal statements. In a sense, we accept and do not accept Paul's gospel, that is we allow some elements normative value, but deny that status to others. I may be misunderstanding Beker's procedures but I think that he is selectively "demythologizing" Paul and with this Bultmann's first hermeneutical question has returned through the back door. Bultmann would ask how it is possible to make these selections if the whole is of one

15. *Paul s Apocalyptic Gospel,* p. 105.

16. Beker's own suggestion is that we understand the Pauline message as a catalytic function for our time. In his most recent book *Suffering and Hope* (Philadelphia: Fortress, 1987) the difficulty is more succinctly stated. As Beker notes, the language of an apocalyptic myth is not only obsolete but also misleading. He asks: "For how can we, in the midst of suffering, rejoice in the 'already' of God's victory over evil and death, when the 'not yet' keeps on being delayed and seemingly reduces the 'already' to a 'never'?" (pp. 88-89).

17. *Paul's Apocalyptic Gospel,* p. 114.

18. *Ibid.,* pp. 114-115.

19. *Ibid.,* p. 115.

20. *Ibid.,* p. 118.

21. *Ibid.,* p. 117.

apocalyptic cloth and on what grounds is the selective adjustment justified?[22]

I must admit that at this point I am a listener caught between the power of two voices. On the one hand, I must agree that Beker's description of what Paul thought is more sufficient than Bultmann's because it gives proper attention to Paul's apocalyptic orientation. On the other hand, Bultmann's argument that such an orientation is untenable for the modern situation is equally powerful. We are agreed that we want to hear Paul so we must listen carefully to Beker, but because we want to hear Paul we must listen with equal care to Bultmann. In other words, having put one's hand to Beker's plow can one look back to Bultmann's field?

Thus we are faced with a major dilemma: How can we interpret Paul without remainder? Even if we grant that Bultmann has overstated the case concerning Paul's apocalyptic framework and language, we are still faced with the major problem of the temporal framework in which Paul conceived of things. We want Paul to inform us about our present situation, especially the crisis facing our creation's continued existence; however, exegetical and theological integrity require that Paul be given his due as an apocalyptic thinker. Any proper reading must retain Paul's thought and be true to its mode, including its temporal nature. Yet, any reading which seeks to address the modern situation must be produced in terms which are understandable. Paul's mode of thought is so significantly different than ours that this is extremely difficult to do.

III. A Grammatical Reading

It appears that what is needed is a system comprehensive enough to incorporate Paul's thought while remaining benevolent towards his mode of expression. Such a system must also provide us with forms of expression that are comprehensible to the modern listener. Not surprisingly, with what follows I do not propose to solve this question, for before such a system can be introduced we must first find guidelines which will serve as norms by which to judge the adequacy of the system, both for Paul and for the present interpreter. It is clear that the system cannot simply be imposed upon Paul, for we would once more be faced with a system which communicates, but does not communicate Paul. The system must arise from within Paul's own expressions of thought and from those convictions which gave rise to them.[23]

What follows is a hypothesis open to your significant revision. I propose that developing a grammar of Paul's expression may serve as the control for the incorporation of a hermeneutical key to Paul. By this term "grammar" I mean a set of principles which explain how various expressions are constructed, interrelated, and understood. I have in mind a discourse grammar which moves to progressively deeper levels, each one composed of the elements which generate the elements of the level above it. Thus I take grammar to refer to the structures which inform, and to a degree, control surface expressions.[24]

22 Bultmann, "New Testament and Mythology," *Kerygma and Myth* (New York: Harper, 1961) p. 9.

23 Cf. Boers, "The Foundations of Paul's Thought," (p. 20) concerning the grammar of Paul's thought.

24 My terms and initial thoughts are drawn from the work of A. J. Greimas (Greimas and Courtes, *Semantics and Language* (Bloomington: Indiana University Press, 1982), but I cannot claim that I have followed his procedure. The field of semiotics remains a complex one, open to significant criticisms. Cf. the discussion in Ronald Schleifer, *A.J. Greimas and the Nature of Meaning* (Lincoln: University of Nebraska Press, 1987), pp. 164-208. Here I have only used Greimas' terms and, to some extent, his idea of a text

A grammatical reading of Paul's texts allows for two of our more pestering problems to be addressed: the clarification of real and apparent ambiguity and the eventual description of the relationship among Paul's terms of expression. I am not arguing that Paul used language with the precision of a mathematician or a symbolic logician. Indeed, I am sure that he did not, for there must have been times when his expressions would have suited his purposes better if they had been formed differently.

No doubt, this ambiguity between statements is sometimes attributable to the context in which Paul is writing, as Beker notes, but it is also the case that these contradictory statements may sometimes be the result of more complex factors. It is conceivable and, I think probable, that some ambiguity in Paul's surface statements arise from his use of the same terms to express deeper structures. Thus ambiguity at the surface level may result from at least three factors: 1) two terms might be used to express the same deep structure, 2) one term might be used to express two deeper structures, or 3) Paul may be adapting his thoughts due to audience conditions which would affect a change in his expressions, *e.g.* where he feels restricted in the use of his language choice because of the understandings which his audience holds.[25]

Thus, ambiguity on the surface level could be due to any of a number of factors or a function of many. But it is precisely at these points that we must make reference to a deeper grammar for explication. When faced with ambiguity in Paul's thought expressions, a grammar would be employed to help us relate and understand them. The point here is that we would distinguish those expressions which are the result of ill-formed writing from those which Paul has made deliberately ambiguous or even contradictory or from those which actually display a deeper level of contradiction.

If such a grammar could be constructed, then we might attempt to rephrase the sentences by first looking to the structures which brought them to this particular expression. Those which were the result of surface contradiction could be differentiated from those which display contradictions at the deeper level. Presumably, following that process would help clarify the relationship between two or more surface expressions and eventually the whole of Paul's thought.

arising from deeper structures. Cf. also H. Boers, "Polarities at the Roots of New Testament Thought," *Perspectives on the New Testament: Essays in Honor of Frank Stagg*, ed. C. H. Talbert, (Macon, Georgia: Mercer University Press, 1985), pp. 55-76. A similar proposal for analysing Paul's thought is made by D. Patte, *Paul's Faith and the Power of the Gospel* (Philadelphia: Fortress, 1985). However Patte's procedure is not entirely clear, especially his distinction of the levels which underlie convictions and the manner of determining them. See the critique in Boers, "Foundations of Paul's Thought," pp. 16-17.

25. It is this third factor which Beker makes the most of in his initial book. He points to the interaction of the contingent aspects of Paul and his audience with Paul's understanding of the primary gospel events. I would suggest that this interplay needs further delineation since, in light of rhetorical procedures which recognize a difference between an actual situation and the rhetorical situation which an author introduces, we should recognize that the letters of Paul only make us partially aware of the contingencies which he faced. Although scholars have debated with Beker about the adequacy of his analysis of the coherency of Paul's thought, it may be that knowing what the contingent factors are pose an even greater problem for us.

I am aware that terms for Paul are context conditioned, for he can and does use the same term to express different, even contradictory, thoughts. A case in point: Paul's remarks about the law and its worth for a community or an individual. At times Paul seems to suggest that the law is of no benefit (*e.g.* Rom. 3:20), at others that it is for the good (Rom. 2:13). Read as straight surface statements such remarks appear contradictory and unless scholars want to consign Paul to the area of muddled thinkers they have no choice but to look for a deeper sense for the meaning of the expression.

In a manner of speaking, this is what Bultmann, Käsemann and Beker have recommended already, by their attempts to correlate Paul's thought. Beker alone makes this clear in his discussion of deep and surface structure; however, one must admit that this conceptual framework receives little expressed attention in the analytic part of Beker's work. It is a heuristic device more that an actual working grammar. Thus in suggesting this procedure I am simply following farther his prior work with the hope of giving it more controls and specificity.

I am aware that such a proposal for considering Paul's sentences is fraught with difficulties. For starters we are aware that all grammars are constructs which come after the fact. That is, they are conscious efforts to make sense of the expressed language. As secondary constructs they do not completely satisfy our desire for precision. Nevertheless, even in its imperfect state we would benefit from such a tool because it enables us to ask why scholars have argued for the connection of various terms and syntactic units. I am also aware that as one moves from simple sentence to construction to discourse grammar the difficulty of producing such a grammar grows exponentially. Nevertheless, the promise of understanding *why* a text coheres as well as what it says, appears to me to make such an attempt worthwhile.[26]

Just as with other discourse grammars, a grammar of Paul's expressed thought will need further clarification, for what we require is a conscious effort to make his expressed thought clear. We want a way to translate Paul from one language to another, but we want a translation without remainder. We are faced with a number of scholars who consistently refine our knowledge of Paul's single terms, but we also have the sense that further exegetical nuance, while helpful, will not break through the barrier which is before us.[27]

Thus, I think that we need to explore not only surface expressions, but those deeper structures and functions which caused them to be written. Paul's thoughts, particular expressions, and employed forms are governed by a deeper set of structures. To arrive at them one pays attention not only to syntagmatic relationships, *i.e.* syntactic continuity, but also to paradigmatic relationships, *i.e.* semantic continuity.

[26]. The philosophical problem of the existence of base polarities or universals which underlies semiotic systems is beyond my scope here. In fact the debate is not new to structuralism, but is a firm element in Western philosophical discourse. (See the editor's foreword to Schleifer, pp. ix-xvii and Jonathan Culler, *Structuralist Poetics* [Ithaca: Cornell University Press], 197 pp. 75-95.) I only want to use the process in helping us to uncover the factors which contribute or hinder a search for coherency in Paul's thought. Should contradictions arise at the deeper levels I do not think that "pushing to deeper levels" will alleviate them. Eventually one would see that the contradictions are real and not apparent. At that point we would ask how Paul holds such contradictions. Thus we note that Paul may have a coherent system of thought, but not a consistent one. Cf. the last sentence of Boers' SBL paper: "Thus we end with the paradox that what gives *coherence* to Paul's thought is contradiction at its most fundamental level." (p. 22)

[27]. I am not contesting the validity of historical research. Indeed this set of procedures is essential for help in determining contingent settings in which Paul wrote; however, such a process tells us about the text's elements, not what makes it readable. We are looking for those principles or structures which are logically anterior to this surface reading. Further, I am not saying that historical research should not be done, but that it must be done in a manner cognizant of those structures which produced the text in the first place. Simply summing the meanings of a discourse's individual sentences will not reveal the meaning of the discourse. In a nutshell, the coherency of Paul's thought will not be achieved by narrower and narrower exegesis. It is the interrelatedness of the terms which we seek to know, not just more about them in isolation and for this we must move to a level underneath the text.

These latter relationships reveal certain patterns of thought which might not surface in the same way, but which are related at the deeper level. It is here that we would begin to find the grammar that informs the formation of our surface texts.

At these deeper levels we would notice patterns of relationship which did not necessarily become apparent on the surface level of the text. Sometimes the expressions, figures or themes would be grouped by their similarities, at other times by their oppositions. As we begin to notice these types of connections, as well as those themes, figures and expressions which are separate, we would begin to realize which expressions Paul is bringing together as equivalent, which are antithetical for him, and which thoughts he considers to be products of others. Finally, we might also begin to derive a sense of the even deeper set of convictions which generated these themes.

Procedures on all of these levels have been attempted before. Most frequently biblical scholars have been involved in the first type of procedure, grouping like terms and trying to find forms which are related. Occasionally we also venture into the second procedure and attempt to describe the coherence of these surface themes. In the past we have called this Biblical theology. One recognizes that such attempts meet with varying degrees of success and failure. It is the move to the third level that is infrequent although scholars like Daniel Patte and Hendrikus Boers have made initial attempts.[28]

Meaning at this convictional level becomes a function of value.[29] We discover those things which the author considers real or unreal, worthy or unworthy, desirable or undesirable, good or evil, etc.[30] Obviously at this level connections and coherence differ from our sense of coherent meaning on the surface level. At the surface we are concerned with logical or cognitive relations, but here the relations seem to have a logic of a different order. If we consider such a connective system then we can begin to consider those modes of thought which began with such convictional patterns and generating principles. It would be in such terms that we could express Paul's thought so that it could be heard by the modern listener.[31]

28. Beker's work appears as a hybrid form somewhere between procedures two and three. The footnote to his work on Paul's coherent center shows that he is aware of the need to identify structural coherency. *Paul the Apostle*, p. 16.

29. The term value, as used by Greimas, is not necessarily linked to aesthetic or moral value but refers to the motivation of expressions. See Greimas, "Values," *Semiotics and Language*, pp. 365-366.

30. Cf. Patte, *Paul's Faith and the Power of The Gospel*, pp. 18-19.

31. So also Patte's considerations in *Paul's Faith and the Power of the Gospel*, pp. 1-25. As we move from the surface level down we move to increasing levels of generality and abstraction. Ultimately it appears that base polarities might be reached from which the generative convictions could be reached, but at this level we have moved from Christianity or any given religious system to the more general category of human existence. The debate here becomes one of determining how to deal with the particularity of Paul's gospel. That is, are the apocalyptic expressions of Paul's gospel the deepest generative force or does a coherent core exist at a deeper level? For Beker moving to this deeper level proves difficult because the apocalyptic facet of the thought is minimized. In contrast to this Boers would maintain its necessity since he considers the apocalyptic part of Paul's expressions to be a manifestation of that which constitutes Paul's core thought. In other words, for Beker apocalyptic expression of the Christ event is Paul's coherency, however plastic that coherency might be; for Boers the apocalyptic expression is an intermediary level. In either case, the grammatical reading would help in determining where the apocalyptic expressions are generative. (See, "Foundations of Paul's Thought," p. 12.) For a different critique of Beker's apocalyptic orientation see Vincent Branick, "Apocalyptic Paul?," *Catholic Biblical Ouarterly* 47 (1985), pp. 664-675, who emphasizes Paul's participation language.

One might have suspicion about the third level since it moves to an even further degree of abstraction; however, one thing may be said in its defense. As things now stand our debates are lacking resolution because we have no Archimedean point which allows us firmly to adjudicate between a Beker and a Bultmann. We can consider the adequacy of their treatment of individual passages, but we are at an impasse in trying to analyse whether their organizing principles are sufficient or necessary. Moving to the third level could provide such a viewpoint and allow the interpreter to see whether those expressions which appear to be crucial forms at the second level can be transformed without remainder at the deeper level. At this deeper level we could consider these more abstract generators of Paul's thought, in order to reveal more of the coherency which Beker seeks. Intersections would become more obvious here, since we would recognize those themes which cohere, but perhaps more importantly we would clearly delineate those themes which are not reconcilable, which remain in tension or outright conflict. In this case, our task becomes explaining why it is important for Paul to maintain such contradictions for his thought, rather than reconciling them.

For example, in the present instance, Beker has argued persuasively that the temporal aspect of Paul's thought cannot be released, but he is faced with the problem of the meaningfulness of that aspect for the modern audience. Perhaps the move to the deeper level will reveal the convictional patterns which explain Paul's insistence on cosmic identity and temporal hiatus, but which also suggest the manner of presentation which confronts the modern listener in the way both Bultmann and Beker wish the gospel message to occur.

IV. Expressions and Themes in Romans 1-8

To be sure such a procedure is risky and fraught with difficulty. Obviously I cannot proceed on the scale I have suggested above, and for the present paper I restrict myself to surface expressions about creation as they appear in Rom. 1-8.[32] First I will consider some of the expressions Paul uses, and then suggest certain figures which help group them. After this I suggest that one may find these as reflections of deeper themes in Paul's thought which may or may not be compatible. Even this is inadequate, since fully to understand the matter we would need to consider its relationship to the other surface figures and subthemes but it serves to test the viability of the procedure. I end with some tentative suggestions about Paul's thoughts about creation and their possible statements to us.

A. Expressions

The expressions arise easily enough from a syntactic reading, a list follows:

[32] A more provocative analysis might occur if one were to work with I Cor., since it is the most "horizontal" of Paul's texts. Paul uses many creation figures in the letter and when this is compared with their use in II Cor. the result would be very interesting. The contrast of the two letters could suggest how creation, as a reflection of God, and as a formative part of Paul's thought would arise in different contingent situations. In I Cor. the theme is closer to the surface, whereas in II Cor. it forms an underpinning for his deliberations in chapters 4-6. However, since the majority of Paul's overt expressions about creation are found in Rom., this section of his letters proves to be a good starting point.

1:19-20 God displays characteristics of power and deity through the creation.
1:23 The glory of the immortal God is exchanged for the images of mortality.
3:23 Through sin all fall short of the glory of God.
4:17 God calls into being that which does not exist.
5:12 Death came through one person.
5:14 Death is now a part of this existence.
7:13-20 Sin infuses the human being's body, frustrating its will.
8:11 The mortal body is given life through the indwelling Spirit.
8:17-18 During the present time we suffer along with the creation.
8:18 The glory is to be revealed to us.
8:19 The creation awaits the revealing of the children of God.
8:20 The creation has been subjected to futility.
8:21 The creation is in a state of bondage and decay.
8:21 The creation will be released from this state to obtain the glorious liberty of the children of God.
8:22 The creation groans in travail.
8:23 The awaited adoption is the redemption of the *soma*.
8:38 Nothing of the created order is sufficiently powerful to separate the believer from God's love.

An interesting feature of this list is that it suggests that Rom. 1 and Rom. 8 are linked. Nils Dahl has already noted that chapters 5 and 8 are connected thematically, but it appears to me that this may be extended back to chapter one, thereby adding to the coherence of the themes in 1 through 8.[33] Only in these two chapters does the term for creation come to the surface, although the motif is evident in both chapters 4 and 5. The concern with creation frames the argument of the first eight chapters. Thus, we would have the interesting case where Paul, contrary to his habit, opens a letter's argumentation by grounding it cosmically, rather than ecclesially or theologically. What one is to make of this remains to be seen, but it does suggest initially that creation motifs and doctrines can be formative in his theological constructions.[34]

B. Themes:

As we move to the next level these expressions can be grouped according to the following themes connected to the figure, creation:

1. God as Creator.
2. Christ as the Redeemer of Creation.
3. Redemption remains a thing of the future.
4. The created order is in a state of nonredemption.
5. The redemption of creation and of human beings is linked.
6. Suffering is connected to creation, the human, and redemption.
7. The glory of God as revealed in creation and the human is affected by the human's actions.

33. N. Dahl, "The Missionary Theology in the Epistle to the Romans," *Studies in Paul* (Augsburg: Minneapolis, 1977), pp. 81-85.
34. As per private discussion with J. Christiaan Beker, October, 1987.

This frame, created by chaps. 1 and 8, involves the relationship between the creation and the Creator as it is manifested in the human response to its created status. It is especially the case that the idea of rebellion can be seen in chap. 1. As a result of the human refusal to recognize the creation as God's, and itself as part of the created order, the human removes itself from proper relationship to God and the created order. It is in this state of rebellion where the Christ encounters us (chap. 5), and it is from this state of rebellion from which we will ultimately be redeemed (chap. 8). In chap. 1 the creation is the arena in which the opportunity for the rebellion occurs, but as chap. 8 makes clear, the creation is also subjected to frustration, from which it cannot be released until the final redemption of the rebellious ones is a fact. Hence there is an interesting symbiotic relationship between creation and human beings. We are intrinsically part of the problem for creation and necessary for its final release from bondage. It was in the revelation of God's power and godliness to humans that the creation had its purpose. Now, it is the redemption of humans for which creation awaits so that it may obtain its freedom. In the former case the creation is for the service of humanity, in the latter it depends upon humanity for its redemption.

Another prominent theme in this section is the use of the expressions referring to glory. In 1:23 the glory of the immortal God is exchanged for the image of the mortal human, but in 8:18 this is reversed. There Paul argues that the glory is to be revealed to us, and we are to be revealed as children of God. This is encapsulated in the expressions found in 3:21ff.; the failure to attain the glory of God is founded upon the sin of humans, which Paul has recognized in chap. 1 as a failure by humans to understand their rightful positions in the created order. To be sure the term is used throughout the first eight chapters, however, only in chaps. 1 and 8 is this contrast of immortality and corruptibility found in Romans. These connections imply that glory is linked to immortality, while its loss is connected with mortality. In chap. 8 the loss of glory is reversed, and when it is ultimately revealed, the creation will be released from corruptibility. Thus, it appears that the redemption to come is the reversal of the rebellion which occurred when people refused to see God in the creation, but also the re-establishment of the creation to its rightful state, freedom from decay and obtainment of glorious liberty.

The argument of Rom. 1-8 suggests that for Paul the history and state of the creation and the human are intertwined in such a way that redemption necessarily includes both. In chap. 1 it was the action of God in creation which was to affect humans positively, but it did not. In chap. 8, however Paul argues that it will be the action of God directed to humans which affects the creation. Further in chap. 1 Paul maintains that humans sought autonomy and so creation was reduced to a state of bondage. Then in chap. 8 he states that the restored human is one who recognizes theonomy; when this state of restoration by God is revealed then creation receives its liberty.

Of the above mentioned themes the controlling theme is that of reversal. The human reverses the place of the created and Creator by refusing to see that the creation reflects such an order. The result is that humans are now in a state of rebellion and loss. They are lacking the glory to come because they have exchanged the glory of God for the mortal image. Further the state of creation has been affected by this reversal. It is now in a state of frustration, decay, and bondage. God, however reverses these states: the verdict against the humanity is reversed, for it will gain the glory to come, and the state of creation is reversed, for it will regain freedom, a freedom which is the product of the coming glory.

The theme of reversal becomes even more distinct when we note how Paul relates the various statements. On a temporal axis one can place present existence - the creation in travail, decay, frustration, suffering, and hope,opposite the theme of future existence - glory, revelation of the children of God, freedom from bondage and decay. Those on the present side of the axis have a negative valuation for Paul, those on the future side a positive value. Changing our orientation to a spatial one, and using a vertical axis we can place the present status of creation - present body, suffering and groaning on the lower side of the axis, and Christ - release from travail, liberation, glory, and redemption on the upper side. Those on the bottom receive a negative value, those on the top a positive one.

Thus far, nothing is irregular about such groupings; however, a distinctive shift can be found with 8:17. Suffering, which on the vertical axis had a negative evaluation, moves from a negative to a positive pole. To be sure Paul is not arguing for a Christo-masochism, but it is clear that the Christ-event reorients his evaluations. In vs. 18 sufferings are conceived of as negative even though they are not worth comparing with the coming glory. Doing this Paul creates a larger nexus for understanding, and hence evaluating,the present sufferings; nonetheless, Paul does not deny that these sufferings are real and experienced painfully. But, with vs. 17 we find that these same experiences are allotted a positive value because of their necessary relationship to glory. Somehow sufferings become sufferings with Christ and so form part of our necessary relationship with him. An interesting "contradiction" occurs: on the horizontal axis suffering is negative, but on the vertical axis it has moved to the positive side with glory. Its value is reoriented by its being placed with Christ.

The two values for suffering remain in tension at the present time. In the future this tension may be resolved, but for now the value of suffering occupies an ambiguous position, since it is both positive and negative. On the horizontal axis of humanity it is on the negative side and on the vertical axis of life and death it is on the side of death, and so negative. Yet, on this same axis it can receive a positive value, since it is connected to the Christ and to the final redemption of humanity and creation of positive. Clearly, Paul creates and maintains such a tension in his evaluation. Further he insists that it is only with the advent of God's triumph that this ambiguity will be replaced with the resolution of the inherited glory.

V. Some Concluding Thoughts

It should be clear by now that an appropriation of Paul's thought poses major problems for the interpreter. Even if the present attempt is found to be abortive, there is much to be gained by such a procedure. Granting its difficulties and mis-steps, such a move needs to be made, for any search for coherence and translation needs to travel a route of this type. Comparing terms or asserting theological coherency creates impasses which cannot be resolved by more comparison or assertion. In the final analysis we will inevitably become involved in assaults on the letters rather than explanations of them. A philosophical or mythological anthropology that does justice to temporal and cosmic aspects of human existence remains to be found. The difficulties in finding such keys are quite daunting, but that does not relieve us of the responsibility if we desire to allow Paul his own voice.

At this point I will not claim to have solved the difficulty with the temporal hiatus in Paul's thought nor to know exactly what the system which could do so might look like. Nevertheless, some of its components are clear to me. First, a sufficient system must recognize that as humans we exist in a state of otherness. There is a separation between ourselves and that which surrounds us, both seen and unseen. But, for Paul, this separation is not an occasion for negation of the other or for its domination. Second, Paul also wants to maintain a position which realizes that this otherness cannot be violated; for, should we forget this, we transgress our limits as a created self. Third, Paul's positioning of the figures on various evaluative axes and his occasional shifts between the positive or negative poles they occupy, suggest that he wants to maintain a tension between the heavenly and the earthly, between now and then, between full identification and separateness. Perhaps these tensions are maintained because Paul is reflecting fundamental polarities, those which drive all human effort and thought. Perhaps, in the end, what we are called to is an acceptance of our humanity: our status as those who are individuals and social beings, those who are cognizant of our earthly origins and who imagine our metaphysical destiny, as Hendrikus Boers has recently maintained.[35] Whatever the case, I maintain that only a full and relentless attempt to move to the core of his thought will reveal what Paul sought. There is a fear in pursuing this course that we may reach levels which lose a Christian sound. This I cannot deny. Still, I do not see that we have a choice, because, in the final analysis, our only task is a pursuit of that which is true. This course lies before us, it is all that we may rightfully claim and its paths are as yet unknown, but a claim to trust God must mean to risk our ideas and convictions.

At the risk of unraveling Paul's garment myself, I would venture three observations about his remarks on creation. First, there is a connection between the created order and the church, and so a call for a correct maintenance of that order in, and by, the church. Thus, there is a responsibility for our environment, social and physical, which comes with our claim to be God's people. But here Paul also cautions against a misunderstanding of our relationship to creation, for this is an impermanent world awaiting its transformation by God. Even those with the highest ecological ideals and desires must submit to the fact that this is God's creation, and so ultimately his responsibility. To act otherwise, even in an effort to save the earth, would be idolatry. The desire will be to save "our world," to save "our rivers," to leave a legacy for "our children." But, in the end, this will simply be an extension of our egos; an unbounded narcissism. With this, once more, we will have exchanged the created for the Creator and, ironically, in the name of being God's stewards we will have become those who have rebelled.[36]

35. Boers, "Polarities at the Roots of New Testament Thought," pp. 73-75. So in the discussion afterwards, Peter Stuhlmacher reminded me that this is part of the debate between Käsemann and Herbert Braun.

36. Cf. C.E.B. Cranfield, "Some Observations on Romans 8:19-21," *Reconciliation and Hope*, ed. R. Banks (Grand Rapids: Eerdmans, 1974). "We have an obligation to the sub-human creation for men's sake, for the sake of living men and also for the sake of those not yet born. Of this truth we must not for a moment lose sight. But the verses indicate that this truth is by no means the whole truth of the matter and that to value the sub-human creation solely as man's habitat, man's environment, man's amenities - even if we do think of 'man's' as meaning 'our neighbor's' rather than "our own" - is to be guilty of idolatry. If the sub-human creation is part of God's creation, if to it also he is faithful, and if he is going to bring it also (as well as believing men) to a goal which is worthy of himself, then it too has a dignity of its own and an inalienable, since divinely - appointed, right to be treated by us with reverence and sensitivity." (pp. 229-230)

Of course a concern for the environment is of great significance and consequence for Christians, since, as God's representatives of the presence of order amid chaos it is a primary responsibility to live out such order as well as proclaim it. But, unless this is carried out with the realization that the future of the earth resides ultimately in the decisions and power of God, as God chooses to express them, we will have failed to recognize our own finitude, our own creatureliness.

Thus, my second suggestion is that from Paul comes a call to live as if our actions have ultimate significance, and to live as if they ultimately have no significance. His insistence on not collapsing the tension between the present and that which is to come, warns us not to choose between these options ourselves. For Paul, to live with a sober sense of our solidarity with creation requires of us a decision to live in hope for the resolution of all things in a just way. His call to await the fulfillment of God's justice requires of us hope in the midst of suffering. This, to be sure is not what we would wish, but it is all that we are given. However, he also exhorts us to live as if all things are resolved, *i.e.* in a "new creation." To do this we can only live as if our actions are of no significance cosmically, for in the new creation actions only have efficacy when they are empowered by God. We are those in whom the treasure exists, but we are as fragile as the jars made of earth. This is, of course, without logic and we must admit it, but we must also confess that we will live in such a manner nevertheless.

I return to those first questions raised such a long time ago. Yes, Paul does have a word which he speaks to the present situation, and we should listen to it, because, when he speaks of creation Paul is referring to a web of relationships in which we exist. These relationships to the seen and unseen, to the future and past, he seeks to understand, and to help others understand, but he knows that his understanding is not complete. Hence he will not release us from ambiguity or the unknown. He provokes thought, exposes shallow reasoning, reveals insufficient thinking, engages us in the discussion. In this sense Paul's thought is catalytic, to use Beker's term, it is creative in its own right, causing us to reconsider our own situations and to respond to them, forcing us to live with as much fidelity as Paul displays when he responds to his situations. Perhaps it is this catalytic, provocative, and challenging stance which enables Paul to be interesting for us, prompting us to ask if he has anything to help us live responsibly in our world. This perhaps is what we have in mind when we argue that Paul should remain an authority for us.[37]

Paul speaks to us because he insists on our humanity and defines it as that which is in relationship with what we only know as other. This relationship of ourselves to the other is still cloudy, its resolution not sharply seen. Paul believes that this ambiguity will be resolved one day, but the operative word here is *believes*. That is why, when he speaks of salvation, he whispers of hope with the same breath. Paul believes in the coming resolution, but he resides in the present ambiguity. Because of this, he argues that we respect the otherness of creation. He argues further, that such respect arises from a solidarity with the creation in its suffering. We, along with the creation must await the moment of resolution, the final redemption.

[37]Cf. the intriguing suggestions of Jeffrey Stout about why philosophy professors continue to use philosophers they no longer consider correct as required reading: "The Relativity of Interpretation," *Monist* 69 (1986), pp.111-112. See also his "What is the Meaning of a Text?," *New Literary History* 14 (Autumn, 1982), pp. 1-12.

Creation, Logos and the Son: Observations On John 1:1-18 And 5:17-18

Peder Borgen

Introduction

John 1:1-18 is the well-known Prologue of the gospel of John. Its dependence on the creation story, Genesis 1:1 ff., is obvious, since the opening words, *en archē* (John 1:1), corresponds to *br'šyt* in Genesis 1:1. The other passage referred to in the title, John 5:17-18, reads: "But Jesus answered them: 'My father works up to now. I am also working'. This was why Jews sought all the more to kill him, because he not only broke the sabbath, but also called God his Father, making himself equal with God." John draws here on Jewish exegetical debates on Genesis 2:2-3: "And on the seventh day God finished his work which he had done, and he rested on the seventh day from all his work which he had done. So God blessed the seventh day and hallowed it, because on it God rested from all his work which he had done in creation." John 5:17-18 is part of the section 5:1-18 about the healing of the paralytic on the sabbath and the subsequent debate on the sabbath question.

Our observations will be guided by the following questions:

1. How is material from the Old Testament used, especially with reference to the creation story?
2. What is the relationship between the particular and the universal aspects? In other words: What is the relationship between the specifics of persons, events, the laws of the sabbath observance on the one hand and the general and universal perspective of creation on the other hand?
3. Since John 5:1-18 tells about a growing conflict between Jesus and his fellow Jews, are there traces found in Jewish sources to indicate that corresponding controversies on the particular and universal took place also elsewhere in Judaism?

The word "observations" in the title must be emphasized. Thus, the two passages will mainly be analysed in their present form in the Gospel, and the paper will deal only with some aspects.

John 5:17-18. The sabbath gives witness to the Creator and the Upholder of creation, i.e. to the Father and the Son.

All four gospels tell about Jesus being involved in sabbath controversies. Often the controversy is presented in the form of a case-story being followed by a legal, halachic, debate.[1] The same form is used in John 5:1-18. The story about the healing of the paralytic on the sabbath, vv. 1-9, presents the legal case. Then in vv. 10-18 a halachic exchange about this case follows. In vv. 10-13 the carrying of the mat on the

[1] See Matt. 12:1-8; Mark 2:23-28; Luke 13:10-17, etc.

sabbath is the issue.[2] Then in vv. 14-16 the healing on the sabbath is included in the violation of the sabbath laws.[3] In both sections the focus is placed on Jesus as the unknown healer who told the man to carry his mat (vv. 10-13), and then in vv.14-16, as the one identified as the person who healed the man. Then in vv. 17-18 the real identity of Jesus is given. He has acted as the Son of God, and in his sovereignty God works on the sabbath. The term "sabbath" from the case-story, v. 9, is repeated throughout the debate, in vv.10, 16 and 18. This shows that John 5:17-18 is an integral part of John 5:1-18. Then in vv. 19-47 there is an elaboration on the relationship between the Father and the Son, and the way in which the Baptist, Jesus' works, the Law of Moses, etc. serve as witnesses to Jesus identity as the Son.

When it is said in v. 17 that God works up to now, that is, including the sabbath, a widespread exegetical debate on Gen. 2:2-3 is presupposed and utilized. The problem was the conviction that God cannot stop working. Consequently, the notion of the sabbath rest of God, as stated in Gen. 2:2-3, stands in tension with this working. Evidence for such exegetical debate of the sabbath rest of God is found as early as the second century B.C., in Aristobulus,[4] and more material is found in Philo and in rabbinic writings.[5]

According to rabbinic exegesis, the sabbath commandment does not forbid one to carry something about in one's house on the sabbath. But God's homestead is the upper and the lower worlds. He may thus create within it without coming into conflict with the sabbath (*Gen. R* 30:6). Philo, relying on the LXX rendering of sabbath, *katepausen,* not *epausato* says that God " caused to rest , 'not rested'; for He causes to rest that which, though actually not in operation, is apparently making, but He himself never ceases making" (*Leg. All* I:5-6). Thus, the meaning of the Seventh day to Philo is that God, who has no origin, is always active. "He is not a mere artificer, but also Father of the things that are coming into being." (*Leg. All* I:18) All created beings are dependent and really inactive in all their doings:"...the number seven ... Its purpose is that creation, observing the inaction which it brings, should call to mind him who does all things invisible." (*Heres.* 170)

An interpretation of Gen. 2:2-3 similar to that of Philo, seems to be presupposed in John 5:1-18. The Son of God brings the Father's upholding and providential activity to bear upon the case of the healing of a person on the sabbath. And the healed person is dependent and inactive, even, in the carrying of the mat on the sabbath. Jesus told him to do so; that is, God's Son told him to do so.

One other aspect of the exegesis of Gen. 2:2-3 might also be presupposed. In various ways it is stated that the sabbath both marked an end to something, and a new beginning. In *Gen. R* 11:10 it is said that God's activity as physical creation came to an end on the sabbath, but not his moral activity. Correspondingly Philo draws the

[2] Jer. 17:19-27; Neh. 13:15-19; cf. Exod. 21:2-17; Num. 15:32-36; Jub. 2:29f; Philo, Migr. 91; Shab. 7:2; 10:5.

[3] Healing on the sabbath is only permitted if the person is in danger of death. See C.K. Barrett, *The Gospel according to St. John*. 2.ed.(Philadelphia, 1978), p. 320. See Luke 13:14 (Jesus could have waited until another day).

[4] N. Walter, *Der Thoraausleger Aristobulus* (Berlin, 1964). pp. 170-171; P. Borgen, "Philo of Alexandria," in M. Stone (ed) *Jewish writings of the Second Temple Period. CRINT* II:2, (Assen, 1984) pp. 277; *id., "Paul Preaches Circumcision and Pleases Men" and Other Essays on Christian Origins* (Trondheim, 1983), pp. 180, 184-185, and *id., Philo, John and Paul. Brown Judaic Studies* 131, (Atlanta, Georgia, 1982) p. 12.

[5] Philo, *Leg. All* I:5-7 and 16-18; *Cher* 86-90; *Migr.* 91; *Heres.* 170; See further Gen. R 11:10; Exod. R 30:6.

distinction in this way: when the seventh and perfect light, the truly divine light of virtue, has dawned, the creation of that whose nature is of the contrary kind comes to a stop (*Leg. All.* I:18); furthermore, whenever there comes upon the soul the holy Logos of which seven is the keynote, six together with all mortal things *(hosa thnēta)* that the soul seems to make therewith comes to a stop (*Leg. All* I:16). Here we notice that the Logos is God's agent in bringing into man's life a new beginning in accordance with the meaning of the sabbath. Again, corresponding to this idea of a new beginning, the healing of the paralytic on the sabbath, performed by the Son, marked the new beginning of resurrection. From John 5:21 we learn that the term "rise" *(egeire)* spoken to the paralytic in v. 8, points to the raising of the dead *(egeire tous nekrous)*, and moreover the healing itself marks a new beginning.

From this analysis of John 5:1-18 it is seen that the sabbath served as witness to God's providential activity brought near through His Son. On the basis of this universal activity of God in his creation, the specific sabbath observances could be abrogated.

It is of importance to notice that Philo gives evidence for a similar controversy taking place, probably within the Alexandrian Jewish community.[6] In *Migr.* 89-93 he refers to some fellow Jews who search for the inner meaning of the laws to the extent that they ignore the external and specific observances. They are taught by the sacred word to let go nothing that is part of the customs fixed by divinely empowered men (*Migr.* 89-90). Against this background Philo gives the following advice and warning:

> - *It is quite true that the Seventh day is meant to teach the power of the Unoriginate and the nonaction of created beings. But let us not for this reason abrogate* **(luōmen)** *the enactments laid down for its observance, and light fires or till the ground or carry loads or demand the restoration of deposits or recover loans, or do all else that we are permitted to do as well on days that are not festival seasons.*
>
> - *It is true also that the keeping of festivals is a symbol of gladness of soul and of thankfulness to God, but we should not for this reason turn our backs on the general gatherings of the year's season.*
>
> - *It is true that receiving circumcision does indeed portray the excision of pleasure and all passions, and the putting away of the impious conceit, under which the mind supposed that it was capable of begetting by its own power: but let us not on this account repeal the law laid down for circumcising.*
>
> - *Why, we shall be ignoring the sanctity of the Temple and a thousand other things, if we are going to pay heed to nothing except what is shown us by the inner meaning of things.*
>
> - *Nay, we should look on all these outward observances as resembling the body, and their inner meaning as resembling the soul, so we must pay heed to the letter of the Laws.*

6. See P. Borgen, *"Paul Preaches Circumcision and Pleases Men" and Other Essays on Christian Origins*, pp. 87-88; *id., Philo, John and Paul*, pp. 65-68.

> - *If we keep and observe these, we shall gain a clearer conception of those things of which these are the symbols; and besides that we shall not incur the censure of the many and the charges they are sure to bring against us.*

Here we find a conflict between two ways of reasoning, both relying upon the Laws of Moses. *Philo's view* might be characterized in this way: the universal principles and activity of the Creator are tied to the specific external observances of a particular nation, the Jewish nation. On this basis this particular nation has a universal function. *The view which Philo criticises* seems to be: The Laws of Moses and the specific observances give witness to the universal principles and activity of the Creator. These universal principles can then be followed apart from the particular external laws and observances of the Jewish nation. Consequently, God's activity and universal principles can be present also when one works on the sabbath just as one does on other days. Philo warns that the Jewish community will incur censure and place charges against those who champion such views.

John's Gospel shows kinship with the spiritualizing and universal views which Philo criticizes. Similar to their views, John holds that the Laws of Moses and the specific observances, such as sabbath, festivals and circumcision, give witness to the activity of the Creator. Since they serve as witness in this way, they do not have importance in themselves and are not binding as external observances any longer.[7] There is a basic difference, however, between the spiritualizing Jews whom Philo criticizes, and the views expressed in John. According to John, the Laws of Moses and the specific observances give witness to the activity of the Creator through his Son, the specific historical person, Jesus of Nazareth. Therefore, this person has a universal function.

Philo warns that those who held the views he criticized will be subject to censure by the community which will bring charges against them. Correspondingly, John 5:16 and 18 tell that Jesus' fellow Jews persecuted him and sought to kill him.

Those who sought to kill Jesus hold a view corresponding to that of Philo. They agreed with the interpretation presupposed in John 5:17 that God worked also on the sabbath, but they combined this understanding with maintaining that specific observance of the sabbath should be kept. They rejected the view that these laws were to give witness to the ongoing work of God in such a way that they were not binding as observances any more, and they rejected the judgment that God's upholding and providential work was carried out by Jesus, as the Son of God. To them this was blasphemy.

It is worth stressing that *Migr.* 91 has striking points of similarities with John 5:1-18. Both places deal with the sabbath. In both places the exegesis of Gen. 2:2-3 is presupposed and utilized, although this Old Testament passage is not quoted and therefore not interpreted in a direct way. And in both places the understanding that God is always active is witnessed to by the sabbath in such a way as to give freedom from the specific observances, such as the prohibition against carrying a load.

[7] Cf. S. Pancaro, *The Law in the Fourth Gospel*, (Leiden, 1975). p. 160: "Jesus' work of revelation (in the concrete case at hand: the healing of the paralytic on the sabbath, which signifies the "gift of life" by the Father in Jesus) puts an end to the sabbath by bringing to perfection and completion the divine purpose which lay behind the OT sabbath." As for circumcision, referred to by John in 7:19-24, Pancaro writes: "The Jewish rite of initiation, which made man a member of God's people, was unable to give man what Jesus came to bring. Jesus alone gives men the power to become children of God and to have life in abundance, and this is what was prefigured by circumcision" (p. 165).

It is probable that John in 5:1-18 has interpreted the Jesus tradition under the influence of some Jews who entertained views similar to those against which Philo warns himself and his readers.

John 1:1-18: The creation story and Jesus of Nazareth. The witness of John the Baptist and of the Law of Moses.

Again it must be stressed that no source analysis as such will be discussed in this study.[8] The analysis will be based upon the Prologue in its present form and in its present context as part of the Gospel.

In John 5:1-18 we analysed a controversial legal case which took place on the sabbath. The debate that followed this specific case broadened the perspective even up to the actitivy of the Creator. The healing on the sabbath gave witness to God's activity through His Son towards His creation. In John 1:1-18 creation is in the center, but also here specific factors in history give witness to aspects of creation. John the Baptist is a witness to the primordial light, v. 9. He also testifies that Logos/the Son, identical with Jesus Christ, was pre-existent, v. 15. Most important, the Law given by Moses points to the divine reality brought by Jesus,v.17, or, as said in 5:46: Moses wrote about Jesus as the Son ot God, the Father. Thus, one might look upon John 1:1-18 as a passage which formulates how Moses in the creation story wrote about Jesus, as the Logos before creation, as agent of creation and as light for the created beings.

How then is the creation story utilized?[9] John 1:1-2 follows the exegetical tradition which makes *br'št/en archē* in Gen. 1:1 refer to what existed prior to the creation of the world. The term *ho logos* in vv. 1-2 and v. 14 is an expository development based on the phrase "God said," in Gen. 1:3.[10] Philo in *Somn.* I:75, demonstrates how this phrase in Gen. 1:3 can be interpreted as Logos in the absolute sense, and he can at times attribute to Logos personal features (*Conf.* 146), just as is the case in John 1:1-2,14.

In John 1:3 the words *br''t hšmym w't h'rṣ,* "created the heavens and earth", Gen.1:1, are replaced by a traditional formula for the creation: *panta di autou egeneto, kai chōris autou egeneto oude en ho gegonen,*" all things were made through him and without him was not anything made that was made." A variant of the formula is found in v.10: *ho kosmos di autou egeneto,* "the world was made through him." Finally, the term "light" and "darkness" *(phōs* and *skotia)* in John 1:4-5 are taken from Gen. 1:2-5, *'wr* and *hšk*. The term "light" is repeated in John 1:7,8,9, and both terms are frequently used in the Gospel.[11] John 1:1-5 thus draws heavily on Gen. 1:1-5, the verses which deal with the beginning and the first day of creation.

On the basis of these observations on John 1:1-5 three themes will be sketched:

1. Logos before creation, and the Epiphany with the coming of Jesus.

8. Concerning the source analysis of the Prologue, see the survey of Johannine research in H. Thyen, *ThR.* NF 39, 1974, 1-69, 222-252; J. Becker, *ThR* NF 47, 1982, 305-347; *ThR* NF 51, 1986, 1-78. A recent analysis is O. Hofius, "Struktur und Gedankengang des Logos-Hymnus in John 1:1-18," *ZNW* 78, 1987, 1-25.

9. For the following analysis, see P. Borgen,*"Logos was the Light" and Other Essays on the Gospel of John,* (Trondheim, 1983), pp. 13-22 and 95-110; (also in *NTS,* 14, 1972, pp. 115-130, and *NT* 23, 1976, pp. 67-75); in revised form in *id., Philo, John and Paul,* pp. 75-101.

10. See also Ps. 33:6.

11. John 3:19ff; 8:12; 9:5; 12:35, 46.

2. The creator and owner who came and was not received.
3. The primordial light and the coming of light.

1. Logos before creation, and Logos' epiphany as Jesus, the Son. Corresponding to the thought model applied to the Torah, - that it existed before creation and was revealed at Sinai - Logos, who existed before creation, became flesh and existed as Jesus Christ, John 1:14. In this verse, the relationship between Logos and God is explained further as that of the Son to the Father. Thus, the appearence of Logos is seen as an epiphany of the Father's glory. In this way John 1:14-18: at several points draws on the theophany at Sinai.[12] Moses was not allowed to see the face of God, whom no one has ever seen, Exod. 33:20. This is alluded to in John 1:18. Logos, as Son, or even God, who is in the bosom of the Father, has made him known, 1:18. And the disciples saw the glory of Logos in flesh, glory as of the only Son to his Father, 1:14. In this way the Law given by Moses told about creation and the Sinai-event as a witness to Jesus as Logos, the Son of God, 1:17.

2. The Creator and owner who came and was not received. In John 1:3 it was stated that all things came into being through Logos. This is repeated in v.10: cosmos came into being through him. This is seen as a background for cosmos' rejection of him through whom it came into being. In v.11 the historical appearance of Jesus is stated: "He came to his own and his own human beings received him not." The debate whether *ta idia* refers to the world or to Israel seems to miss the point. Israel is rather to be seen as the centre of the world and therefore represents the world.[13] A motif from Wisdom tradition is reflected here, such as stated in Enoch 40:2: "Wisdom came to make the dwelling place among the children of men and found no dwelling place."[14] This rejection motif in John 1:10-11 formulates in a general and summary fashion that Jesus was persecuted and that they sought to kill him, John 5:1-18, and other places.

3. The primordial light and the coming of light. The light is mentioned in John 1:4-9, its coming being referred to in v.9. The translation of v. 9 is difficult, however, and is much debated. I have elsewhere defended the grammatical understanding, that the participle *erchomenon,* coming, refers back to the subject of *phōtizei,* enlightens, i.e. to the subject *to phōs,* light. The participle without the article thus expresses what happens simultaneously with the action of the verb. The translation is thus: "He [*Logos*] was the true light, which enlightens every man when it (light) enters the world." Freely rendered the verse goes thus: Logos was the true light which enlightens every man by coming into the world.[15] What provides the thought-model for this coming of light?[16] One might attempt to interpret light against the background of ideas of Messiah's light, but since Logos in John is the light, it is more probable that

12. See especially M.E. Boismard, *St. John's Prologue,* (Westminster, 1957), pp. 136-140; S. Schulz, *Komposition und Herkunft der johanneischen Reden,* (Stuttgart, 1960), pp. 40f; N.A. Dahl, The Johannine Church and History," in W. Klassen and G. F. Snyder, *Current Issues in New Testament Interpretation,* (New York, 1962), pp. 32-133.

13. See especially N.A. Dahl, "The Johannine Church and History," esp.p. 129; P. Borgen, *Bread from Heaven.* 2. ed. (Leiden 1981), pp. 148f, 175-179; *id.; "Logos was the True Light" and Other Essays,* p. 17; *id., Philo, John and Paul,* p. 83.

14. See R.E. Brown, *The Gospel According to John, I-XII,* (Garden City, N.Y., 1966), 30 and 523.

15. P. Borgen, *"Logos was the True Light', and Other Essays on the Gospel of John,* pp. 102-103; *id., Philo, John and Paul,* pp. 86-87.

16. For a more comprehensive discussion of the following interpretation, see P. Borgen, *"Logos Was the True Light" and Other Essays,* pp. 103-106, *id., Philo, John and Paul,* pp. 87-89.

the thought-model behind v. 9 is the coming of the primordial light with the lawgiving of Moses. Among the several points which support this interpretation, it should be mentioned that the lawgiving of Moses was for all men, so also in John 1:9 the light shines for every man by coming into the world. Of particular note here is the Wisdom of Solomon 18:4 where it says that the law's light will be given to the world. Thus, in John 1:9 it is stressed that Jesus as the primordial Logos/light, has a universal importance and has a universal role. He enlightens every man.

The three themes which we have sketched show us three aspects of the connection between creation (and before) and the revelation in history, i.e. in Jesus Christ:

1. The epiphany which brought men to see God's glory;

2. The appearance of the creator and owner of cosmos and the rejection of him by his own people; and

3. The universal role of the primordial light which shines as the historical person Jesus Christ.

As shown in our analysis, John draws here on the Old Testament and on exegetical traditions. Thus, the Prologue demonstrates how Moses wrote about Jesus, the Son of God, John 5:46.

Logos **ensarkos** *and Logos* **asarkos?** *Some indications.*

In John's Gospel there is a strong concentration on the historical person and event of Jesus. Thus, creation ideas are applied to him as we have seen in John 1:1-18 and 5:17-18. The question should be raised, however, whether John also has a more general use of creation ideas. Are there indications that divine activity is taking place within a broader perspective?

There is a long exegetical tradition which interprets John 1:9 on the basis of the following translation: "He (the Logos) was the true light which enlightens every man who comes into the world." Then the meaning would be that there are elements of light in every human being. Even though a rabbinic formula about becoming man seems to lend support to this approach, the translation does not seem satisfactory. The context, as well as John 3:19 and 12:46, shows that the word *erchomenon* concerns the coming of light, and not the birth of every man. On this basis the translation which gives best meaning and which is grammatically defendable, is "He (the Logos) was the true light, which enlightens every man when it enters the world."[17] The conclusion is: John 1:9 does not give us insight into divine activity in creation beyond the event of incarnation.

There is an opening for a broader perspective in John 5:17, however. When it says that the Father works up to now, i.e. including this particular Sabbath, it means that the Father is active in his upholding and providential work all the time in all of His creation. The word *arti* (up to now) refers to the activity of the Father from creation and up to the present. According to John 5:20-21 the Father is the one who gives life, here specified as the raising of the dead. This activity of the Father has been handed over to the Son. Compare the fact that in rabbinic exegesis God has in his own hand the key to rain, the key to the womb, and the key to the resurrection of the dead (*Taanith* 2a).

[17] See further P. Borgen, "*Logos was the True Light and Other Essays*, pp. 102-103; *id., Philo, John and Paul, 86-87.*

Within this context the healing of the paralytic by Jesus on the Sabbath as an example of the lifegiving activity given to the Son by the Father, is a specific demonstration of God's upholding and providential care for His creation. In other words, salvation seems to be seen as making God's providence manifest. This particular manifestation of God's providence anticipates the eschatological resurrection.

Two points from the Prologue indicate a similar kind of universal perspective. First human beings are seen as a part of the created "all things," *panta,* John 1:3. R. Bultmann[18] interprets *panta* to refer to mankind, but this understanding does not do justice to the emphatic statement that "without him (Logos) was not anything made that was made." Moreover, the background in the creation story, Gen. 1:1ff, shows that all of creation is meant. Thus, anthropology is part of cosmology in John, although it is not absorbed by cosmology since Logos became flesh and brought life to human beings.[19] John does not spell out further the relationship between the salvation of human beings and of all of creation.[20] Nevertheless, phenomena within creation, such as the wind (John 3:8); day and night (9:4; 11:9-10); bread (6:26-27); a grain of wheat that falls into the earth, dies, and grows up and gives fruit (12:24); birth (16:21; 3:3ff.); the vine (15:1ff), etc. can serve as "symbols" of the work of the Son among men.

John 1:4 goes behind the coming of light in Jesus (v.9) to light as a cosmic light of human beings. Verse 4 deals with the ideas of life and light in relation to Logos and mankind from the creation and onwards with no direct reference to the incarnation. This thought serves as cosmic background for the coming of light, v. 9, but its actual functioning among human beings prior to the coming of light in Jesus Christ is not clearly defined.[21] Although the perspective is cosmic and thus broader than being a reference to redemptive history, still it is relevant in this connection to mention that persons in biblical history saw the Logos/Christ prior to the incarnation.[22] The vision of Isaiah 6 is thus interpreted as a vision of the Logos who was in the beginning and became flesh, John 12:41. Moreover, when John 5:37b refers to the vision of the form of God, it probably refers to the epiphany at Sinai. The "form of God" seems then to mean the Logos who became incarnate as Jesus Christ, since the rejection of Jesus implied that they had not seen God's form at Sinai.

Moreover, in John 1:10-11 it is said,that Logos came to his own (property). The basis for Logos' ownership is the view that he served as agent in the creation of the world, v. 10 and v. 3. He came to the world which he had himself created.[23] Thus, the relationship of Logos to the world was that of ownership, even prior to the incarnation.

A central point in the Prologue of John is the view that the creator and redeemer are one and the same. Logos is both agent in the act of creation and the Logos who

18. *The Gospel of John,* (Philadelphia, 1977), pp. 36-37.

19. See G. Siegwall, "Der Prolog des Johannesevangelium als Einführung in eine christliche Theologie der Rekapitulation," *Neue Zeitschrift für systematische Theologie,* 24, 1982, 150-171.

20. A cosmic dimension can be seen in John 12:31, "the ruler of this world," but also here the relation to mankind is in the center.

21. Cf. C.K. Barrett, *The Gospel according to St. John,* 2. ed., *157:* "The Prologue . . . sets first in a cosmological what later will appear in a soteriological." Cf. B. Lindars, *The Gospel of John,* (London, 1972), pp. 85-86, and P. Borgen, *Philo, John and Paul,* pp. 89-92.

22. Cf. N.A. Dahl, "The Johannine Church and History," pp. 130-136.

23. See B. Lindars, *The Gospel of John,* p. 90.

became flesh. Against this background one might analyze the particular and general aspects of "flesh", *sarx*. In John 1:14 "flesh" refers to the particular historical person, Jesus of Nazareth. Thus, one cannot in John's Gospel talk about a general incarnational principle. Nevertheless, "flesh" is a concept which applies to every one born by a woman, John 3:6, and is part of that which was created. When it is said that "Logos became flesh", John 1:14, this means that there is unity between, on the one hand the one who was before creation and through whom all things came into being, and on the other hand the creatures in the woman-born historical person Jesus of Nazareth. Accordingly, the fleshly or bodily aspect of the raising up of human beings on the last day, John 6:39 and 54, must be taken seriously.[24]

Conclusion

Now we can answer the questions which were raised at the beginning. *First,* how is material from the Old Testament used, especially with reference to the creation story? Both in John 5:17-18 and 1:1-18 John draws on Jewish exegetical traditions relating to the creation story, mainly Gen. 1:1-5 and 2:2-3. In 5:17 a problem-solving exegetical tradition is used. How could it be said that God rested on the Seventh day, Gen 2:2-3, when he was always active and at work? John 1:1-5 follows the exegetical tradition of referring "in the beginning," Gen. 1:1,to what existed prior to the creation of the world, and replaces the words in Gen. 1:1, "created the heavens and the earth," with a widespread creation formula, and finally follows the tradition of interpreting light and darkness as dualistic principles or forces. Several words from Gen. 1:1-5 are paraphrased by John, in passages other than John 1:1-5.

In John 1:14-18 words are taken from the story about the theophany at Sinai, Exod 33:17-34:9. These words are paraphrased in John.

Second, What is the relationship between the specifics of persons, events, the laws of sabbath observance on the one hand, and the general and universal perspective of creation on the other hand?

The Law of Moses, (the Sabbath observances, the creation story, the theophany at Sinai, etc.) is a testimony to the Logos, the Son, the agent of creation and the primordial light, and to the Son's providential/salvific activity even on the Sabbath. The healing of the paralytic points to the resurrection of the dead. John the Baptist gives witness to primordial light and to the pre-existent Logos/Son.

This witnessing function of the Law and the observances meant that the specific observances as such were not binding any more. The Law pointed beyond itself and ceased to have importance in itself.

Central to John, however, is the idea that the Law of Moses and thus the specific observances give witness to the activity of the Creator through His Son, the specific historical person, Jesus of Nazareth. This historical person, therefore, has a universal function, corresponding to the idea of Torah existing before creation and being revealed in history at the theophany at Sinai.

There are indications that the divine activity, with its center in the Incarnation, is seen within the broader perspective of cosmos and redemptive history. Salvation, exemplified by the healing of the paralytic, is seen as making God's providence

[24] Cf. C.K. Barrett, *The Gospel according to St. John*, pp. 68-69, 262, 283f, 294; P. Borgen, *Bread from Heaven*, pp. 166-172. 188-192.

manifest. Anthropology is part of cosmology, although man has a special relationship to God and his Son. Logos, who became flesh in Jesus Christ, could be seen already by persons in biblical history, and the relationship of Logos to the world was that of ownership, even prior to the Incarnation. Finally, the Incarnation means that in Jesus of Nazareth there is unity between Logos, who was in the beginning and through whom things came into being, and the creatures in the woman-born historical person Jesus Christ.

Third, since John 5:1-18 tells about a growing conflict between Jesus and his fellow Jews, are there traces found in Jewish sources to indicate that corresponding controversies on the particular and universal took place also elsewhere in Judaism?

Philo, in *Migr.* 89-93 gives evidence for a similar controversy. *Philo's own view was:* the universal principle and activity of the Creator are tied to the specific laws and observances of the Jewish nation. Therefore, this particular nation has a universal role in the world. *The view criticized by Philo was:* The Laws of Moses and the specific observances give witness to the universal principles and activity of the Creator. These universal principles can be followed apart from the particular observances of the Jewish nation. Since these observances are not binding as such, one can do away with them, and work on the sabbath, such as carrying loads, etc.

The views of those who persecuted Jesus and sought to kill him were akin to those of Philo himself. The views of the Johannine community seem to have as background an understanding similar to the one criticized by Philo: the Laws of Moses point beyond themselves to the Creator and his activity in creation. Distinct to John is the crystallization of all these creation concepts around the particular historical person, Jesus of Nazareth.

Philo warns that those who held the views he criticizes would be censured by the community, which would bring charges against them. Jesus was persecuted, and his fellow Jews sought to kill him, according to John 5:16.18; cf. 1:10-11.

John 5:1-18 can be understood as an initiation story which served as paradigm for the entry into the Johannine community. Those who entered would see the law of Moses and the whole Jewish context as a witness to Jesus, the Son of God. Thus, creation, the theophany at Sinai, etc. pointed to the epiphany in this Logos/Son. The observances of sabbath, Jewish festivals, circumcision, etc. were not binding, since the divine purpose which is behind these specifics was now present in Logos *ensarkos,* Jesus as the Son of God.

THE BIBLICAL UNDERSTANDING OF CREATION AND THE HUMAN COMMITMENT

SHEMARYAHU TALMON

I

It would appear that the present discussion of the meaning of creation has been timed for a very propitious moment in the Jewish cultic year. About two weeks ago, Jews all over the world observed Rosh Hashanah, the festival which marks the beginning of the new year. A Jewish tradition ascribed to Rabbi Eliezer ben Hyrcanus (second century C.E.) has it that this season coincides with the time of the year in which creation occurred.[1] While this synchronization obviously cannot be taken at face value, yet it highlights an idea on which I will comment, namely that creation merges at some juncture with history and transcends it, ultimately flowing into metahistory. Thus creation can yet be observed in actual human life experience. One way or another this linking of creation with history reflects the concept of a *creatio continua* which is debated by Jewish thinkers, and not by them alone.

The linkage of creation with history by synchronizing the beginning of the world with the beginning of the calendar year was especially accentuated in a dissident Jewish tradition, which came to our knowledge barely forty years ago. I refer to the discovery in the Judean Desert of ancient manuscripts which constitute the "Library of the Covenanters of Qumran."[2] An investigation of the most ingenious solar-lunar calendar of 364 days to which the Covenanters adhered proves that their first day of the year always fell on the fourth day of the week, the day on which the Creator God is said to have fashioned the great luminaries (Genesis 1:16).[3] There can be little doubt that in this instance the synchronization of the flow of time in the actual life of the individual and of society is highlighted by harnessing the calendar to the timetable of the biblical creation story. Thus history is riveted to a time pattern which was divinely established for eternity from the very beginning of the world.

I am inclined to see in this view of creation as merging into history an expression of the meaning which can be attached to creation: it serves as a guideline for a human commitment to principles of individual and societal behavior, such as can be extra-polated in essence from the biblical traditions concerning the beginning of the world.

II

I propose to structure my presentation as follows: I shall approach the matter at hand from two viewpoints which are indeed connected, but nevertheless are subject to different modes of description and analysis.

1. Rabbi Joshua ben Hananiah holds that the world was created in the months of Nissan in which Passover falls (b.RHSh 10b-11a).

2. F. M. Cross, *The Ancient Library of Qumran and Modern Biblical Studies,* rev. ed. (Grand Rapids: Baker Book House, 1980).

3. See S. Talmon, "The Calendar Reckoning of the Sect from the Judaean Desert," *Scripta Hierosolymitana* 4, ed. C. Rabin and Y. Yadin (Jerusalem: Magnes, 1965), p. 176.

The first part of my presentation is determined by the exegetical methods, developed and perfected in contemporary biblical scholarship. Here we must bring under scrutiny a variety of creation traditions which are presented in the Hebrew Scriptures, albeit merely in bits and parts. It goes without saying that on that level one may expect a high degree of similarity both in analytical techniques and in the results at which scholars would arrive irrespective of their creed or confession: objectivity, determined by scientific reasoning, outweighs or should outweigh subjectivity.

The restrictions imposed upon the professional scholar by the demand for objectivity become less stringent when he approaches the problem of creation as an interpreter who aims to extrapolate from the biblical tradition guidelines for human behavior in the present time. At this stage of his investigation he necessarily speaks "from within the credal fold" of his persuasion, and is actually called upon to bring into play his religious beliefs. In doing so, he will integrate himself into the ongoing process of interpretation of the seminal biblical texts in his particular tradition as it developed over the ages. Therefore, in the second part of my deliberations, decidedly speaking as a Jewish Bible scholar, I shall direct my remarks exclusively to the creation story in the book of Genesis which became normative in Jewish tradition. That is to say, only in passing shall I mention allusions to other depictions of creation found in the Hebrew Bible which reflect ancient Near Eastern myths that were still current among the Hebrews, had been absorbed into their cultural heritage and infiltrated their sacred writings.

While it is desirable to separate the *objective* approach from the *subjective*, it would be preposterous to maintain that this separation can be always neatly achieved. At times the "two souls that dwell in our breast" will strive to be united. At this or the other juncture the realm of scholarly objectivity will be invaded by subjective ideological or religious considerations which arise from the *condition humaine*. This seems to be acceptable as long as the merging occurs under control, that is to say as long as subjective interpretation is not given full dominance over scholarly objectivity, thus turning the exegesis of biblical texts into an eisegesis.

The duality of approaches outlined above is linked with two further phenomena which must be taken into account. One pertains to the matter under investigation, the other to the investigator.

(a) We should first highlight a difficulty which confronts the student of the Hebrew Scriptures, irrespective of his credal affiliation, who sets out to extract from the factual accounts of events which predominate in biblical literature the never fully-explicated principles and concepts which supposedly inspired them. It may be considered a characteristic of this literature that rarely, if ever, will a biblical author present his reflections on matters which then were current in the Israelite marketplace of ideas in a systematic fashion and in conceptual terms.

From this results a dilemma which is the common experience of all students of the Hebrew Bible: the investigator who sets out to present an integrated picture of any aspect in the biblical world of ideas must resort to conjoining fragmentary bits of mostly factual information, extracted from a diversity of texts. Scholars have called attention to the narrative-dramatic tenor of the biblical creation account and the concomitant paucity of abstract vocables in the biblical as well as the post-biblical Hebrew vocabulary pertaining to creation.[4] Conceptualization does not surface in the

[4] *E.g.* H. H. Rowley, *The Growth of the Old Testament* (New York: Harper and Row, 1963, p. 137; J. Vajda, *Introduction a la pensée juive du moyen âge* (Paris: Librairie Philosophique, 1947), p. 12.

texts themselves. Rather can it be achieved, to a restricted degree, by the scholar's endeavor to distill from the reported "facts" elements which will assist him in revealing the presumed cogitation and conceptualization of the ancient writers. The result of this labor will perforce always be a mosaic in which many pieces are missing.[5]

(b) The Jewish scholar faces an additional limitation which impedes his attempt to delineate the specifically Jewish appreciation of conceptual matters pertaining to the Bible, such as the understanding of creation and the imperatives of human commitment which can be elicited from it. Judaism is not monolithic in the interpretation of its heritage. In the present framework it would be impossible to do justice to the diverse nuances, some even varying on principles, which can be discerned in Jewish tradition in reference to the issue under review. As is the case in regard to other aspects of speculative thought, also the varying interpretations of creation to a large degree depend directly upon the specific historical situation in which this or the other interpretation is offered. The application of biblical ideas to the changing realities of successive generations of Jewish thinkers bears the imprint of contemporary political-religious conditions. It follows that in an attempt to define the essence of the Jewish understanding of creation selection is imperative. Even then, what will emerge is the view of a Jew and not of Jewish tradition in its comprehensiveness. Therefore, one can only hope to recapture some pivotal aspects which guide, or should guide, Jewish thinking on creation and on its demands on human commitment in the present age.

Let me add that in reality Judaism diverged and still diverges from the principles which seemingly can be distilled from the basic normative sources of the Hebrew Bible. Reality seldom dovetails with ideal concepts which bear upon them the stamp of Utopia. To put it in a nutshell, in the words of T. S. Eliot: "Between the idea–And the reality–Between the motion–And the act–falls the shadow." Here arises in full force the problem of relating ideas to actualities. On the one hand, we may run the danger of altogether subjecting actualities in their relativity to visionary absolute morals. On the other hand, immediacy and expediency can cause short-range deliberations of practicality to gain the upper hand over principles. Judaism is fully aware of this predicament and tries to steer a middle path. We may apply to our problem, *mutatis mutandis,* a statement by Martin Buber relating not to creation, but to the execution of perfect justice in the world of reality: "it is true that we are not able to live in perfect justice, and in order to preserve the community of man, we are often compelled to accept wrongness in decisions concerning the community." But, he continues, and here lies the applicability of this dictum to the issue of Creation and the human commitment: "what matters is that in every hour of decision we are aware of our responsibility and summon our conscience to weigh exactly how much is necessary to preserve the community [and possibly humanity], and accept just so much and no more."[6]

5. See S. Talmon, "Kingship and the Ideology of the State," in *King, Cult, and Calendar in Ancient Israel* (Jerusalem: Magnes, 1986), pp.9-12.

6. M. Buber, "Hebrew Humanism," *Israel and the World: Essays in a Time of Crisis* (New York: Schocken, 1948), p. 246.

III

Let me now turn to a consideration proper of the issue which is under review. I aim at offering an understanding of some pivotal texts which in some way differ from points of view which were put forward in our symposium. I intend to probe the frame of mind of the biblical writers to the best of my ability, rather than using their texts as props for underpinning one or another modern theology of creation. Toward this end, I shall endeavor to highlight some aspects of the pertinent texts which in my view are essential for gauging the conceptual bases of the biblical tradition:

(a) Creation is seen as the first and fundamental constituent in a time scheme which encompasses primordiality together with experienced history and comprises as well the uncharted future.

(b) The multiformity which inheres in and characterizes creation constitutes the immutable basis of the plurality and diversity of phenomena which man observes in human life and in the cosmos altogether and which he is duty bound to preserve.

(c) From here it follows that the biblical creation tradition, like the biblical literature altogether, addresses the question how the earth goes and how to go about on earth, rather than how the heavens go and how men can go to heaven, as Dr. Jaki put it paraphrasing St. Augustine.

Not unlike cosmogonies which were transmitted by diverse people in many cultures all over the world, the biblical creation tradition gives expression to a pre- or proto-scientific endeavor on the part of men of faith to fathom the quintessence of the universe, chart the place of man in it and define the tasks and functions allotted to him. This tradition has necessarily a retrospective thrust. It may enlighten us on the understanding and the intellectual stance of the biblical author or authors, rather than reveal the factualities of creation which remained hidden to the ancients not less or possibly even more than to modern man. It is because of this deficiency, namely the fact that "Scripture does not give us definitions of things any more than nature does," that Spinoza held the Hebrew Bible in low regard.[7]

It is from here that any attempt to define a human commitment to creation in the framework of the Jewish, and similarly in the Christian world of ideas, must take its departure.

It should be stressed that like its ensuing interpretation in postbiblical Judaism, scriptural tradition concerning creation is not monolithic. There is no need to engage here in a detailed investigation of this well-known fact. Some remarks will suffice to put the issue in perspective. Above all, two quite diverse creation traditions can be discerned:

(1) the major tradition, embedded in the first part of the book of Genesis, which, as will yet be spelled out, scholars consider to be itself composite; and

(2) diffuse residues of ancient Near Eastern tales of creation.

Let me first refer to these vestiges of ancient cosmogonies which had been current in Mesopotamia and the Canaanite expanse on the coast of the Mediterranean. Of special importance in this respect are survivals of epic texts in the Bible which echo sources that have been known to scholars for approximately half a century. These texts were inscribed on tablets discovered at Minet-el-Baida, a small seaside town on

7. *The Chief Works of Benedict de Spinoza*, Vol. I, transl. R. H. M. Elwes (London: G. Bell and Sons, 1883-84). p. 101.

the Phoenician coast. Until the thirteenth century B.C.E. the kingdom of Ugarit had occupied this territory. The geographical proximity of the site, and the linguistic similarity of Ugaritic, a west-semitic language, and biblical Hebrew facilitated the absorption of Ugaritic phraseology and imagery into the ancient Israelites' literature.[8] But the pagan substance of those mythopoeic works was obviously rejected by the biblical authors. Therefore, they play an only secondary role in their writings and in the present context do not require more than cursory attention.

These mythological residues pertain predominantly to two features of ancient cosmogony:

(a) We find recurring references to a creator deity who battles against shadowy forces, represented by primordial monsters that oppose him in the act of creation: Mot, lord of the netherworld, and his allies Yam, Tiamat-Sheol, Behemot, Leviathan, Rahab, the Rigid[9] (rather than: Fleeing) and the Twisting Serpent. It will suffice to quote only a few passages in biblical literature which reflect these mostly epic tales.[10] These residual references were, in fact, intended by the biblical authors to highlight the impotence of those fiends when their futile opposition is viewed in the framework of the monotheistic biblical tradition which portrays the acts of the sole and sovereign Creator God:

Job 7:8:	He alone stretched out the skies, trampled upon **Yam's** carcass;
Job 26:12-14:	With his might he subdued **Yam,** with his wisdom he crushed **Rahab,** with his will he fashioned heavens, his hand transfixed the **Rigid** [fleeing] **Serpent;**
Job 9:13:	God will not let his fury rest [until] **Rahab's** minions are brought to their knees;
Job 38:8-10:	[I, God] locked in **Yam** [the sea] behind [closed] gates. . . , I marked the bounds it was not to cross and kept it behind bolted doors;
Jeremiah 5:22:	I set the sand [of the shores] as a limit to **Yam** [the sea], as an everlasting barrier it cannot pass (cf. Job 7:2);
Psalm 74:13-14:	By your power you split **Yam,** you smashed the heads of the **Taninim** upon the waters, you crushed **Leviathan's** heads.

Similar terminology is used in passages in which the writer entreats God to re-enact his victory over inimical powers in his future battles against them:

8. I can absolve myself from dealing in detail with these texts since they were extensively discussed by Gerald Janzen. See his paper in the present issue.

9. The rendition of Heb. *nāhāš bārīah* by 'rigid serpent,' connecting it with *bārīah* = bolt, shaft, rather than deriving it from *brh* = flee, escape, accords better with the designation of its companion as *nāhāš 'aqalātōn* = 'bent or twisting serpent.'

10. The recent study by Carola Kloos, *YHWH's Combat with the Sea* (Leiden; Brill. 1986) provides a succinct discussion of the issue, together with a comprehensive bibliography to which may be added: J. B. Geyer, "Twisting Tiamat's Tail: A Mythological Interpretation of Isaiah XIII 5 and 8," *VT* xxxvii (1987), pp. 164-79.

Isaiah 27:1: That day, YHWH, with his hard sword, massive and strong, will bring punishment upon **Leviathan,** the **Rigid** [fleeing] **Serpent,** and upon **Leviathan** the bent **[Twisting] Serpent,** he will kill the **Tanin of Yam** [the sea].

It can be confidently surmised that all these mentions had already lost their original pagan content, and that the biblical writers employed mythological terminology as figures of speech, drawing from a storehouse of well-known Canaanite, or rather, ancient Semitic mythopoeic phraseology. This is borne out by the fact that the same vocabulary is also employed on a quite different plane by biblical authors who implore God to vanquish his enemies, who are the enemies of Israel in history:

Isaiah 51:9: Arise, arise! Clothe yourself in strength, arm of YHWH, arise as in the past, in times long ago, when you transfixed **Rahab,** pierced **Tanin,** dried up the Sea [**Yam**], the waters of the great abyss [**Tehom = Tiamat**].

It is of interest to observe that such borrowed mythopoeic imagery is found mainly in prophetic and wisdom literature, and in Psalms, in which poetic license facilitates their employment. They are practically absent from biblical historiography and also from the Pentateuch, in which historical narratives and legal materials preponderate. The one mention of **Taninim** in the normative Creation tradition in Genesis, actually substantiates the claim that this pagan terminology had lost its cosmogonic connotations for the Hebrew writers. The biblical tradition emphatically denigrates the primordial monsters whom mythology could present as opposing the creator-deity, to the status of creatures which like all creatures were sovereignly fashioned by the one and only God: "He created the great **Taninim** and every kind of living creature with which the waters teem" (Genesis 1:21).

Mark the insistence on referring to these primordial deities in the plural, thus denying to them any presumed original "divine" singularity. Their reduction to mere creatures is further developed in God's famous reply to Job, who rebelled against the injustice that he had suffered: no human has a right to question the mystery of God's acts of him who alone created the world. In this context, the ancient myth of a primordial monster opposing the creator-deity is given a most interesting twist: the "mighty Leviathan" is turned into a pet that can be paraded in public:

Job 40:25-29 [RSV, 41:1-5; JB, 40:20-24]: Can you catch **Leviathan** with a fish hook, or put a line through his tongue? Can you put a ring through his nose, or pierce his jaw with a hook? Will he plead and plead with you, will he coax you with smooth words? Will he make an agreement with you to become your eternal slave? Will you play with him like [with a] pet bird, tie him on a leash for [the amusement] of your maids?

The comparison of this Job passage with the text of Isaiah 37:36 on which Bennie Ollenburger commented,[11] provides a persuasive illustration of the "historization" of mythic materials in the biblical literature. Some of the imagery in which is depicted

[11] See B. C. Ollenburger, "Isaiah's Creation Theology," in the present volume.

the subjection of the mighty Leviathan in creation myths, is used in Isaiah to announce God's humiliating the proud Assyrian king Sennacherib whose forces threaten to storm the city of Jerusalem: "I will put my hook in your nose and my bit in your lips."[12] The mythopoeic nature of this phraseology is brought in full light by the preceding reference to the days of yore: "You must have heard it: I fashioned all this long ago from days of old; I created it (then–*yesartīhā),* now I brought it" (Isaiah 37:26), obviously--to have it acted out in history.

It is probable that also the portrayal of the snake in the Garden of Eden which cunningly persuades man to violate the Creator's commandments and in punishment is reduced to "eating dust" (Genesis 3:1-15), is meant to ridicule the primordial serpent that had dared to oppose the mythological divine creator.

We may, in fact, have here a two-register "verbal portrayal" of the Canaanite twin-monsters, the "Rigid" and the "Twisting" Serpents. The ending of the Garden of Eden episode which has the snake crawling on its belly and winding in the dust (3:14), not unlike the *nāhāš ʿaqalātōn,* evidently presupposes that in its first encounter with Eve the snake stood straight and then resembled the *nāhāš bārīah* (3:1-4). Rabbinic tradition indeed pictures the snake as standing initially upright and approaching Eve like a human being, actually as a man. Thus interpreted, the Eden episode would contain one other indirect reduction of mythological deities to dust.

The biblical Garden of Eden story actually may be altogether an adjusted ancient Near Eastern mythological tale. What looks like an early pagan version of the Genesis account is yet preserved in an oracle against the King of Tyre in the book of Ezekiel. There (Ezek. 28:11-19), that king is depicted strutting proudly among sundry precious stones which abound in God's "Garden of Eden," located on God's "holy mountain" (Ezek. 28:13, 14). This conception was clearly corrected in the Genesis version of the Eden story, in which the garden is established from the outset to house man, whom God puts there to "cultivate and take care of it" (Gen. 2:15). Normal vegetation replaces the mythical abundance of precious stones in the presumedly pagan version which is reflected in Ezekiel (an echo of this motif reverberates in Gen. 2:12): the human king of Tyre, swollen with pride, aspires to become godlike, saying, "I am sitting on the throne of God" (Ezek. 28:2). He considers himself "an exemplar of perfection, full of wisdom, perfect in beauty" and actually wishes to play the role of the "guardian cherub" in charge of the mythical garden (Ezek. 28:12-14; cf. 3:24 and also 2:15).

How different the depiction of Adam and Eve in the Hebrew version: man and wife whom God had placed in the garden of Eden for their own enjoyment (Gen. 3:1-20). Both Adam and the King of Tyre are punished for their transgressions: one, for his overbearing *hubris*, his aspiring to divinity; the other, for disobeying a divine command. The first is consumed by a fire bursting forth from his own body (Ezek. 28:18); the other is condemned to live in the realism of human life, toiling with sweat on his brow to win sustenance from the soil to which he will return after death (Gen. 3:17-19). The message seems to be obvious: myth is rejected by means of completely

12. A close reading of the two passages shows the Isaiah text to be a contracted version in which one term stands for three to four synonymous expressions in the Job wording, unless one prefers to view that wording as a poetic amplification of the shorter Isaiah text. In both are employed the terms *śym*--' put in,' *'ap*--'nose' and *hah*--' hook' which serve as catchphrases. The Job text exhibits three additional coterminous verbs for *śym* namely *šq*', *ngb*, and *mšk*. For *meteg* it provides the three synonyms *hakāh*, *hebel* and *'agmōn;* and for śāpāh the synonyms *lehy* and *lāšōn*.

revamping its essential content, and by substituting human-existential reality for mythopoeic imagery.

As a result of this "watering-down," such literary residues which give evidence to the currency of pagan mythology in ancient Israel in some instances could be combined with references to the normative Hebrew tradition of creation. For example, God's above-mentioned reply to Job's complaints brims with mythological imagery (Job 40, 41). We find there a detailed description of the mighty *Behemot* of yore (40:15-24) and of the incomparably powerful *Leviathan* (40:25-41:26) that stirs up *Yam* (the sea) like a bubbling cauldron (41:23), while "firebrands shoot from his mouth, and sparks come streaming out" (41:19-20). But preceding this, God is said to reject Job's rebellious outcries by referring to creation in terms which clearly echo the creation pericope in Genesis 1 (Job 38, 39): "Where were you when I laid the earth's foundations . . . Who settled its dimensions . . . Who stretched its measuring line over it?" (38:4-6) The terminology immediately brings to mind similar phraseology in (Second) Isaiah: "Who has gauged the waters in the palm of his hand, or with its span set limits to the heavens? Who has held all the soil of earth in a bushel, or weighed the mountains on a balance and the hills on a pair of scales . . . ." Once again, this Creation imagery is historicized in the immediately adjoining passage in Isa. 40:15. The primordial waters which only God himself could measure become here "drops from a bucket" to which image all peoples of the earth together are likened. The "dust of the earth" which only the Creator could "weigh in a balance" is transformed into "the nations of the world" who are like "the specks which cling to the scales." And the well-known Mount Lebanon takes the place of the primeval mountains and hills which God laid out and measured when He created the universe:

> *To him nations are but drops from a bucket,*
> *no more than specks on the scales;*
> *He lifts up islands as if they were feathers.*
> *All Lebanon does not yield wood enough for fuel*
> *and the beast in it not enough for a sacrifice.*

And as if to ensure that the point is not missed, the author ends that entire section on a string of creation terms and imagery. Somewhat freely rendered, the passage would read:

> *You surely know this, you surely heard it, it certainly*
> *was told you from the very beginning;*
> *you surely are knowledgeable of the founding of the earth,*
> *of God being enthroned above the vault of the earth . . .*
> *unfolding the heavens like a curtain,*
> *stretching them out like a tent. (Isa. 40:21-22)*

Side by side with this "normative" biblical vocabulary, there turns up in the Book of Job an imagery which is altogether mythopoeic:

> *He enclosed Yam within doors . . . put it behind gates*
> *and bolts and said, "thus far shall you come and no*
> *farther." (Job 38:8-11)*

IV

We can now turn our attention to an analysis and evaluation of the normative Hebrew creation tradition in Gen. 1-2. Even though traditional exegetes, both Christians and Jews, insist that this pericope is a unit, differences in language and content leave little doubt that the passage indeed is made up of originally independent creation accounts, as is commonly agreed by modern Bible scholars.

There have been various ways of identifying its major components, but the overwhelming majority of students would ascribe one account to the priestly (P) and the other to the yahwistic source (J).[13] However, for our present considerations the division is of little consequence. We have to relate to the text as it is, taking a holistic approach, somewhat along the lines set by the emerging new school of "canonical criticism."[14] The question that confronts us is this: what is the message which the final arranger of the pericope wished to convey to his audience? The answer is obvious. The biblical account of creation, in all its presumed subdivisions, propounds one pivotal idea: the universe was established by a sole and sovereign Creator, who went about his task unaided by any helpers, and unimpeded by any opposing forces.[15] It could not have been otherwise, since "before the world was created, the Holy One, blessed be He, with His name alone existed."[16] To put it differently, before the creation of the universe, God was the only reality, and the nonexistence of other beings or powers, serves to highlight the divine unity which is the very opposite of the diversity which is to characterize the created world.

The biblical text, though, does not offer any help for solving a problem which has exercised the minds of later theologians and philosophers: is the formation of the universe viewed as *creatio ex nihilo* or does the account rather conceive of the Creator as giving form to pre-existing matter? The Hebrew Bible simply relates facts, and not all the facts, and does not interpret them. To a degree, this method of a factual presentation of "events" is followed by most later Jewish commentators, theologians and philosophers. They do not endeavor to explain, creation, nor will they occupy themselves with revealing the mysteries which preceded the acts of creation.[17] Says the medieval exegete Nachmanides: "This is one of the mysteries of the Torah. If its author would have wanted to be better understood, he surely would have been more explicit. [But since he did not do so,] we have no right to fathom what he covered with a veil." The same idea is again expressed by a different image. In reply to the question

13. Scholarly publications on this matter are much too numerous to be listed here. An up-to-date survey may be found in C. Westermann, *Genesis 1-11* (Neukirchener-Vluyn: Neukirchener Verlag des Erziehüngsvereins, 1966-1974).

14. See: B. Childs, *Introduction to the Old Testament as Scripture* (Philadelphia: Fortress 1979), esp. pp. 109-160; R. Rendtorff, *Das Alte Testament: Eine Einführung* (Neukirchen-Vluyn: Neukirchener Verlag des Ersiehungs-vereins 1983, 1985).

15. An excellent discussion of the main features of the Jewish concept of Creation is offered by E. E. Urbach, *The Sages - Their Concepts and Beliefs: "He Who Spoke and the World Came into Being"* (Jerusalem: Magnes 1979), pp. 184-213.

16. Midrash Pes. d'R. Eliezer, ed. Friedländer, 10.

17. See, for example, S. W. Baron, *A Social and Religious History of the Jews,* Vol. 8, *High Middle Ages, Philosophy and Science* (New York: University of Columbia Press) pp. 87 ff.; E. Dantinne, "Création et Séparation," *Le Muséon* 74 (1961); pp. 450-451.

why does the Hebrew Bible begin with the second letter of the alphabet, the *bet* in the initial word *b'rēšīt*, it is stated: the *bet* is "open" on its left side, but "closed" on its right. This implies (for the Hebrew reader) that one may investigate what follows upon the first letter of the creation story, but one should refrain from exploring what precedes it. The Sages do not delve into questions about what was before the world was created. They never ask "what is above, what is beneath, what was before time was created, what will be thereafter?" (m.Hag. 2,1; Tos. Hag. 2,7; p.T. Hag. 2,1 p.77c).

Jewish traditional exegesis indeed does not entirely disregard some discrepancies between various passages of the present creation account but tends to get around the problem by conceiving of the entire pericope as a developing tale; the overall presentation of cosmogony in chapter one (which critical scholars ascribe to P), leads to the fashioning of man in chapter two (which critical scholars ascribe to J), as the crowning piece of creation.[18]

But some discrepancies and the internal tension which surfaces in the account cannot be glossed over. Let me illustrate this with just a few examples:

(a) Himself perfect and omniscient, the Creator-God nevertheless could not prevent his work from going awry. Therefore he destroys it (Gen. 6:5-8), and has to fashion a new universe. He is hailed as the sole and sovereign ruler of the cosmos, the only source of the laws by which it is governed. And yet, after the Flood, he submits to his self-imposed restriction never again to destroy the work of his hands. He sets the rainbow in the skies as a memorial and a reminder both for him and for mankind that the once-established order of creation should never be disturbed again (Gen. 8:22; 9:12-16). We may add here that midrashic Jewish tradition has it that the present world was established after God had destroyed a series of successive previous creations (Gen Rabba 3:7,9; Qoh Rabba 3:11; Midr. Psalms 34).

(b) A similar internal tension can be observed in the depiction of man. On the one hand, it is stressed that "God fashioned man of dust from the soil" (Gen. 2:7) and to "dust he will return" (Gen. 3:19). This idea is taken up in numerous passages in biblical literature, became a prominent motif in postbiblical Jewish thought, and beyond that was accepted in all civilizations that acknowledge the Hebrew Bible as a cornerstone of their culture. On the other hand, God appoints man as ruler of the universe, delegating to him authority over the entire creation: "be fruitful, multiply, fill the earth and conquer it. Be masters of the fish of the sea, the birds of heaven and all living animals on the earth. . . I give you all the seed-bearing plants that are upon the whole earth and all the trees with seed-bearing fruit; this shall be your food" (Gen. 1:28-29).

Man's mastery over creation is further evinced by his giving "names to all the cattle, all the birds of heaven, and all the wild beasts" (Gen. 2:20). This act clearly symbolizes his assumption of authority over all living creatures, since in doing so, man emulates God's giving names to the diverse components of the cosmos which he had created before fashioning man: "He called the light day, and the darkness night . . . and God called the vault heaven . . . God called the dry land earth, and the gathering of the waters he called seas" (1:5-10). There is here indeed, as Patrick Miller says, "an apparent paradox." Ignoring, for the moment, the division into sources, we could state

[18] See E. E. Urbach, "Man", *op. cit.*, pp. 214-254.

with him: "To be *'elohim*-like is God's will for his creatures; to become *'elohim*-like is to go precisely counter to the divine will. . . In a very real sense the whole narrative of the Primeval History flows out of this tension."[19]

The discrepancy between the portrayal of man as being but dust of the soil, on the one hand, and ruler of the universe, on the other hand, which appears to be a *contradictio in se,* disturbs the modern, rationalistic mind, controlled by the "law of non-contradiction." But it was viewed with apparent equanimity by the biblical writers and by later Jewish thinkers alike. We may, in fact, discern here the imprint of thought processes that acquiesce in the plurality which inheres in human experience and governs human life.

This phenomenon was accurately discerned by Gershom Scholem in relation to the intellectual world of postbiblical Judaism. Modified and adjusted, his observations can be applied to biblical literature in general and to the creation narrative in particular: "It is precisely the wealth of contradictions, of differing views, which is encompassed and unqualifiedly affirmed by tradition. There were many possibilities of interpreting the Torah, and tradition claimed to comprise them all. It maintains the contradictory views with astounding seriousness and intrepidity, as if to say that one can never know whether a view at one time rejected may not one day become the cornerstone of an entirely new edifice."[20]

V

Generally speaking, the biblical creation traditions mirror an adjusted perception of three stages in the making of the universe. A similar conception underlies the creation myths of so-called preliterate cultures, for example in the South Seas or in South America. More importantly, it is preserved in literatures of the ancient Near East, in Egypt and Mesopotamia: *theogony*–the creation or emanation of deities, precedes *cosmogony*–the fashioning of the universe, which for its part is succeeded by *anthropogony*–the creation of man. It is obvious that the notion of a pre-existent, unique and only, immanent God which permeates biblical monotheism ruled out any possibility of Israel's developing a *theogony.* The total and absolute rejection of any reflection on the origin of God is seen in the fact that even the aforementioned residues of pagan creation myths preserved in the Bible never pertain to theogony. The primordial deities enter the stage when they are already engaged in their primeval battle over the creation of the universe and of man, and no thought is given to the question of how they themselves came into existence.

One is inclined to perceive in this absence of any discernible trace of theogony one other indication of the basic biblical orientation toward man and his place in the world. It appears that rather than being theocentric, the Hebrew creation tradition is first and foremost anthropocentric, then ethnocentric. From here follows that in order to fathom the intrinsic meaning of the biblical creation tradition, we must go beyond Gen. 1 and 2 and bring under scrutiny also the ensuing block of texts (chaps.

19. P. D. Miller, Jr., *Genesis 1-11, Studies in Structure and Theme, JSOT* Suppl. Ser. 8 (Sheffield; University of Sheffield 1978).

20. Gershom Scholem, "Revelation and Tradition as Religious Categories in Judaism," in *The Messianic Idea in Judaism and other Essays on Jewish Spirituality* (New York: Schocken, 1971), p. 290.

3-11) which precedes the narrowing of the focus on the history of the people of Israel, beginning with Abraham's exodus from his native land (Gen. 12:1 ff.).[21]

Viewed in this larger framework, the biblical account tells of two successive creations which exhibit manifest similarities:

(a) Both accounts emphasize the basic principle on which the universe is founded: the cosmos was created as an all-embracing organism consisting of diverse and differentiated natural phenomena, creatures and species. They should remain distinct forever. All mixed breeds are anathema. There is to be no crossing the lines which divide species, above all the borders which set apart animal from man, and the human world from the divine sphere. This principle embodies a concept of particularity which is characteristic of the biblical world of ideas. Mythological cosmogonies, entertained by ancient Near Eastern and classical societies or current among preliterate peoples, do not proclaim this total separation of beast and man, of man and deity. Quite the contrary. In such mythic tales, crossbreeds of many colors and shapes roam the scene: heroes and centaurs, demigods, nymphs and flying dragons serve as welcome objects for depiction and plastic representation.

(b) The story of the primordial creation (Gen. 1:1-6:12) comprehends cosmogony, leading up to anthropogony (Gen. 1:2).[22] Then it depicts the first man's fate and thus presents to the reader what could be viewed as an insipient biblical anthropology (Gen. 3-6). In the account of the history of the first *men,* there surfaces a literary pattern which will repeatedly recur in biblical literature: a father begetting three sons, the youngest of whom will surpass his brothers. After Abel's murder at the hands of his brother Cain and the ensuing disqualification of Cain, and Adam's death, the last born Seth is destined to ensure the continuance of the human race.

This same pattern becomes apparent in the postdeluge account of the second creation which is in fact tantamount with the creation of the prehistoric world. Noah indeed takes center stage in the report on the destruction of the world by the Flood and its re-creation. But already in his lifetime, his two sons, Ham and Japheth, serve as a foil for the third, Shem. Shem is accorded ascendancy over his brothers. He is a precursor of Abraham, on whose descendants and their fate biblical literature will focus: "Cursed be Canaan (the son of Ham), slave of slaves shall he be to his brothers . . . Bless, 0 Lord, the tents of Shem, may Canaan be his slave. May God extend Japheth's bounds, let him dwell in the tents of Shem, may Canaan be their slave" (Gen. 9:25-27).

(c) Both accounts culminate in reports of the destruction of the created world as punishment of the human race for transgressing the fundamental principle of the absolute differentiation between God and Man.

But against this background of similarities, some telling differences between the two tales emerge.

(a) The immediate cause for the annihilation of the primordial creation is the cohabitation of the "daughters of men" with the "sons of God," which produced the "heroes of old" (Gen. 6:1-4), evidently semi-divine creatures. The reported intermin-

[21] The conceptual and structural unity of this text-complex has been recurrently underlined in recent publications. See, *e.g.* K. Westermann, *op. cit.;* D. J. A. Clines, "Theme in Genesis 1-11," *CBQ* (1976); pp. 483-507; M. Fishbane, *Text and Texture - Close Readings of Selected Biblical Texts* (New York; Schocken 1979) pp. 3-39; P. D. Miller, *op. cit.* (n. 19), and others.

[22] See R. Albertz, *Weltschöpfung und Menschenschöpfung. Untersucht bei Deuterojesaja* (Stuttgart: Calwer, 1974).

gling of humans with celestial beings suggests an underlying quest of man for the attainment of divine status. The prehistoric world is nearly destroyed for a similar reason. The tale of the Tower of Babel gives evidence to the attempt of depraved mankind to "reach heaven," i.e., to arrogate to itself divine status (Gen. 11:1-4; cf. Isa. 14:13-14). But in this instance judgment is mitigated. The punishment meted out to the offenders consists in the dissolution of the "one-ness," which had generated their *hubris*. "Unity" is God's alone, from before creation. Mankind is scattered over the earth (Gen. 11:1-9) and resultingly humanity's reproachable unity dissolves into a plurality of peoples, countries, and languages. Thus, the divinely established differentiation of the first creation, between species and within a species, is reconstituted (Gen. 11:11 32), providing the backdrop for the ensuing particular history of the people of Israel.

(b) Viewed from another angle the comprehensive tradition complex of Gen. 1-11 can be subdivided into two components, one of which (Gen. 1-2) is determined by the concept of either *creatio ex nihilo* or of creation which consists of giving form to pre-existing amorphous matter, with the Creator functioning as a demiurge, as he is conceived in Gnosticism. In contradistinction, the other component, also consisting of two subunits (Gen. 3:1-6:8 and 6:9-11:32), is characterized by the concept of emanation: the reconstituted world evolves by way of self-perpetuation out of extant matter. The difference can be partly explained by the fact that in the primordial, i.e. in the first creation all plants and living beings had been invested with the faculty to procreate, which faculty ensured the continued existence of all creatures after the Deluge. The disastrous flood did not totally annihilate the universe. Nature had been subjected to a mere temporary eclipse. When the waters receded, the peaks of the mountains emerged, followed by the treetops, until the earth, freed from the last sheets of water, was again revealed in the form it had been given in the primordial creation (Gen. 8:1-14).

All living species were reduced to the barest minimum. But after the disaster had passed, this minimum allowed for a regeneration. According to one tradition, the animal world was cut back to one pair of every species (Gen. 6:19-20). According to another, seven pairs of all ritually clean animals were preserved, and one pair of all ritually unclean animals.

Similarly, mankind was reduced to one other "first couple," Noah and his wife, replacing the primary "first couple," Adam and Eve. Adam and Eve had been placed by God in the Garden of Eden; Noah and his wife were saved from destruction by being put into the Ark. Adam and Eve became the forefathers of "all those who live" (Gen. 3:20), "procreating" whereas God had "created." But biblical Hebrew uses one and the same vocable–*qnh*–for describing these diverse manners of creation. Having given birth to her firstborn, Eve had proudly proclaimed: "I have [pro-]created–*qānīti*–a man like YHWH" (Gen. 4:1). This proclamation echoes a statement in Deut. 32:6, where it is said of God: "Is not he your father, your creator–*gānēka,* he made you–*'āsekā*–and fashioned you" (cf. also Gen. 14:19, 22 and Prov. 8:22-30). After the first creation, procreation was obviously considered an outstanding human achievement, notwithstanding the birth pains which went with it as a divine punishment (Gen. 3:16). After the post-Flood re-creation of the world it became commonplace. The production of offspring by Noah and his wife is recorded matter-of-factly. The post deluge account moves from the plane of primordial history to the plane of prehistory, which will serve as a backdrop for the ensuing presentation of history proper.

prehistory, which will serve as a backdrop for the ensuing presentation of history proper.

VI

The biblical text exhibits an almost bewildering variety of vocables pertaining to creation. Terminology signifying technical acts of creation is freely mixed and combined with a vocabulary which connotes emanation: *'śh,* make; *bnh,* build; *yṣr,* fashion. All these terms apply equally to God the Creator and to man, his regent on earth. One other term used both in reference to God and to man, *hivdīl,* separate, should be mentioned here only in passing, since we will yet refer to it in detail.

Two terms are reserved for the description of God's acts alone. One is *'mr,* speak. As is well known, this verb has a much wider application in biblical literature generally, but in the context under review it signifies the act of creation by divine fiat. The other is *br',* the most significant vocable in the biblical creation complex. While the prevailing translation "create" is acceptable, there are grounds for viewing *br'* as a parallel to *hivdīl* = separate, like it signifying creation by differentiation. *br'* occurs altogether forty-nine times in the Hebrew Bible, and has exclusively God as its subject. No certain etymological derivation can be established for *br',* nor were equivalents of it found so far in other Semitic languages.[23] The exclusive association of *br'* with the creative acts of the one Creator-God is highlighted by the fact that this term is never used in biblical passages which contain terminological residues of ancient Near Eastern cosmogonies.

Equally, *bārā'* is not used to describe man's creative activities, with two exceptions:

(a) with the connotation of *cutting down* trees–for "creating" arable land (Josh. 17:15, 18); and

(b) with the connotation of *cutting up* men with swords (Ezek. 23-47; Ezek. 21:24b is unintelligible and therefore may be left out of our consideration).

The suggested technical connotation of the term *br',* "create by separation," colors the meaning of the more general term *'śh,* "make." In the context under review also *'śh* signifies creation by separation (Gen. 1:26, 27; 2:3, 4; cf. 1:25 with 2:19; cf. other passages which echo creation terminology, such as Isa. 45:7; Amos 4:13; see further, Exod. 34:10 and Isa. 41:20, 48:7).

This compressed survey of the most prominent verbs in the "normative" biblical account of cosmogony lends substance to the proposition that "differentiation" is considered the pivotal aspect of creation. "To create" means essentially to give peculiar character and specific form to the diverse phenomena which *in toto* constitute the universe. A glance at the unfolding stages in the biblical account of creation proves the point.

The first major step in the process is the separation of heaven and earth (Gen. 1:1: *bārā'*). Then follows the separation of light from darkness, identified with day and night respectively (Gen. 1:4, 5; cf. 1:18). This sets the stage for the emergence of the earth as man knows it. Thereafter, the division of day and night with respect to the upper spheres is achieved by God's fashioning, *'āsāh,* the two great luminaries: the sun

[23] For a discussion of the issue see A. Angerstorfer, *Der Schöpfergott des Alten Testaments. Herkunft und Bedeutungsentwicklung des hebräischen Terminus (bārā') "schaffen". Regensburger Studien zur Theologie* 20 (Frankfurt: Peter Lang, 1979).

governing day and the moon governing night. The two together are set apart from the minor luminaries, the stars. Again, as in respect to the differentiation between the (day)light and the darkness (of night) on earth, the distinction between the diverse heavenly bodies is indicated by *hivdīl* (Gen. 1:14-18; cf. vv. 4-5; Jer. 31-35; Psalms 136:5-9).

Once "night" had been separated from "day," a distinction was introduced into "day" itself. The Creator sets apart the seventh day of this and every week, from the preceding six "workdays," declaring it to be a "holy day of rest" (Gen. 2:1-3). It should be pointed out that the root *qdš,* by which the special character of the seventh day is singled out, *wayeqaddēš 'ōtō* (cf. Exod. 20:8 = Deut. 5:12), in biblical and also in later Jewish tradition can again signify separation.

The principle of differentiation, applied to the luminaries in the upper spheres, is given further expression in that heaven is conceived of as a flat sheet *'rāgīa',* Gen. 1:8), which divides the supracelestial from the infracelestial waters (1:7). Also this act of separation is defined by *hivdīl.*

Ensuingly, the dry land is segregated from the seas (*yammīm*). By God's gathering the terrestrial waters (*mayīm*) in one mass or place it becomes earth (1:9-10). This detachment of the seas from the dry land (*yabāšāh*) seems to reflect mythological imagery (see above): having vanquished his primordial foes, the creator deity puts **Yam** (the sea) in fetters by setting the sands of the seashore as his eternal bounds.

Once the sea has been set apart, the earth (Gen. 1:10) can produce vegetation–plants and trees, again differentiated from the very beginning into their various and distinct kinds, each one–*lemīnō* (1:11, 12). Parallel to that, the seas bring forth various kinds of creatures by a divine fiat (*'amar*) (Gen. 1:20, 21b). These evidently natural beings are distinguished from the originally mythological great *tanīnīm,* whom God creates separately, *bārā* (Gen. 1:21a). Like the seas which are teeming with various species of aquatic beings, *lemīnēhem,* also the heavens are populated by diverse kinds of winged creatures, *lemīnēhū* (Gen. 1:20-21). The same pertains to earth, which is said to have produced "every kind of living creature: cattle, reptiles, and every kind of wild beast" (Gen. 1:24, 25).

The recurring insistence upon diversity cannot be overlooked (cf. 7:14).

VII

Altogether distinct is man. God makes man, *'āśāh./bārā',* in his likeness or his image, *besalmēnū kidmūtēnū* (Gen. 1:26, 27). Resultingly, man differs from all other species of living creatures. But differentiation shows also in the very act of making man. Mankind appears on the scene in two separate sexes, male and female (Gen. 1:27): in one tradition, from the very outset; in another, in a two-stage development, the female being derived from the male (Gen. 2:21-23).[24]

This notion of the separation of mankind into sexes, cannot be reconciled with the former statement of man's being created in the image of God, since God is seen to be indivisible and sexless. While the anthropomorphic thrust of the vocabulary

[24] This particular feature of sex differentiation was not mentioned in reference to any previously created living being. It will apply to the animal world only in the "second creation" tradition, featuring Noah and the Ark (Gen. 6:19-7:16).

cannot be denied, the glaring internal contradiction can be only mitigated if in this context *selem* and *demūt* are not understood in the literal sense of physical likeness, but are given less tangible connotations. To cite E. Jabés: "Le visage n'est ni la face de Dieu ni la figure de l'homme, il en est la ressemblance."[25] And indeed, when interpreted contextually, the likeness implied in the Hebrew terms *selem* and *demūt* appears to aim at the Creator's dominion over the universe, rather than to the visual perception of his "image." Such an understanding of the terms involved can be achieved if we explain the relevant passages by having recourse to an "inbuilt" means of interpretation which traditional Jewish exegesis brings to our attention. Frequently, an obscure or opaque phrase in a biblical verse or in one part of a verse will be clarified by another part or another verse whose meaning is unequivocally clear. This method is especially helpful when we are confronted with a term pertaining to an abstract-conceptual notion which stands in need of clarification or with a sentence structure which appears to obscure the sense of a verse rather than disclose it. Let me give just one illustration of this technique. The pregnant term *'aharīt hayāmīm* which is often invested with an eschatological content by rendering it "latter days" or the like, in Deut. 31:29 is "internally" explained to refer to the much more tangible times of the next generation. There Moses admonishes Israel before his demise to persist in following God's ways since otherwise disaster will befall them *be'aharīt hayāmīm*. The chronological gap between the "now" and "then" is transparently circumscribed at the beginning of the verse in Moses' own words: "For I know that *after my death* you will take to degrading practices."[26]

Drawing upon a scriptural phrase in Job 36:33 *yāgīd 'ālāw rē'ō*, "his friend will tell of him," this method of interpretation was construed by early commentators[27] to mean "one verse may help in ascertaining the (inherent) sense of another."[28] Applied to the texts under review, the crucial passages would be best read as follows: "God said: Let us make man, like us to assume mastery over the fish of the sea, the birds of heaven, the cattle, all the wild beasts and all the reptiles that crawl upon the earth. God created man in his likeness . . . blessed him and said to him: Be fruitful and potent, fill the earth and subdue it. Be master of the fish in the sea, the birds of heaven and all living animals on the earth" (Gen. 1:26-28).

25. Quoted by J. Derrida, "Violence et metaphysique," in *L'Ecriture et la différence* (Paris,1967) 160n., 161n.

26. The NEB translates *be'aharīt hayāmīm* in this verse correctly: "in days to come," thus avoiding eschatological implications.

27. Modern commentators and translators usually emend the MT so as to achieve a reading which is better suited to the storm imagery which prevails in the context. Thus NEB: "In his anger he calls up the tempest."

28. The method has also been defined by the phrase *mimerhāq tābī' lahmah*, said in praise of a 'capable wife' who "brings home food from far off" (Prov. 31:14). From this basic principle are derived several of the thirty-two exegetical rules laid down by R. Eliezer ben Yosei the Galilean, *e.g.* "the meaning of an expression can be established with the help of another (similar) passage (rule 22); 'some texts shed light on others' (rule 23) et sim." See: *The Baraita of the 32 Hermeneutic Rules of R. Eliezer* (Vilna, 5685/1025) 77b.45 (Hebrew); *t. Parah* 10,4 (ed. Zuckermandel 639.4); *Gen.Rab.* 16b (ed. Theodor-Albeck 143). See also W. Bacher, *Die exegetische Terminologie der jüdischen Traditionsliteratur* (Leipzig; J.C. Hinrichs 1899-1905) I, 55-56; II, 64, s.v. *hsr;* idem, *Die Aggada der Tannaiten* (Strassburg: K.J. Trübner, 1890) II, p. 295; idem, *Die Aggada der babylonischen Amoräer* (Hildesheim: G. Olms, 1967) III, ,68. Further: S. Talmon, "Emendation of Biblical Texts on the Basis of Ugaritic Parallels," *Studies in Bible, Scripta Hierosolymitana* xxxi, ed. S. Japhet (Jerusalem: Magnes, 1986), pp. 279-300.

Thus, the "likeness" of which the text speaks would not pertain to the physical image, but rather to the similarity of functions. It would appear that it was thus understood by the Psalmist: "thou hast made him (man) little less than (a) god, crowning him with glory and honour. Thou makest him master over all thy creatures; thou hast put everything under his feet . . ." (Ps. 8:5-8). This portrayal of man shows him to be king of all created beings and brings to mind "Akkadian Prophesies" (*Pr.A* no. 5) which state: "The kings of Uruk will exercise their sovereignty like gods."[29] The mastery over the world accorded to man indeed reflects God's rule over the universe. However, being but a reflection of the divine omnipotence, man's mastery amounts in fact to stewardship: he is called upon to preserve the world and to refashion it only within the limits of what God has singularly created (*bārā'*). By stressing its derivative nature, the biblical tradition severely circumscribes man's power and actually denies him the right to subject creation to fundamental changes. Man is doubly bound by God's promise after the destructive flood that creation will not be anymore affected by radical upheavals: "Never again will I strike down every living being as I have done. As long as earth lasts, sowing and reaping, cold and heat, summer and winter, day and night shall cease no more" (Gen. 8:21-22, cf. Jer. 33:20, 25-26).[30]

These texts cannot be construed to serve as a detailed blueprint for personal and societal behavior. But they offer the possibility of extracting from them principles which can be adapted to novel situations in which humans, individuals and societies, find themselves.

VIII

The appointment of man as "master of the universe," symbolized also in his giving names to all living beings (cf. Gen. 2:20), leads, almost unavoidably, to the emergences of human *hubris,* man's aspiration to achieve a status beyond what had been accorded to him in the divine plan. "When man began, *lārōb,*[31] to assume mastery of the earth" (Gen. 6:1; cf. 1:28), he also began to mix with celestial beings: "The daughters of men" cohabited with the "sons of God" (Gen. 6:2).[32]

Hebrew *tārōb* is mostly translated: "When mankind began to increase" (NEB). I believe, however, that we have here a *double-entendre.* The root *rbb* expresses increase in both quantity and quality. Thus, e.g. in Isa. 5:9 where *bātim rabbīm,* qualified as it is by *gedōlīm wetōbīm* in the parallel stitch, should be translated "mansions" (cf. Amos 6:11) rather than "many houses" (NEB). Accordingly, the Genesis passage speaks of an increase in power which corrupted mankind to aim at transcending its humanity by interbreeding with superterrestial beings. The Bible emphatically rejects this commingling of superhumans with humans. Although the episode does not pertain to creation itself, but rather is given as the reason for its undoing (Gen. 6:1-7), it should

29. H. Hunger, *Spätbabylonische Texte aus Uruk* (Berlin: Mann 1976) 21b.

30. See: N. Lohfink SJ, "Der Schöpfergott und der Bestand von Himmel und Erde," in: G. Altner u.a., *Sind wir noch zu retten?* (Münster: Regensburg, 1978) pp. 15-39.

31. See: S. Herrmann, "Die Naturlehre des Schöpfungsberichtes - Erwägungen zur Vorgeschichte von Genesis 1," *ThLZ* (1961), pp. 413-424.

32. See: R. S. Hendel, "Of Demigods and the Deluge: Toward an Interpretation of Genesis 6:1-4," *JBL* 106 (1987), pp. 13-26.

nevertheless be viewed and evaluated in the context of the basic motif of separation which permeates the creation account. In the condemnation of the fusion of categories which the Creator had intended to be separate, we may discern a concomitant rejection of any positive attitude toward demigods, heroes, and other beings who blur the impenetrable border between this, the human world, and the heavenly spheres. Such belief in the existence of intermediate beings found a prominent expression in ancient Near Eastern cultures in the self-aggrandizement and the popular veneration of royalty. The biblical repudiation of these offensive notions is highlighted in the prophecies of Isaiah against the King of Babylon (Chap. 14) and of Ezekiel against the King of Tyre (Chap. 28) respectively. Both rulers had aspired to divinity; each wanted to set up his throne next to, if not in place of, the throne of God (Isa. 14:13-14; Ezek. 28:2, 13-14). God smashed both to earth, and thus they were reduced to their proper position of human inferiority.

The biblical creation tradition, especially the account in Gen. 1, reads altogether like an ancient treatise which conceives of the universe as one comprehensive whole, made up in orderly fashion of clearly defined categories. It resembles didactic wisdom literature which offers information in the form of onomastica in which are enumerated diverse species and subdivisions of species of various phenomena observable in the universe. The Bible ascribes the composition of such rosters to King Solomon, whose wisdom is said to have surpassed that "of all the sons of the East and of Egypt . . . he composed three thousand proverbs and his songs [of instruction] numbered 1005. He could talk about plants from the cedar in Lebanon to the hyssop, and he could talk of animals, and birds, and reptiles and fish" (1 Kings 5:9-13; cf. Prov. 30:15-31; further, Job 38:-39, et al).

Therefore, the Biblical creation account can be viewed as an attempt on the part of ancient man to overcome taxonomic confusion and to grasp in an orderly fashion the bewildering number and variety of phenomena which confront him in his world, without blurring their differences. Indeed, "Genesis I personalizes the classification of the world."[33]

Equally, postbiblical Jewish tradition insists on keeping apart what had been created differently. It has been surmised that this principle could explain the large number of injunctions against the mixing of species.[34] Biblical law proscribes the interweaving of wool and flax and the cross-breeding of different kinds of animals (Lev. 19:19; Deut. 22:9,11). Dietary laws forbid the consumption of creatures which exhibit characteristics of more than one basic species, such as aquatic mammals (Lev. 11:9-12; Deut. 14:9-10) or insects which both fly and crawl (Lev. 11:19, 23, 27, 42).

Applied to the human sphere, this principle underlies the interdiction of intermarriage between members of different ethnic and/or religious groups. The objection essentially evidences a positive intention to preserve distinctions and relations rooted in creation–actually in the, re-Creation of the universe after the Flood–rather than a negative, overbearing attitude towards outsiders.

There emerges in the Jewish tradition a structured universe in which each species, different and separate from others, is accorded its appropriate place in the divine economy. Particularity and an all-embracing universality are seen as complementary, rather than mutually exclusive. Judaism recognizes particularity not only as

[33] K. Burke, *The Rhetoric of Religion. Studies in Logology* (Los Angeles: University of California, 1970), pp. 201 ff.

[34] See Mary Douglas, *Purity and Danger* (London: Routledge & Paul, 1966).

an undeniable principle of human existence. Conceiving of it as divinely decreed, it also confers a spiritual dimension upon actual particularity, such as is experienced in all life situations: it is a basic phenomenon of the human condition from the days of creation–anthropologically, ethnically, socially and politically. Particularity implies diversity of all beings and, therefore, also separateness of men under the unifying overlordship of the Creator who reigns supreme over all mankind. The underlying tenet could be defined with Jacques Maritain as "distinguer pour unir." Judaism affirms the resulting diversity in the realm of the human spirit. It considers multiformity as a reality of human history, in the physical world as in the world of ideas and beliefs.

IX

The taxonomic character of the biblical creation account, apparent in the principle of categorization, can further be discerned in the presentation of the progressive socialization of man.

(a) As already pointed out, the story begins with defining the relation of man to other species and to nature in the wider sense of the word by his being appointed as their master.

Then we are translated to another plane. Now, man as an individual is depicted in the most basic interhuman relationships, primarily within the framework of the nuclear family: husband with wife (Gen. 2:22-24; cf. 3:6, 12, 16-17), sibling with sibling (Gen. 4:1-16).

Thereafter, the canvas is enlarged. "The roll of Adam's descendants" or possibly "the account of man's origins" (Gen. 5:1-2), actually endeavors to reveal the progress of "history" in the form of a series of interconnected genealogies. Such genealogies, based on the generation-cycle, the issue of a son from his father, may be viewed as an early attempt to capture the causal interdependence of events in their chronological sequence. At this stage, family relations, birth, marriage, and procreation, pertain not any more to the individual alone. They are, rather, means for expressing relationship between social units. The story of "first man" as a prototypical individual, becomes the story of "first men," who are but personified collectivities (5:3-32).

(b) The account of the progressive socialization is further refined by connecting man's basic occupations and crafts to the very beginnings of the world. Man starts out as a "food gatherer" in the "Garden" provided for him by the Creator (Gen. 2:8-17). When expelled from the Garden in punishment for his transgression, he becomes a "horticulturist," working the recalcitrant soil "by the sweat of his brow" to extract from it his daily bread (Gen. 3:17-19). Further categories are introduced in the confrontation of Cain, "the agriculturalist," and his brother Abel, "the herdsman" (Gen. 4:2 ff.). One of Cain's descendants, Jabal, removed from Cain by several generations, and considered "the ancestor of the tent-dwellers and owners of livestock" (Gen. 4:20), obviously continues his forefather's occupational line. Jabal's half-brother Tubal-Cain is presented as the progenitor of "all metalworkers in bronze or iron" (4:22), a technical trade which appears to have been closely affiliated with the growing of livestock. Jabal's brother Jubal represents the finer arts: "he was the ancestor of all who play the lyre and the flute" (4:22).

The crafts which are missing from that list are not less interesting than the occupations recorded as having arisen in the primordial stage. There is, e.g., no mention of a first fisherman or a first sailor. This dovetails with the fact that biblical writers considered seagoing highly hazardous. In their writings, the sea and everything connected with it stands for "danger." Think, for example, of the Psalm of Jonah (Jonah 2). The imagery pertaining to the "sea," carries over notions of destruction and peril that go with the primordial deity *Yam* of ancient semitic cosmology. Normally, seafaring was not an occupation in which the ancient Hebrews commonly engaged. When they did engage in it, the results were disastrous. This is demonstrated by the report on the attempted maritime enterprise of Jehoshaphat, King of Judah, which ended with his ships being wrecked at Etzion-Geber (I Kings 22:49 = II Chron. 20:37). Solomon's seafaring undertakings had been successful because his men teamed up with the men of Hiram, King of Tyre, "sailors who knew the sea" (I Kings 9:27 = II Chronicles 8:18). Thus, it would appear that the curtailed roster of trades in the cluster of genealogies pertaining to the primordial times reflects the existential experience of the ancient Israelite writers.

We should highlight the fact that biblical tradition places also the beginnings of Yahwism in the primordial age. Scripture states that in the days of Adam's grandson, Enosh, "the name of YHWH was first invoked"; the LXX reads: he [Enosh] was the first "to invoke the name of YHWH" (Gen. 4:46).[35]

(c) In the ensuing stage of man's development, set in the world recreated after the Flood, wider aspects of social organization come to the fore. The "table of nations" (Gen. 10) visualizes the emerging "peoples" in their mutual relations, each implanted in its "country." Thus the diversity of ethnic entities and their attachment to particular geographical areas is recognized and affirmed. By being included among the cosmological "firsts," the ethnic and political compositeness of humanity is given an almost prescriptive authority. This conception of man's basic constitution, colored indeed by an Israelite ethnocentric bias, is reflected in the Song of Moses which declares: "When the Most High gave the nations [their] appointed lands, when he divided mankind [lit.: sons of man], he fixed their boundaries according to the number [read: the needs] of the sons of Israel [LXX, Qum.: sons of God]" (Deut. 32:8; see also Num. 23:10).

(d) It is worthy of mention that while the Bible registers the diversity of man in terms of ethnic, geographic, and political particularity, there is no reference to a differentiation by color. Indeed, such a differentiation subsequently emerges in biblical records which pertain to historical actualities. This late emergence suggests that in the biblical world of ideas the differentiation of man by color is considered secondary and in no way has the fundamental value which attaches to particularities that are considered to be rooted in the constitutive phase of the primordial aeon.

(e) I tend to interpret similarly the absence of any reference to forms of socio-political organization in the biblical creation account. Other ancient Near Eastern civilizations conceived of "kingship" as being part and parcel of cosmogony. From the very inception of the world kings were known to have ruled in an orderly succes-

35. This statement contradicts other texts which maintain that God did not make himself known by his name YHWH even to the Patriarchs: "To Abraham and Isaac and Jacob I appeared as El Shaddai; I did not make myself known to them by my name YHWH" (Exod. 6:3). The first revelation of this specific divine epithet is reserved for Moses, and from that time he shall be invoked by this name for all generations to come (Exod. 3:13-15).

sion, amounting to what might be defined as dynasties. Lists of primeval kings were preserved in Sumerian and Babylonian texts. Also in other parts of the world, as *e.g.* on Madagascar and Tongareva, traditions concerning societal organization from the beginning are couched in terms of royalty. Their very primordiality conferred a measure of sanctity on monarchy and on the person of the king. In contradistinction, such an ideological dimension did not attach originally to kingship in Israel. Rather is the institution of monarchy presented as having arisen out of specific historical circumstances, it emerged at a time when the sporadic and diffuse rule of the Judges-Saviors could not stem the advance of the Philistines, whose much more efficient political organization was superior to that of Israel. It was only at a later stage that one tried to undergird the *de facto* advantages of dynastic royal rule by providing it with a *de jure* or ideonic basis, emulating conceptual foundations of political structures which prevailed in surrounding nations. This appears to be the thrust of Micah's prophecy concerning the house of David: "You, Bethlehem in Ephratah, the youngest among Judah's clans, out of you shall come forth a ruler in Israel, whose roots are far back in the past, in the time (of the beginnings) of the world" (Micah 5:1; NEB: in days gone by).[36]

The recognition of the basically realistic view of the world which inspires the biblical tradition of creation, leads us back to some remarks made at the outset of this presentation; the blending of creation with history. The acquiescence in the bewildering multiformity of natural phenomena, the dissimilarity of human beings, and above all, the acceptance of the diversity that marks human society, seems to reveal a process which could be defined as "historization of creation." The Hebrew Bible tends to view creation in historical terms, and to conceive of history in imagery drawn from the creation accounts. In his daily prayers, morning and evening, a Jew praises God "who alone effects mighty deeds, makes new phenomena . . . master of wondrous acts who in his benevolence forever renews Creation day after day." This understanding of creation as forever being present in the life of the individual and the community culminates in a prayer which is recurrently offered on the New Year festival after each sounding of the Shofar, the ram's horn: "This day the world was called into being. This day all creatures of the universe stand in judgment before thee as children or as servants. If as children, have pity upon us as a father pities his children; and if as servants, we call upon thee to be gracious unto us and merciful in judgment of us, O revered and holy God."

This riveting of "creation" to "history" makes for an inbuilt mechanism of "accommodation." The historicizing of cosmology causes creation to become subjected to the relativity which governs human existential experience. The creation tradition is couched in the terminology of biblical narrative style and therefore can be assessed by the ideonic yardsticks which apply to biblical historiography in general. To put it differently: the wording of the creation account has the same and no more authoritative force than the wording of the records pertaining to the "historical" times of the biblical kings, like David, Solomon and Ahab or, for that matter, of the period of the Saviors, like Gideon, Jephtha and Samson. There is no insistence in Judaism as a whole on an unqualified literalists' acceptance of the biblical creation tradition in its transmitted wording. Jewish thinkers seldom got exercised over the defense of a credal understanding of creation springing from a literalness which embraces the Genesis

36. See S. Talmon, *King, Cult, and Calendar*, (n. 5) pp. 16-37.

text as it stands, vis-à-vis alternative theories based on secular, scientific reasoning. While never doubting the divine inspiration which permeates the creation pericope, as all biblical writings, one finds in the Jewish sources a recurring insistence on the principle that these records were worded to fit human comprehension: "the Torah (Bible) speaks in the tongue of men." The tale of God's deeds in the context of "creation" was adjusted to the intellectual capabilities of biblical man, the human recipient of the message which it contains. And this human language tends to encapsulate abstract thought and absolute principles in metaphors and imagery which cannot be taken at face value but must be recurrently interpreted in line with man's expanding comprehension of the universe. Just as the world is seen to be divinely recreated every day, the phenomenon of creation must necessarily be reinterpreted by every generation.

Nature and the Theater of Redemption: Schleiermacher On Christian Dogmatics And the Creation Story

B.A. Gerrish

Quite simply, I have interrogated the feeling common to all devout Christians and have only tried to describe it.
Any dogma that represents an actual element in our Christian consciousness can be so conceived as not to get us mixed up with science.

-*Schleiermacher*

The question I want to address in this paper is what one does with the creation story in dogmatic, as distinct from biblical, theology. More exactly: What is the *place* of "creation" within a dogmatic system? The answer will of course turn around the answer to a prior question: What is dogmatic theology, and how does it differ from biblical theology? As my title indicates, I propose to take my bearings from Friedrich Schleiermacher's understanding of Christian dogmatics, although, as is my habit, I shall also mention John Calvin by way of comparison and contrast with Schleiermacher. I shall not try to give a detailed, prudently qualified account of either one, or of all the likenesses and differences I find between them on our theme. A great deal will have to be left unspoken, some of it obvious enough, some perhaps not so obvious. My limited aim is to indicate briefly what I take to be the pertinent features of Schleiermacher's dogmatics and the corresponding treatment of creation that they lead him to; then, after putting in a good word for him against his latest critics, to conclude with a suggested revision of his approach. It seems to me to be a modest revision. But I should admit in advance that Schleiermacher himself might possibly consider it a surrender of one of his fundamental claims: that the essence of piety lies neither in knowing nor in doing, but in feeling or immediate self-consciousness. Moreover, the dogmatic revision I am proposing is two-sided and carries with it a historical corollary he certainly would not have liked: that the New Testament must be understood as far more deeply rooted in the Hebrew scriptures than he was willing to admit. It is precisely here, I believe, in his attitude to the Old Testament, that we find one of his most far-reaching departures from the Reformed school, to which he professed allegiance.

The Task of Christian Dogmatics

Calvin's *Institutes* and Schleiermacher's *Christian Faith* have both won a secure place among the masterpieces of theological literature, and it seems natural to compare them as classics of dogmatic theology. And yet, so striking are the differences of style and approach between them, that one may finally wonder whether they really belong in the same literary genre. Comparison, though natural, could be misleading. In the interval between Calvin and Schleiermacher, theology divided into fields, and the fields into sub-fields. Hence, for instance, that Schleiermacher's work is not so full of biblical texts as Calvin's is an obvious remark, but it is beside the point if one forgets to add that by Schleiermacher's day dogmatic theology and biblical (or exegetical) theology had become two separate fields. Schleiermacher had to ask: What are the dogmatic theologians doing, if they are *not* expounding the oracles of God?

This is not to suggest that in Calvin's day biblical theology and dogmatic theology were indistinguishable. One might wish to argue that Calvin's biblical commentaries are just as much "theology" as the various editions of his *Institutes*, and yet that the commentaries and the *Institutes* represent different kinds of theological literature. True enough. But the point is that the *Institutes*, though something other than a collection of commentaries, nonetheless proceed largely by marshalling biblical evidence, and Calvin believed that the soundness of his "dogmatics" (if we may so call it) was to be judged by the correctness of his exegesis. In this sense, dogmatics remained for him biblical theology. Indeed, the *Institutes* became even more explicitly a biblical theology in its later editions. By the time he published the second edition (1539), Calvin had moved away from the catechetical model of the first (1536) toward something much closer to the *Loci Communes* ("theological topics"; first edition, 1521) of Philip Melanchthon. The serious student of the Bible meets with certain constantly recurring theological themes: sin, law, grace, and so on. Calvin had come to view his *Institutes* as a useful companion for such students to read along with his commentaries. The discussion of recurring themes could be kept much briefer in the commentaries if the reader had the wisdom to keep the *Institutes* close at hand.[1]

But then, of course, the question arises: How do you arrange the topics? Calvin evidently devoted a great deal more thought to this question than did his friend Melanchthon, whose topics were initially suggested to him by his lectures on Paul's Letter to the Romans. Calvin's systematic instincts called for a tighter organization, and when the definitive edition of the *Institutes* finally appeared (1559), he had given the work its familiar arrangement under the two main themes "The Knowledge of God the Creator" and "The Knowledge of God the Redeemer in Christ."[2] The new arrangement, however, did not indicate any change in the purpose of the work; the *Institutes* remained a companion to Bible studies, and Calvin accordingly kept the preface to the earlier, second edition, although with a number of changes.

Schleiermacher also worked with a two-part system of dogmatics, which dealt in turn with creation and redemption, and like Calvin he devoted a great deal of thought to the arrangement of his material. The very first proposition of his *Christian Faith,* in the first edition (1821-22), defined dogmatics as "the science of the coherence *(dem Zusammenhange)* of the doctrine current in a Christian church at a given time."[3]

[1]John Calvin, *Epistola ad lectorem* (preface to the *Institutes*), in *Ioannis Calvini opera selecta,* ed. Peter Barth and Wilhelm Niesel, 5 vols. (Munich: Chr. Kaiser, 1926-52), 3:5-7. Barth and Niesel give the 1559 version of the preface and indicate variations from the earlier text in their notes.

[2]See Edward A. Dowey, Jr., *The Knowledge of God in Calvin's Theology,* 2nd ed. (New York: Columbia University Press,1965), esp. p. 41.

[3]This became proposition 19 in the second, revised edition (1830-31). See Friedrich Schleiermacher, *Der christliche Glaube nach den Grundsätzen der evangelischen Kirche im Zusammenhange dargestellt,* 7th ed., based on the 2d, ed. Martin Redeker, 2 vols. (Berlin: Walter de Gruyter, 1960). The revised edition of Schleiermacher's *Glaubenslehre,* as he liked to call his dogmatic work, is cited hereafter as *Gl.* by section and (where pertinent) subsection. The page numbers in parentheses refer to the English translation, though I have

Both Calvin and Schleiermacher, then, aimed at a comprehensive, logically ordered presentation of the Christian religion (or Christian faith), and at point after point the overall structure of their respective works really does invite comparison between them. Nevertheless, with respect to the data, the status, and the use of dogmatics, Schleiermacher departed significantly from Calvin's model.

In the first place, Schleiermacher understood dogmatics to be a descriptive, rather than an exegetical, field of study. Like Calvin, he wanted a comprehensive statement of Christian faith, and to this extent they held a common view of their subject matter. But whereas Calvin tried to get at the subject through interpretation of the Bible as the authoritative statement of what Christian belief should be, Schleiermacher thought of dogmatics as empirical understanding of an actual, present way of believing (a *Glaubensweise*).[4] He did acknowledge the possibility of what he called a "scriptural dogmatics," and he never claimed that his was the only way to practice dogmatic theology, or even that any system had to follow one model exclusively. It is just that he himself preferred to regard exegetical theology and dogmatic theology as two distinct, coordinate fields.[5] One reason he gave for his preference is that he wrote his dogmatics expressly for the church of the Prussian union between Lutherans and Reformed, and while the scriptures are the norm of what is Christian, a Protestant dogmatics has to ask more specifically what is evangelical. For this purpose, the most immediate data will be the Reformation confessions of faith, used less as tests of orthodox belief than as the primary expressions of the evangelical Christian "spirit". Schleiermacher's method, too, like Calvin's, is inescapably hermeneutical insofar as it works with texts, albeit different texts. But it is also, as has often been said, psychologizing: what he is after is a description of a particular variety of religious affections, or a specific religious consciousness. The method is not individualistic, however, as is sometimes further supposed, since it is a collective consciousness that occupies his attention. And it cannot be a merely statistical method either, but remains, in its own manner, normative. Dogmaticians do not distribute questionnaires; they turn to the earliest sources of the evangelical faith, where the waters presumably flowed most purely.[6]

not always followed its wording: Schleiermacher, *The Christian Faith,* Eng. trans. of the 2d German ed., ed. H.R. Mackintosh and J.S. Stewart (Edinburgh: T. and T. Clark, 1928). The "propositions" *(Leitsätze)* of the first edition, included by Redeker in an appendix, are cited by volume and page; for proposition 1, see Redeker, 2:498.

[4]*Schleiermachers Sendschreiben über seine Glaubenslehre an Lücke* (1829), ed. Hermann Mulert, Studien zur Geschichte des neueren Protestantismus, Quellenheft 2 (Giessen: Alfred Töpelmann [J. Ricker], 1908), pp. 20-21, 25-26, 28, 33; Schleiermacher, *Kurze Darstellung des theologischen Studiums zum Behuf einleitender Vorlesungen* (1811; 2d ed., 1830), 3d, critical ed., ed. Heinrich Scholz, Quellenschriften zur Geschichte des Protestantismus, vol. 10 (1910; reprint ed., Darmstadt: Wissenschaftliche Buchgesellschaft, 1961), §§ 1, 26, 97, 188, 195. The procedure of dogmatics is "empirical" in that it describes actual facts of experience (*Sendschreiben*, pp. 20-21). Cf. *Gl.*, §§ 28.2 (p. 121), 33.3 (p. 136), 64.1-2 (pp. 265-266), 100.3 (p. 428).

[5]*Gl.,* §§ 19 (postscript, pp. 92-93), 27.3 (p. 116), 27.4 (pp. 116-17). Dogmatic theology strives for completeness (*Gl.,* §§ 18.3 [p. 87], 20.1 [p. 94], 29.2 [p. 124]), but completeness can be attained in more than one way (*Sendschreiben,* pp. 46-49; cf. p. 41).

[6]*Gl.*, § 27.1-2 (pp. 112-15); *Gl.*, §§ 15 (p. 76), 16 (postscript, p. 81), 31 (p. 127); *Kurze Darstellung,* § 83. For Schleiermacher's view of the Reformation confessions, see further his "Über den eigenthümlichen Werth und das bindende Ansehen symbolischer Bücher" (1819), reprinted in Schleiermacher, *Kleine Schriften und Predigten,* ed. Hayo Gerdes and Emanuel Hirsch, 3 vols. (Berlin: Walter de Gruyter, 1969-70), 2:141-66, esp. pp. 143-44. 159-62. His intention to do the science of a *collective* religious consciousness is plainly conveyed in his ecclesial norm (*Gl.*, § 17.1 [pp. 83-84]) - indeed, in the very title he gave to his dogmatic work (see n. 3 above).

In the second place, precisely because he understood dogmatics to be descriptive, Schleiermacher was more modest than Calvin about the status of dogmatic assertions. Calvin took it for granted that Christian truth was the whole of sound religion. Schleiermacher acknowledged that those for whom a Christian dogmatics is written, being Christians, will presuppose the truth of Christianity; that is the nature of the faith being described, and it is the task of dogmatics to explicate faith, not to defend or to doubt it. But it does not follow that truth is wholly lacking in other religions.[7] There are many faiths. In his introduction Schleiermacher tries, as a preliminary task, to locate Christianity among them - to define Christianity's essence - and at the same time to indicate the place of dogmatics among the empirical sciences. He proceeds, as everyone knows, by arguing that each historical religion is a particular modification of the feeling of absolute dependence; Christianity is distinguished from other monotheistic faiths (*Glaubensweisen*) by the fact that everything in it is related to the redemption accomplished by Jesus of Nazareth. The task of Schleiermacher's dogmatics is to describe this faith in its Protestant form.[8] He does not have to deny the authenticity of other forms of Christianity, or even of other religions. As a dogmatic theologian of the evangelical church, he believed Christianity to be the highest form of monotheistic faith. But as at least an amateur philosopher of religion, he recognized that what dogmatic theology does - and so, the status of the discipline as a science - can only be understood from a neutral point "above" the various religions.[9]

In the third place, while both Calvin and Schleiermacher wrote dogmatics mainly to educate pastors, Schleiermacher did not think of his work as a companion to Bible study (although it could conceivably be so used), but rather as a treatise on what we might call "the dynamics of faith." Pastors need a firm grasp on how the faith they are to nurture actually functions. Of course, they need *biblical* theology for that, too, which is why exegetical theology must be regarded as a coordinate field of theological study along with dogmatics. The primary usefulness of *dogmatic* theology is that it shows how the Christian way of believing "hangs together" (its *Zusammenhang*), and this in turn makes it easier for the pastor to sort out the great wealth of biblical images - an abundance that, without the discipline of dogmatic training, might occasion one-sided teaching, false teaching,or conflicting teachings in the

[7]Schleiermacher asserts that his presentation is relative to dogmatics, and that dogmatics is only for Christians (*Gl.*, § 11.5 [pp. 59-60]). But presumably a descriptive Islamic dogmatics could be written on Schleiermacher's principles by a Mohammedan, who, of course, would write for Moslems and would presuppose the truth of Islam.

[8]Schleiermacher's definition of the essence of Christianity is given in *Gl.*, § 11 (p. 52). The connection with Jesus brings about a modification of the feeling of absolute dependence: the fundamental *Christian* feeling is of the need for redemption and its satisfaction in Christ (*Sendschreiben*, pp. 31, 47), and these are facts of experience *(erfahrungsmässige Tatsachen)*, not facts of consciousness antecedent to experience (*ibid.*, pp. 21-22). On the notion of a "placement" *(Ortsbestimmung)* of Christianity, see *Sendschreiben*, pp. 53-56.

[9]*Gl.*, §§ 7.3 (p. 33), 8.4 (pp. 37-38), 10 (postscript, p. 52), 11.5 (pp. 59-60). That the argument of the introduction was intended to define the place of dogmatics among the sciences, as well as the place of Christianity among the religions, is clearly indicated in *Sendschreiben*, pp. 58-59. On the vantage point "above" Christianity, see *Kurze Darstellung*, § 33, and *Glaubenslehre*, first edition, § 6 (Redeker, 2:500). Schleiermacher makes it abundantly clear that this vantage point is only provisional; it is not the standpoint of the dogmatic theologian, since the entire introduction lies outside dogmatics proper (*Sendschreiben*, pp. 55-56; *Gl.*, 1.1 [p. 2]).

church.[10] The times also called for pastors who clearly understood how to relate the dynamics of faith to the rapid dissemination of knowledge from the natural sciences. The doctrine of creation provides us with an excellent test case for this conception of dogmatics. The double question the dogmatician asks is: Where does the belief in creation fit into a description of the Christian consciousness, and can that belief be so presented as not to get us mixed up with natural science?[11]

CREATION AND REDEMPTION

In premodern Christian dogmatics, the place of "creation" was automatically dictated by the assumption that the creation was one act in a sequence of divine acts. The dogmatic order was supposedly historical or chronological: in accordance with his eternal decrees, God first created the world and humans; then, when Adam and Eve fell through their disobedience, God intervened in human history by the election of a chosen people; in the fullness of time, he became incarnate in Jesus of Nazareth; and now he continues to establish his kingdom through the spread of the church. If we remove the divine decrees beyond time, then creation appears as act one in a divine drama. Presumably Calvin, for instance, required no lengthy reflection to make "The Knowledge of God the Creator" the theme of the first book of his 1559 *Institutes*. In the temporal sequence of divine works, creation is where everything begins; redemption is where it is going, at any rate for the elect.

Already in Calvin, however, there is the possibility of an alternative order. If, as he argued, the knowledge of God the Creator was lost, or at least suppressed and distorted, by the fall, then in the order of Christian experience - as distinct from the order of divine works - redemption actually precedes a true knowledge of the Creator; or perhaps we could say that since the fall knowledge of God the Creator depends on, and is contained in, knowledge of God the Redeemer.[12] Calvin, to be sure, did not decide to follow the experiential order,or he would have written the four books of the *Institutes* backwards, so to say, beginning with what is now the last book and ending with what is now the first. But the experiential perspective apparently leads him to make two distinct (though not incompatible) claims about creation and revelation.

[10]Dogmatics *(das dogmatische Verfahren)* only exists for the sake of preaching (*die Verkündigung; Gl.*, § 19.1 [p. 88]). What is needed is a clear and stimulating description of a shared inward experience, and "doctrine" is only a means to this end (*Sendschreiben*, p. 16; cf. *Gl.*, § 18.3 [p. 87]). Dogmatics has its usefulness as a guide to teaching in the pulpit (*Sendschreiben*, p. 29), though the language of dogmatic theology is not designed to be carried over into the sermon without translation (*ibid.*, p. 59). On the regulative and systematic function of dogmatics in sifting biblical imagery, see *Gl.*, §§ 16.3 (pp. 80-81), 17.2 (p. 84), 20.1 (p. 94), 28.2 (p. 120), 50.1 (p. 195), 61.4 (p. 253). Not dogmatics only, but every branch of theology serves the leadership of the church directly (*Gl.*, § 19 [postscript, p. 92]).

[11]The two quotations that serve as my epigraphs at the beginning of this paper will be found in *Sendschreiben*, pp. 25, 40. Cf. Calvin's interesting attempt to exclude from the doctrine of the Virgin Birth matters that belong not to theology but to philosophy and medicine. Calvin, *Institutio Christianae religionis* (Geneva, 1559; cited hereafter as *Inst.* by book, chapter, and section), 2.13.3 (1:479). Volume and page numbers in parentheses refer to the standard English translation: *Calvin: Institutes of the Christian Religion*, ed. John T. McNeill and trans. Ford Lewis Battles, 2 vols., Library of Christian Classics, vols. 20-21 (Philadelphia: Westminster Press, 1960).

[12]*Inst.*, 1.5.14 (1:68), 1.6.1 (1:70-71), 2.6.1 (1:341).

On the one hand, Calvin thinks that the Scriptures, though given to counteract the effects of sin, actually provide such information about the beginning of the world as we could not possibly have had, without special revelation, even if Adam had never fallen. The narrative of creation, to be sure, is not a strictly scientific account; nevertheless we are informed, for instance, that God created the world and humans over a period of six days, which we certainly could not know had God not chosen to reveal it to Moses. Notice what this implies about the nature of revelation: it is information, not otherwise available, imparted in a supernatural manner.[13] On the other hand, Calvin can also say that through the revelation of Scripture we are enabled to view nature with a clearer vision and to perceive what we should and would have known but for the fall: that nature is the handiwork of the Creator. The Scriptures are like reading glasses: they aid our weak vision and focus the otherwise confused knowledge of God in our minds. Of course, the Scriptures teach us to perceive God as Redeemer; but without the Word, we would not even recognize him as artificer of the universe. Revelation, from this perspective, is not supernaturally conveyed information; it is divinely restored vision. And only those whose blindness has been healed by God the Redeemer can recognize God as Creator.[14]

Calvin provides us, in effect, with two quite different dogmatic approaches to creation. Schleiermacher was well aware of them both. He admits that Christians have commonly linked creation with the opening chapters of Genesis, understood as a factual narrative about the beginning of all spatial and temporal existence. But the Mosaic account of creation is mythical rather than proto-scientific; and Schleiermacher notes that many eminent Jewish and Christian thinkers, including Calvin, did not treat it as biblical science. The time has now come to turn over to the natural scientists the entire question of how the universe first took shape. Dogmatic theologians can await the results calmly, because it is not really their business.[15]

Naturally, Schleiermacher was apprehensive that the Mosaic narrative might lend itself to anthropomorphic images of the divine activity, as though God made the entire temporal and spatial universe the way a human craftsman fashions some artifact within time and space.[16] But his fundamental objection to basing a doctrine of creation on the Mosaic narrative was more directly related to his preference for the second methodological option. Even if the Mosaic description *were* a historical account, it could only give us natural science communicated in an extraordinary way; it would tell us little or nothing about the real content of faith in creation, and so would have little or no interest for dogmatics. Hence the development of a strictly dogmatic account of creation cannot take the form of an exegesis of the Mosaic

[13]*Inst.*, 1.14.1-2 (1:160-61). Calvin does not doubt that the history of creation is revealed truth, but because Moses presents it in language accommodated to the unlearned, anyone who wants to learn astronomy must look elsewhere. See his commentary on Genesis 1:6, *Ioannis Calvini opera quae supersunt omnia*, ed. Wilhelm Baum, Edward Cunitz, and Edward Reuss, 59 vols., *Corpus Reformatorum*, vols. 29-87 (Brunswick: C.A. Schwetschke and Son [M. Bruhn], 1863-1900), 23:18. Cf. *Inst.*, 1.14.3 (1:162).

[14]*Inst.*, 1.5.14 (1:68), 1.6.1 (1.70), 1.14.1 (1:160-61). Cf. the "argument" to the commentary on Genesis (*Opera omnia*, 23:9/10).

[15]*Gl.*, §§36.2 (p. 143), 40.1-2 (pp. 150-51).

[16]*Gl.*, §§41 (p. 152), 46..1 (p. 173). Strictly speaking, there is only one divine activity: namely the creating, sustaining activity that forms the whole world (*Gl.*, § 100.2 [pp. 426-27]).

narrative. The crucial question must rather be: What does belief in creation mean as an element in the Christian religious consciousness?[17]

Now the most important consequence of this approach is not that the Genesis account of creation need not be taken literally, but that the doctrine of creation is not, strictly speaking, about how the world got started at all; rather, it is about the way the devout mind perceives the natural order. This is Schleiermacher's first major contribution to our theme. He turns our attention from the creation "in the beginning" to the creature-consciousness that every Christian has in the present. Hence, as he expressly points out, there is no essential reason for distinguishing an act of creation from the activity of providence (or, as he prefers to say, "preservation"). He thinks there is even a strictly historical warrant for not separating creation from preservation as though they were two divine works or activities: the original creedal formula in the Roman Symbol was, "I believe in God the Ruler of all things *(theon pantocratora),*" and this is also the original, simple expression of the consciousness that the world exists only in absolute dependence on God.[18]

Given Schleiermacher's dogmatic method, creation tends to collapse into providence, providence being the more fitting of the two expressions for the feeling of absolute dependence. The problem with the idea of creation is not merely that in itself it affirms absolute dependence only for the beginning of things, but also that, insofar as it refers to a remote past, it cannot possibly represent anything immediately given in the present religious consciousness. If we say that it *is*, after all, an item of faith, that can only mean faith in the improper sense of assent to extraordinarily communicated items of information. It does not follow that curiosity about origins is wholly inappropriate, only that the origin of finite being is of no interest to Christian piety or Christian dogmatics and can safely be left in the hands of scientific theorists. Even the debate over eternal creation, as distinct from a temporal beginning, has no bearing on the content of the feeling of absolute dependence, and it is a matter of indifference how it is decided. If the correct dogmatic procedure is consistently followed, there will be no temptation for theology to lose itself in foreign territory, or to pass from the distinctively religious domain to the speculative and the natural-scientific domains.[19]

So what *is* the content of what used to be called the "doctrine of creation"? It is quite simply our consciousness of being in the world as finite beings who are absolutely dependent on God. Here Schleiermacher makes a second contribution that is equally important. To be absolutely dependent upon God cannot be simply identical with our dependence on the world, and yet, he insists, these two relations are inseparable in our actual experience: we become aware of our total dependence on God

[17]*Gl.,* §§36.1 (pp. 142-43), 40.2 (p. 151). Unlike Calvin, Schleiermacher does not assert that *only* the Christian consciousness contains an awareness of creation; on the contrary, he thinks that the doctrines of part one of his *Glaubenslehre* will tend to coincide with those of other religions (see *Gl.*, §§29.1-2 [pp. 123-24], 34.3 [p. 140]). However, monotheistic piety exists only concretely - in connection with the distinctive features of a positive religion (Gl., §32.3 [p. 133]).

[18]*Gl.,* § 36 (note, p. 142). On the term "providence" *(Vorsehung),* see *Gl.,* s 164.3 (pp. 725-26). Schleiermacher's preferred term throughout the discussion in §§46-49 is *Erhaltung.*

[19]*Gl.,* §§ 36.1-2 (pp. 142-43), 37.1-3 (pp. 143-45), 38.1-2 (pp. 146-47), 39.1 (pp. 148-49), 39.3 (p. 149); §§ 40.2 (p. 151), 61.1 (p. 248); § 41.2 (p. 155); §§ 37.3 (p. 145), 39.1-2 (pp. 148-49). Cf. the discussions of the Devil and the origin of sin in §§ 45 (postscript, pp. 169-70) and 72.1-2 (pp. 292-93). In practice Schleiermacher did retain a distinction between "creation" and "preservation," but more for pedagogical than for substantive reasons (*Gl.,* § 39.3 [p. 149]).

precisely as we become conscious of ourselves as part of the world, understood as one causal system. The consciousness of God and consciousness of ourselves as part of a causal nexus tend to rise and fall together. Schleiermacher noted in the margin of his own copy of the *Christian Faith:* "Togetherness of the feeling of dependence and the consciousness of the world." In this way, he forged the crucial link between the religious doctrine of "creation" (as we may continue to call it) and the fundamental presupposition of natural-scientific inquiry: that the world constitutes an orderly whole. God and nature are not, so to say, in competition in the religious consciousness, as though what is assigned to natural causality must inevitably be taken away from God. Divine causality and natural causality, though different in kind, are coextensive; they belong together.[20]

Here Schleiermacher was perfectly aware that his exposition put him at loggerheads with much popular piety, and it may seem as if his entire dogmatic method is jeopardized. No Christian doubts the day to day preservation of the natural order by God's sustaining hand. But there is a common tendency among believers to picture God's *sustaining* activity as interrupted from time to time by special *creative* or *miraculous* acts. Indeed, there is even anxiety that the natural sciences, precisely by reducing the entire course of nature to regular, undeviating patterns ("laws"), constitute a threat to the pious expectation that God can and does intervene in nature when and where he wills. For it is exactly in such extraordinary acts of divine intervention that many devout souls chiefly see the hand of God. Piety thus seems to have a vested interest in opposing the advance of scientific research; conversely, the better the scientists understand the working of the natural order, the less devout they are likely to be.[21]

Schleiermacher's response to this apparent dilemma is characteristic. To be sure, he opposes any thought of divine (or demonic) intervention in the course of nature as destructive of sound scientific procedure. The introduction of an element of irregularity into the natural order undermines the very concept of nature itself - and with it scientific inquiry.[22] But the essential question, he believes, is not whether interventions in the course of natural events are possible or scientifically conceivable but, as far as Christian dogmatics is concerned, what they would mean for the religious self-consciousness. And if the core of the religious consciousness is indeed total confidence in the reliability of the natural order that God sustains, then a suspension of the normal workings of nature can only be judged as much a threat to piety as it would be to science. It is simply wrong to imagine a creative divine activity that enters in at individual moments as *another* activity *besides* God's sustaining activity. Such a perverted notion has its roots not in Christian piety, but in a confused world view that invokes dependence on God as the explanation for events only where the causal nexus is concealed. "We are clearly quite wrong," Schleiermacher concludes, "if we allege, as a general experience, that the incomprehensible as such is more conducive to the awakening of the religious feeling than that which is understood." His reason is plain: because, rightly interpreted, the heart of religion is the feeling of absolute dependence on God that the very regularity of nature evokes in us.

[20]*Gl.*, §§ 32.2 (p. 132), 34 (pp. 137-38), 46 (p. 170), 47 (p. 178), 51.1 (pp. 200-2). Schleiermacher's handwritten note is given in Redeker's edition (1:180). Cf. *Gl.*, § 33 (p. 133): in the feeling of absolute dependence, our self-consciousness represents the finitude of our being.

[21]*Gl.*, §§ 34.2 (p. 139), 38.2 (p. 148), 46.1 (p. 171).

[22]*Gl.*, §§ 46.1 (p. 172), 47.2 (pp. 181-82).

We cannot, of course, draw in advance limits on what is or is not naturally possible; much that we now perceive as "miraculous" may one day yield to scientific explanation. Nevertheless, it can be stated as a general rule that the interests of religion and the interests of natural science coincide.[23]

Schleiermacher's attempt to rethink the doctrine of creation arose, then, from his determination to carry through a strictly dogmatic method - and from his unfailing confidence that the dogmatic method, as he understood it, could not possibly range faith and science against each other. Any appearance of conflict between religion and natural science must be ascribed to one of two causes: either that the nature of genuine piety is being misconstrued, or that the limits of the natural are being too narrowly drawn. Schleiermacher's fear was that if the church refused to undertake the needed reconstruction of the old doctrine of creation, then in the very near future religion would go with obscurantism, science with unbelief.[24] For this reason, he attached great importance to the themes of creation and preservation in the first part of his system of doctrine. But his careful distinction between the two parts of the system should rule out any suggestion that the doctrine of creation, or the feeling of absolute dependence itself, is the real heart of his Christian faith. In itself, the doctrine of creation is only an empty frame, to be filled in, as he puts it, by the subsequent discussion: that is, by his description of the full Christian consciousness of redemption. For what does the omnipotence of the Creator mean to me until I know its purpose, which is disclosed only in the consciousness of the *new* creation? Schleiermacher assumed that the readers of his introduction and first part would supply from their own Christian consciousness what his exposition held momentarily in abeyance.[25] From the critics' reception of his first edition, he realized that he had assumed too much.

Schleiermacher and His Critics

From his own day until ours, a succession of critics have been unwilling to take Schleiermacher's word for it when he claims to be simply describing how Christians believe, and there has been a surprising amount of continuity in the critical tradition. In the first half of our century, the assault came mainly from the side of neoorthodoxy. The most extensive neoorthodox critique, Emil Brunner's *Mysticism and the Word* (1924), alleged that "mysticism" in Schleiermacher's theology supplanted the Word of God. Brunner argued that a general concept of religion, derived from the philosophy of religion, determined the entire content of Schleiermacher's imagined description of Christianity; all that was really Christian in his dogmatics belonged not to the essence of Christianity, but merely to the mode of its historical manifestation. In other words, the feeling of absolute dependence, according to Brunner, was the actual essence of Schleiermacher's Christianity. Only, whereas the Christian has the feeling of absolute dependence accidentally in the form of a connection with Jesus Christ, another monotheist, a Stoic for instance, lacks this special Christian element without thereby missing anything essential in piety itself.[26]

[23] *Gl.*, § 47.1 (pp. 178-79); § 38.2 (p. 148); § 46.1 (p. 171); §§ 47.3 (pp. 183-84), 49 (postscript, p. 193).

[24] *Sendschreiben*, p. 37.

[25] *Ibid.*, pp. 32-33.

[26] Emil Brunner, *Die Mystik und das Wort: Der Gegensatz zwischen moderner Religionsauffassung und christlichem Glauben dargestellt an der Theologie Schleiermachers* (Tübingen: J.C. B. Mohr [Paul Siebeck], 1924); see esp. pp. 129, 132. Karl Barth's lectures on the theology of Schleiermacher (1923-24) were not published until 1978: *Die Theologie Schleiermachers, Karl Barth Gesamtausgabe,* 2, 11 (Zurich: Theologischer Verlag, 1978).

A decade ago, in *Tradition and the Modern World,* I tried to show why Brunner's reading of Schleiermacher's dogmatics would not do.[27] I suppose it could be said that the argument I made there was fifty years late as a response to neoorthodoxy. In any case, it was ten years too *early* to serve as a reply to the present wave of "antifoundationalist" criticisms of Schleiermacher, although, as a matter of fact, the issues remain largely the same. There is no need to repeat my case in detail. But I cannot afford to let the newer critiques pass unquestioned, because if they were right, then my interpretation of where the doctrine of creation belongs in Schleiermacher's dogmatics would be mistaken: "creation," as a thematization of the feeling of absolute dependence, would be not so much a formal presupposition of Christian faith as its essential content.

One of the most vigorous and detailed antifoundationalist critiques of Schleiermacher, which we may fairly take as representative, has come from Ronald Thiemann. In an article on "Piety, Narrative, and Christian Identity," Thiemann argues that Schleiermacher made philosophical theology the key theological discipline, and that he assigned it the pivotal role of justifying Christian faith by uncovering its universal religious content. The price Schleiermacher allegedly paid for this *foundational* method is twofold: the distinctiveness of Christian identity becomes secondary to the universal form of religion, and Christian theology becomes correspondingly abstract and remote from the concrete expressions of Christian faith and life.[28] In his book *Revelation and Theology,* Thiemann's interpretation of Schleiermacher is in some respects more cautious. He refers expressly to Schleiermacher's own statement of what the introduction to his dogmatics was all about, and he recognizes at least the possibility that Schleiermacher's method might well, on a charitable reading, be taken to support just such a *descriptive* theology as Thiemann himself prefers.[29] Nevertheless, in the book, too, Schleiermacher is presented as one of the foundationalists, for whom the central theological task is apologetic: to justify Christian claims, and especially the claim to a prevenient divine revelation, by grounding them in a self-evident, non-inferential belief or set of beliefs, or in a universal religious experience.[30]

It is, of course, what Schleiermacher himself calls the "dangerous introduction"[31] to his dogmatics that gives rise to the antifoundationalist critique. He does indeed

[27]B.A. Gerrish, *Tradition and the Modern World: Reformed Theology in the Nineteenth Century* (Chicago: University of Chicago Press, 1978), chap. 1, esp. pp. 22-39.

[28]Ronald F. Thiemann, "Piety, Narrative, and Christian Identity," *Word and World* 3 (1983): 148-59. Thiemann assigns to Schleiermacher's philosophical theology the task of disclosing the "self-identical essence of piety" (p. 151). Subsequently, he states that foundational theology claims to "discern the unchanging essence of Christianity" (p. 156). Unless the essence of Christianity is taken to be identical with the essence of piety (which is certainly not Schleiermacher's view), these two tasks must be carefully differentiated.

[29]Thiemann, *Revelation and Theology: The Gospel as Narrated Promise* (Notre Dame, Indiana: University of Notre Dame Press, 1985); see esp. p. 28, p. 172 n.5. Thiemann also grants that "demonstration of the essential religiousness of human nature . . . may well be part of an overall apologetic strategy" (*ibid.,* p. 155), and he does not see narrative theology as a *substitute* for a discursive dogmatic theology: theologians are not story tellers ("Piety, Narrative, and Christian Identity," p. 159, n. 25).

[30]Thiemann, *Revelation,* pp. 7, 24-31, 73-75, 158-59 (n. 20). The feeling of absolute dependence is not strictly a belief at all (as Thiemann implies on p. 31); and the reason why it must be a consciousness of *God* is not because it is immediate or precognitive (p. 29) but because our dependence on anything less than God, or even on the sum total of finite existents, is never absolute (see Schleiermacher, *Gl.,* §§ 4.4 [pp. 16-17], 32.2 [p. 132]).

[31]*Sendschreiben,* p. 33.

seek, in the opening paragraphs of *The Christian Faith,* to isolate a self-identical element that underlies all religions and is an essential constituent in human consciousness. But he does not do so in order to offer, as Thiemann asserts of foundationalists in general, a "theoretical justification for Christian belief in God's prevenience." The quest for a "full-scale justification of belief in God's prevenience" is Thiemann's, not Schleiermacher's.[32] If one insists on looking for such a justification in Schleiermacher, one would do better to look at his doctrine of election: Schleiermacher was a supralapsarian Calvinist, and justifications of divine prevenience do not come any more "full scale" than that.[33] But as far as the introduction to his dogmatics is concerned, I see no reason for doubting that he was doing there exactly what he claimed to be doing.

Schleiermacher insists repeatedly that in his introduction he is not trying to justify Christian beliefs or to provide a philosophical foundation for dogmatics. The function of his propositions borrowed from philosophical theology is not to defend Christianity by grounding it in a universal religious consciousness, but, quite the contrary, to show what is special to Christianity - to define its essence and so to draw the boundaries within which appropriate expressions of distinctively Christian faith must be contained. And he tells us expressly that there is no way to justify Christianity (or any other positive religion) by philosophical means, even if we wanted to; he simply assumes that Christian dogmatics is written for those who need no such justification because they are already believers in Christ.[34]

When, therefore, Thiemann writes that for foundationalism "apologetics inevitably emerges as the *primary* theological task" and "the two most important theological activities - the development of a universal justificatory argument and the defense of Christian claims before the bar of rationality - are carried on independent of the internal logic of Christian belief and practice and with little reference to criteria of judgement internal to the Christian tradition," his remarks scarcely fit Schleiermacher.[35] Throughout his dogmatics, Schleiermacher rests his argument chiefly on the Lutheran and Reformed confessions - norms specific to Protestant Christianity. And I think he would be fully justified in asking again, as he did in 1829, that any who doubt whether his method can fairly represent a specific Christian doctrine would at least consider how he actually explicates Christian doctrines in the second, main part of his system. Few of his early critics seem to have troubled themselves with the second

[32]Thiemann, *Revelation,* pp. 7, 69.

[33]*Gl.,* § 120.3 (p. 555); cf. § 79.1 (pp. 325-26).

[34]*Sendschreiben,* pp. 17-18, 31-32, 38-40, 54-56; *Gl.,* §§ 10 (esp. the postscript, pp. 51-52), 11.5 (pp. 59-60), 22.2 (pp. 98-99). On the other hand, see *Gl.,* § 8.4 (p. 38). In the context of the present discussion of foundationalism, it is particularly interesting to find Schleiermacher describing piety as *das Unbegründete* and saying: "Von einem Begründen ist gar nicht die Rede bei mir" *(Sendschreiben,* pp. 17, 20). Cf. *Gl.,* §§ 2.1 (p. 3), 34.3 (p. 136). Thiemann writes of a shift from assumption to argument as theology moves into the post-Cartesian world (*Revelation,* pp. 11-12). But a case could be made for holding that Calvin, at least, was more concerned than Schleiermacher to *argue* for the universality of the religious sense and the divine origin of the Christian revelation (see *Inst.,* 1.3 and 1.8 [1:43-47 and 1:81-92]).

[35]Thiemann, *Revelation,* p. 74. For Schleiermacher the only possible "foundation" for a dogmatic assertion is to establish that it is the *correct* expression of the Christian self-consciousness (*Sendschreiben,* p. 56). In his own terminology, the task of "apologetics" is to defend the *distinctiveness* of Christianity (*Kurze Darstellung,* §§ 39, 44-46; *Sendschreiben,* p. 57; *Gl.,* §§ 2.2 [p. 4], 19.1 [p. 89], 28.3 [p. 122]).

part at all; of those that did, some, to his obvious amusement, were annoyed to see that he could still wear his churchly mantle with a certain natural ease.[36]

Against what he takes to be the foundationalist misconception of the theological task, Theimann calls for a "conception of theology as primarily a descriptive activity, a second-order mode of reflection which displays the logic inherent in Christian belief and practice"; or again, "an interpretive activity which seeks to illuminate the structure embedded in beliefs and practices," eschewing theoretical defenses of Christian doctrine.[37] But that, it seems to me, is a perfect statement of Schleiermacher's own dogmatic aims! Thiemann further calls for a theology that allows for the thoroughly historical character of theological thinking and hence for diverse expressions of Christian faith at any given time. And the nonfoundationalists, he insists, speak from within the religious community, their theology being an exercise of the Anselmian *fides quaerens intellectum* - a quest to understand faith, not to justify it.[38] But these, too, are cardinal points in Schleiermacher's theological program!

Surprisingly enough, then, or so it seems to me, Thiemann's antidote to foundationalism resembles Schleiermacher's theological program much more closely than does the malady he diagnoses. His prescriptions for a healthy theology were expressly proposed a century and a half ago by Schleiermacher. And this ought to promise well for a much better accommodation between Schleiermacherians and the antifoundationalist "narrative theologians" than we seem to have managed in the last few years. Schleiermacher was a pioneer in his recognition that theology is a thoroughly historical discipline and that there will always be a diversity of ways of expressing the common faith. Dogmatics can never be more than the science of the system of doctrine current in *a* church at *a* particular time, and that is why he classified dogmatics as a branch of historical theology. The subject matter of dogmatics is not static but in constant movement and change.[39] And because he could not conceive of anyone doing theology save in the believing community, he wrote boldly on the title page of his great dogmatic system the Anselmian motto: "I do not seek to understand in order that I may believe, but I believe in order that I may understand . . . . For anyone who has not believed will not experience, and anyone who has not experienced will not understand."[40]

[36]*Sendschreiben,* pp. 62-63; p. 33. Some readers treated the introduction as though it were the real kernel of the whole book (p. 31).

[37]Thiemann, *Revelation,* p. 72.

[38]"Piety, Narrative, and Christian Identity," pp. 155-56.

[39]*Sendschreiben,* p. 31; *Gl.,* § 19.2 (p. 89). Cf. *Friedrich Schleiermachers Weihnachtsfeier* (1806), critical ed., ed. Hermann Mulert, Philosophische Bibliothek, vol. 117 (Leipzig: Dürr, 1908), pref. to the 2d ed. (1826), pp. 57-58; *Kurze Darstellung,* § 195 (cf. § 33 from the 1st ed., cited in Scholz's footnote 1 on p. 11).

[40]Anselm, *Proslogium,* chap. 1; *De fide trinitatis et de incarnatione verbi,* chap. 2. Unfortunately, the two quotations from Anselm were dropped from the title page of the English translation. On the role of conviction in dogmatics, see also Schleiermacher, *Gl.,* §§ 13 (postscript, p. 67), 19.1 (pp. 88-89), 33.3 (p. 136), 100.3 (p. 429), 114.1 (p. 529); *Kurze Darstellung,* § 196. It is not dogmatics but philosophical theology that takes its point of departure from "above" Christianity (*Kurze Darstellung*, § 33; cf. proposition 6 of the first edition of the *Glaubenslehre:* Redeker, 2:500). Schleiermacher did think that dogmatics had the right to borrow concepts from philosophy, but only on the same condition that Thiemann finds in Barth (*Revelation,* p. 173 n. 7): that their meaning must then be given by the new linguistic context (*Sendschreiben,* p. 60; *Gl.,* § 16, [postscript, pp. 81-83]).

Although it never occurred to Schleiermacher, as it did to the neoorthodox, to deny that Christianity is one religion among others, the accent in his dogmatics falls unmistakably on the particularity of Christian faith. His instincts were against what he called "the tendency to regard Christianity simply as a means of advancing and propagating religion in general," as though its own distinctive nature were merely accidental and secondary. One critic charged Schleiermacher in his own day with trying to absorb what is distinctively Christian into a universal religious knowledge, and he replied that any such knowledge could only be an *abstraction from* what is Christian. It was not *his* theology but rationalism's that would have surrendered the particularity of Christian faith to a common religion of humanity, which he considered no religion at all but a Teutonic mish-mash of morals and metaphysics; and he thought that this travesty of religion went far to explain why French atheism had made incursions into Germany.[41]

Schleiermacher's distinctive contribution to the doctrine of creation will only be appreciated where he is seen for what he was: a church dogmatician whose main concern was to explicate the peculiarly Christian consciousness of sin and grace. The idea of absolute dependence, articulated in the doctrines of creation and preservation, cannot *ground* or *justify* Christian faith. It is not "an atemporal essence which is prior to all historical and cultural particulars";[42] it is rather an *abstraction from* historical and cultural particulars. If one is to speak of "foundations" or "grounding" at all in Schleiermacher's theology, then it is the particular that grounds the universal, not the other way around. The actual foundation of the Christian's confidence in the divinely governed world-order is faith in Christ. This is why Schleiermacher can only assign the doctrine of creation to the religious consciousness presupposed by and contained in the Christian religious affections. If this is "foundationalism," it is a kind of inverted foundationalism, in which the universal religious consciousness or feeling of absolute dependence emerges in connection with the particular form of a historical faith. This was Schleiermacher's standpoint already in the famous *Speeches on Religion,* in which, after saying a great deal about religion in the abstract, he finally admonished the cultured despisers that only those can finally hope to know religion who are willing to pitch their tent *somewhere*. Why not in Christianity?[43]

Creation and the Moral World-Order

The connection Schleiermacher makes between the universal and the particular elements in Christian faith turns out to be anything but reductive. Christians receive their entire consciousness of God from Christ. Their sense of dependence on God is awakened by him. But they also receive from him the awareness that the world is more than a law-governed causal nexus ("nature"); it is, as Schleiermacher puts it, a "theater of redemption." In the order of exposition, the last word goes to redemption, but it is

[41] *Gl.*, §§ 11.4 (p. 57), 24.3 (p. 105); *Sendschreiben*, pp. 17, 28-29; cf *Friedrich Schleiermacher's Reden über die Religion,* critical ed., ed. G. Ch. Bernhard Pünjer (Brunswick: C.A. Schwetschke and Son [M. Bruhn], 1879), pp. 244, 246-47.

[42] Thiemann, "Piety, Narrative, and Christian Identity," p. 155.

[43] *Reden*, pp. 257, 275, 287. Oman translates the first passage: "Only those who . . . pitch their camp [*sich niederläßt*] in some such positive form, have . . . any well-earned right of citizenship in the religious world." Schleiermacher, *On Religion: Speeches to its Cultured Despisers,* trans. from the 3d German ed. (1821) by John Oman (1894; reprint ed., New York: Harper and Row, 1958), pp. 223-24.

actually the first word in the order of Christian experience: faith in creation, although it brings them closer to other monotheists, is awakened in Christians by the Redeemer.[44]

The way the "feeling of absolute dependence" functions as a concept in Schleiermacher's dogmatics - the way it relates to creation and redemption - thus seems to be free of the difficulties most commonly attributed to it. It is another question, however, whether the concept itself can be sustained. "Feeling," in the sense of "immediate self-consciousness," is by definition elusive: a living movement that stops when you stop to look at it. But as long as you leave it alone, it remains indeterminate and you cannot say what it is. In Schleiermacher's own lifetime, it was argued against him that religious feelings must be byproducts of religious ideas. I think he defended himself successfully against the argument that piety presupposes the idea of *God.* That the feeling of absolute dependence rather gives rise to the idea of God seems to me a defensible analysis. But can you have a feeling of absolute dependence without the idea of *dependence*? And if not, how can it be maintained that the feeling belongs purely to the domain of immediate self-consciousness - unmediated, that is, by reflection? Schleiermacher would patiently reply, I expect, that what he is talking about is something always latent in human consciousness as pure feeling, but it only comes to expression in thought as a feeling of absolute dependence. Indeed, in itself it is an actual existential relationship; piety is its most primitive expression.[45]

A "little introspection" is supposed to reveal all of this to us.[46] But perhaps it is not merely frivolous when one recent author gives us this report:

> *Now I have described the feeling of absolute dependence to a colleague of mine who is thirty years old, lucid of memory, more than astute enough to follow the description, and an enthusiastic member of a developed Protestant community. He stoutly denies that he has ever had the feeling.*[47]

I would not myself be inclined to take this for a conclusive refutation of Schleiermacher. Immediate self-consciousness - a field of consciousness beyond whatever it is that engages our attention at any given moment - is a perennially fascinating notion, and it may have a great deal to do with the specifically human way of being in the world. But the problems are enough to make me doubt the wisdom of beginning

[44]*Glaubenslehre,* 1st ed., § 39 (Redeker, 2:510); *Sendschreiben,* p. 31; *Gl.,* §§ 29.2 (p. 124), 32.1 (p. 132), 169 (p. 735). The efficacy of redemption enables us to assert that the purpose of the divine government of the world is the planting and extension of the Christian church (*Gl.,* § 164 [p. 723]).

[45]*Sendschreiben,* pp. 13-15; cf. *Reden,* pp. 53-56 (2d ed.); *Gl.,* §§ 3-4 (pp. 5-18). That the feeling of absolute dependence presupposes the concept of dependence has been argued recently by Wayne Proudfoot, *Religious Experience* (Berkeley and Los Angeles: University of California Press, 1985), esp. pp. 18-19. Of course, Schleiermacher himself asserts that the feeling of absolute dependence emerges only in conjunction with the feeling of partial dependence on the world (e.g., *Gl.,* §§ 5.3 [pp. 20-22], 60.1 [p. 244]). The question is what this means for the notion of immediate self-consciousness.

[46]*Gl.,* § 4.1 (p. 13). Presumably, "introspection" *(Selbstbeobachtung)* is the method for the entire section, not just for § 4.1. Indeed, Schleiermacher constantly appeals to the reader's introspection also in dealing with the specifically Chistian facts, from which the feeling of absolute dependence is only a logical abstraction; hence the motto from Anselm (see n. 40 above). A similar appeal is occasionally made by Calvin (e.g., *Inst.,* 1.7.5 [1:80-81]).

[47]Robert Roberts, "The Feeling of Absolute Dependence," *Journal of Religion* 57 (1977): 252-66, esp. p. 260.

Christian dogmatics with it or making the thematization of it the content of the doctrine of creation. If one is still willing to try Schleiermacher's *approach*, one may need another *starting point*. And what intrigues me here is something else that he himself frequently says in speaking of creation and preservation: that piety has to do with our sense of being part of a stable, orderly whole.[48] Could the doctrine of creation be more suitably taken to articulate, not the elusive feeling of absolute dependence, but our sense that we exist in an ordered, and therefore meaningful, world?

Perhaps this invites the objection that some of our colleagues never have *this* feeling either. But the problem then is not, I think, conceptual, as though the notion as such were too elusive for us even to know what it means. The problem has to do rather with alienation; we know what a "sense of order" means, but the thing itself sometimes runs away from us. Hence it seems exactly right to assert that the sense of order is *contained in* the Christian's faith in Christ as Redeemer, though others may have it in other ways, and still others may lose it or not have it securely at all. And I would also wish to argue that there is in fact a *conceptual fit* between faith in Christ and the sense of order, because the sense of order too is a kind of faith - a confidence by which we live, but which we cannot prove.

Christian dogmatics is not required to demonstrate that this more general faith is the underlying content of every empirical religion (though it *may* be), but only to explicate its content as an actual presupposition of faith in Christ. No more is asked of the dogmatician than to ensure that all the pieces of the Christian way of believing are there, and in a logical arrangement that makes sense. If the subject matter of Christian dogmatics is indeed Christian faith as a way of believing, then it surely does make good sense to begin with the question: What is believing? Schleiermacher already hovered on the brink of so phrasing the first question of dogmatics when he wrote that "there is something common to all ways of believing *(Glaubensweisen)* by virtue of which we put them together as kin, and something peculiar in each by virtue of which we separate it from the rest."[49] He no doubt had in mind the historical religions. But to communicate what Christian dogmatics is about, it seems to me a natural enough move to go back to less explicitly religious ways of believing, and finally to that "inevitable belief," as A.J. Balfour called it, that we inhabit an orderly world.[50] While not a religious belief as we commonly use the word "religious," it is the presupposition of every scientific experiment and seems to underlie human existence as such. We should try the experiment of putting this "existential faith" (as we may call it) in the place that the feeling of absolute dependence presently occupies in Schleiermacher's dogmatics.[51]

It will not be expected of me to say much more here about the notion of existential faith, which I am currently exploring in a historical study of F.H. Jacobi, the philosopher of faith to whom Schleiermacher would have dedicated the *Christian Faith* but for his (Jacobi's) death in 1819. But I must at least indicate why (in my opening remarks) I described the proposed dogmatic revision as "two-sided." It seems to me that, for all his emphasis on the teleological (or ethical) character of Christian monotheism, Schleiermacher's cosmic vision in his dogmatics, or at least in his doctrine of creation,

[48]See n. 20 above.

[49]*Glaubenslehre,* first edition, § 6 (Redeker, 2:500).

[50]Arthur James Balfour, *Theism and Humanism* (New York: George H. Doran, 1915), pp. 28-32.

[51]Cf. Gerrish, *Tradition and the Modern World,* pp. 36-38, 211-12 n. 77.

remained onesidedly aesthetic, and it was perhaps (for understandable reasons) more dominated by the theoretical problems of religion and natural science than a present-day doctrine of creation can afford to be. At any rate, I should think that if the Christian consciousness presupposes a stable world-order at all, it surely presupposes its moral character, perceiving it as a source not only of security but also of responsibility; and this, too, is something it holds in common with the monotheistic faiths of Judaism and Islam.[52] Schleiermacher includes no ethical moment either in his definition of piety or in his doctrine of creation. This is perhaps the price he had to pay for his determination not to *reduce* religion to ethics but to differentiate it from science and morals alike. And the anti-Kantian strain in his religious thought seems to have been reinforced by his failure to appreciate the religion of the Old Testament, which he always saw in terms of a legalistic and anthropomorphic piety that was wholly distasteful to him.[53]

If we say, as is said often enough, that the concluding propositions on the Trinity constitute a feeble appendix to his dogmatics, then it is with the magnificent vision of the world as the theater of redemption that Schleiermacher's *Christian Faith* comes to its end. His vision represents an interesting variation on the old Calvinistic theme of the manifestation of God's glory. He writes in the very last proposition on redemption: "The divine wisdom is the ground by virtue of which the world, as theater of redemption, is also the absolute revelation of the Supreme Being, and therefore *good*." In effect, this makes the goodness of the world an eschatological concept, lying more in the future consummation of redemption than in a divine creative work of the past. The goodness of the world becomes, in fact, a moral task, and Schleiermacher leaves his dogmatics on the threshold of Christian ethics:

> *For we are now confronted [he writes] with the task of more and more securing recognition for the world as a good world, as also of forming all things into an organ of the divine Spirit in harmony with the divine idea originally underlying the world-order, thus bringing all into unity with the system of redemption.*[54]

I have no quarrel with this eloquent confession. My point is simply that it surely presupposes not just a world-order but (to borrow one of Fichte's favorite expressions) a "*moral* world-order,"[55] and I cannot see why Schleiermacher did not carry the ethical moment back into his doctrine of creation, unless it was because his definition of piety as the feeling of absolute dependence stood in the way.[56]

52For Schleiermacher's own classification of Islam as an aesthetic, rather than a teleological, faith, see *Gl.*, § 9.2 (pp. 43-44). It is significant that he apparently did not consider the distinction between the aesthetic and the teleological types of monotheism to be important for the doctrine of creation (cf. *Gl.*, § 29.2 [p. 124]).

53See, *e.g. Reden*, pp. 275-78; *Sendschreiben*, pp. 28-29, 41-42; *Gl.*, §§ 8.4 (pp. 37-38), 9.2 (pp. 43-44), 12.2 (pp. 60-62), 27.3 (p. 115), 77.2 (p. 321), 94.2 (p. 387), 132.2 (p. 609).

54*Gl.*, § 169.3; trans. in Mackintosh and Stewart, pp. 736-37.

55See, *e.g.* J.G. Fichte, "Über den Grund unsers Glaubens an eine göttliche Weltregierung" (1798), in *Die Schriften zu J.G. Fichte's Atheismus-Streit* (Munich: Georg Müller, 1912), pp. 26, 34-35. For Fichte, the world is constituted by the ego as a *stage* for moral action (pp. 30-31).

56This is by no means to imply that Schleiermacher neglected ethics: for him Christian ethics, like exegetical theology, was a distinct theological field and not a part of dogmatics. He thought that the teleological character of Christianity was better expressed in Christian ethics than in dogmatics (*Gl.*, § 29.2 [p. 124]). The existential relationship that piety "voices" (n. 45 above) gives rise, precisely through

With the revision proposed,Schleiermacher's doctrine of creation still seems to me a sound model for Christian dogmatics. "Creation" is not about the way the world first got started, but about the kind of world that is presupposed by the Christian drama of redemption. The adequacy of this way of presenting the doctrine must be judged precisely by the double test of correctly describing the Christian consciousness while avoiding entanglements with natural science. And while I do not think dogmatics is apologetics, it does seem to me that to interpret the doctrine of creation as an attempt to thematize existential faith puts the apologist in a position of strength. No apologetic can be the ground or foundation on which Christians repose their faith, which is, by definition, faith in Christ. An attempt to rest Christian faith on arguments would be to misconstrue the phenomenon of faith, and for just this reason it would be poor dogmatics. But this is merely to make the common distinction between the context of discovery and the context of justification, and not by any means to deny that there is a place for apologetics.

True, there are Christians who may find it hard to recognize in such a doctrine of creation their actual Christian faith. If their belief is assent to supernaturally imparted information, then for them creation will be about how the world began - one item in a list of Christian credenda. I can only judge their approach to be wrong. But at least the approach I am recommending instead has no need to deny the genuineness of a *faith* in creation that is conveyed by a largely erroneous *doctrine* of creation, such as, for instance, most of us would take creationism to be. Someone who clings tenaciously to belief in the six-day work of Genesis may be mistaken about the status of the biblical story, but nonetheless nurtured by it in a sound confidence toward the world-order and a sense of responsibility for stewardship of its resources. Moreover, is it not the case that the weight of theological opinion since Schleiermacher's time has moved over to his side of the boat? He anticipated that Christians would have to learn to do without much that many of them still thought to be inextricably tied up with the essence of Christianity, including the very *concept* of creation as usually construed, and not just the Mosaic *account* of it. But he risked another prophecy even while admitting that orthodoxy was not then on his side: "I am firmly persuaded that my discussion is an inspired heterodoxy which in its own good time - if not just because of my book and not until long after my death - will become orthodox."[57]

the recognition of it in piety, to specific volitions as well as thought (see, *e.g. Sendschreiben,* p. 19). My question, however, is whether Schleiermacher's ethical emphasis ought not to be reflected also in the *dogmatic* propositions that express the presuppositions of Christian faith concerning the constitution of the world.

[57] *Sendschreiben*, p. 29.

The Universe In The Bible And In Modern Science

STANLEY L. JAKI

The universe as depicted in the Bible and the universe of modern science may seem to belong to two different worlds. A universe of billions of galaxies, each with trillions of stars and measured in thousands if not millions of light years, is staggeringly beyond a tent-like structure floating on waters. Compared with that world-tent even the geocentric world of Ptolemy appears to be rationality incarnate. Worse, rationality, which implies consistency, can hardly be imagined to be at home in a world where mountains (volcanoes) emit their fumes when touched by an overlord and where clouds, hailstones, and rain are sent or withdrawn at his will if not plain whim. Still worse, all this, hardly to boast about, may not even be original.

One cannot deny all sympathy to panbabylonist scholars who, in the wake of the first deciphering of cuneiform tables, rushed to the conclusion that the cosmogenesis of the Bible was a regurgitation of *Enuma elish.* They should have, however, been struck by the classic brevity of Genesis l, a feature wholly absent in its Babylonian counterpart. While in the latter the building of the actual world begins only after a long internecine struggle among gods and goddesses, representing various parts of an animistic nature, the world building in Genesis 1 starts with no hesitation. Nor is it held up at any phase of the process.

Absence of cosmic struggle in Genesis 1 certainly puts it in a class by itself. That throughout the Bible there are but few and tenuous references to a *Chaoskampf*[1] further strengthens the uniqueness of the biblical world view. Yet in more than one glaring respect the world view is Mesopotamian primitiveness. In addition to details given in Genesis 1 the biblical world view contains such quaint particulars as openings in the sky as if it were more a sieve than a vault so that rain and clouds might exit from their heavenly storage and return there after their work was done on earth (Gen. 7:11, Isa. 24:18). The pillars on which the roof rests are in that world view the only parts that were simply postulated (1 Sam. 2:8, Job 9:6, 26:11, 38:6). All the rest is on hand on the basis of direct sensory evidence.

As to the production of a world stretched out like a tent (Ps 104:2), it has details that stultify efforts to explain them scientifically. A roof that exists before there is a ground, a light that shines long before the sun is on hand, have not failed to rebuff those who looked with one eye on science and with another on Genesis 1. Such a look, which can never match a look with both eyes, first on one, then on the other subject, is lurking behind the claim that by days the author meant long ages. In addition to scientific problems the procedure poses also a theological one. Is God's sabbath also

[1] It is precisely the **polemical** character of Genesis 1 that is not proved in E. Hasel's excellent article, "The Polemic Nature of the Genesis Cosmology," *Evangelical Quarterly* 46 (1974) pp. 81-102, which, on the basis of its contents, could have been rightly called the markedly non-Babylonian character of that cosmology. The article lacks any pointer to the significance of the emphasis on "goodness" in Genesis 1.

a geological age? Difficulties remain even if one takes into account results which show the hollowness of the panbabylonists' claim at least with respect to the biblical world-building. Nor are the foregoing difficulties dissipated by the claim that the Bible, to recall an old insight made famous by Galileo,[2] is not about the manner in which the heavens go around but about the manner of going to heaven.

For if salvation history is to be given justice, a message of Genesis 1 is to be found that can be fitted into the patriarchal narrative. Did that narrative need an introduction other than Gen. 2-3? The latter is certainly as picturesque and as dramatic as the story of the patriarchs. On the contrary there is nothing particularly picturesque in Genesis 1 and it is anything but dramatic in a human sense.

A drama or tragedy can only be had if there is a chink in the armor of the hero or if he has antagonists. In Genesis 1 Elohim has no opposition (a subtle evidence of his oneness) and all that he achieves is good, indeed his total achievement is declared to be very good. Moreover, since in Genesis 1 man and woman appear at the end (*Enuma elish* begins with them as personifications of salt and fresh water), the world-building is a purely physical affair. As such it resists parallels with extrabiblical cosmogonies full of forces that are evil in a moral sense.

In Genesis 1 goodness is predicated on plain physical and nonintelligent living things time and again, before the same is done, with no direct reference to moral qualities, about man and woman. Long before 20th-century man achieved a hard won realization about the factor that makes a good car and less frequently good plumbing, ancient people knew what makes a good tent, a bow, a boat and similar artifacts. The factor is reliability, stability, consistency, and endurance -- physical or mechanical qualities not necessarily dependent on "good" intentions. Nor is that factor discredited by better illustrations of it through the growth of knowledge, be it scientific.

Genesis 1 reveals a plainly objectivist thrust by the fact that it is not God's action as such which is declared there to be good but the product of his actions. Once this is kept in mind, the exact meaning of the expression "in the beginning" and of the verb "*bara*" will seem of secondary importance.[3] In fact nothing is so misleading as preoccupation with arcane details of linguistics when one is in view of a lucid proposition: there is one universe of things which is solidly arranged.

Very lucid is the manner in which the author of Genesis 1 offers his very realistic message that can be taken literally with no damage to biblical inerrancy and modern science. The lucidity of the manner is not weakened by the fact that it is couched in a metaphor. Metaphors, which are a dime a dozen in biblical salvation history, do not detract from its most serious reality. If this is not understood by modern man, he only has to blame himself and the overcomplicatedness of his scholarly apparatus that time and again prevents him from seeing the forest for the trees.

Contrary to the prejudices generated by that apparatus, a plain comprehension of the realist thrust of a metaphor is not demythologization. The latter is a denial that God can act on an autonomous nature. Genesis 1 on the contrary states that whatever

[2] In the manuscript of his letter to Grand Duchess Christina (1616), Galileo refers to Baronius as the author of that phrase. See S. Drake, *Discoveries and Opinions of Galileo* (Garden City, NY: Doubleday, 1957), p. 186.

[3] Even *bara*, which presents the far clearer case of the two expressions, does not lend itself to a perfectly clear theological argument. The reason is its use at least three times in connection with human actions (Josh. 17:15 and 18, and Ezek. 23:47).

the solidity of nature, it is not autonomous in a strict sense. Its solidity, expressive of laws of consistent working, is given to it in all its totality. The author of Genesis 1 could have, of course, stated this in a brief general statement. For all its penchant for concreteness, the vocabulary of the Old Testament contains very frequently used abstract notions such as nothing, unlimited, eternal, and all, the latter being particularly elusive to the senses when taken in a most emphatic sense.

Fortunately, the author of Genesis 1 knew better than to write to professional and self-styled philosophers (and theologians, to say nothing of exegetes) who would hardly listen and whose sense of the real is vanishingly small all too often. He wrote to down-to-earth people with a sound poetic sense of which learned scholars are often in short supply. There is a touch of poetry on hand whenever the whole, all too evident in itself, is described by enumerating its chief parts.[4] The whole in question is a tent-like universe with the heaven and the earth (roof and ground) as its chief parts. These two are accounted for on the 2d and 3d days, with the roof coming first, possibly because of the dignity it has on account of its proximity to God's throne above. The appearance of plants and trees simultaneously with the ground is simply a part of the Mesopotamian view (held until the 18th century even in the scientific West) that they spontaneously arise from moist ground.

The listing of the chief parts is followed by the listing of their principal details: sun, moon, and stars on the roof (4th day), animals, birds, and fish by the ground (5th day). That man is introduced into a solid edifice shows of course God's goodness that must be as reliable as human goodness as the latter can certainly be expected to provide safe habitat. God's rest on the 7th day and his providing light in the first day are part of a metaphor secondary to the chief metaphor though intimately connected with it. The chief metaphor is about the world as a solidly arranged whole, which an edifice, be it a tent (Isa. 40:22, 44:24, 45:12), always is. The secondary metaphor is about God as a workman, a builder, who very logically, provides light before setting about a work which is accomplished in seven days, a symbol of perfection. As to the presentation of God as a builder, it should seem hardly less surprising than seeing him presented as a warrior.

Discard the metaphors of edifice and worker and a major loss will be on hand, together with endless difficulties. The loss is the practically inevitable removal of the universe as such from the interpreter's horizon.[5] As to the difficulties, they had started long before Copernicus, Newton, and Einstein arrived on the scene. The Ptolemaic universe had already in patristic times provided headaches that could not be talked away by pious rhetoric. Few interpreters of Genesis 1 have up to now taken to heart Augustine's poignant observation: "It is often the case that a non-Christian happens to know something with absolute certainty and through experimental evidence about the earth, sky, and other elements of this world...It is therefore very deplorable and harmful, and to be avoided at any cost that he should hear a Christian give, so to

[4] Two examples may suffice. In Psalm 115 the total deadness of idols is presented by listing the absence in them of any of the five senses. In Isaiah 24:2 twelve classes of people are enumerated to emphasize the totality of the inhabitants of an earth to be devastated.

[5] See for instance, N. M. Sarna, *Understanding Genesis* (New York: Shocken Books, 1970), P. Beauchamp, *Création et Séparation* (Paris: Aubier Montaigne, 1969), G. von Rad, *Genesis* (Philadelphia: Westminster Press, 1961), that illustrate the point respectively through a Jewish, Catholic, and Protestant exegete.

speak, a 'Christian account' of these topics in such a way that he could hardly hold his laughter on seeing, as the saying goes, the error rise sky-high."[6] Unfortunately, he himself did not fully digest the medicine offered by him. Post-Newtonian science had to come before a major dent was made (not without some shock) in concordist interpretations of Genesis 1.

Did Genesis 1 and similar messages in the Bible about the universe come through that shock without losing their credibility? Before taking up this question, a further look is necessary at the biblical teaching about the universe. The first to be noted is that there is something unnatural about the chief characteristic of that teaching, or the goodness, that is, the solidity, reliability and consistency of all physical or material things. In Mesopotamia as well as in Egypt, to speak only of Israel's immediate great neighbors, the opposite was true. Apart from *Enuma elish,* where strife is the rule, Babylon offered the yearly Akitu festival, a week-long public frenzy whereby the rulers and the populace imagined themselves to be caught in the cosmic disorder and to secure, as if by magic ritualism, orderly conditions for another year.[7]

If Genesis 1 is assumed to have been written in the wake of Babylonian captivity, its interpretation should seem straightforward. It is a calm, solid assertion of cosmic order, the basis of all certainty about anything else, but above all about salvation history. This assertion which, as will be seen shortly, is a most biblical preface to the patriarchal narrative, could have been voiced half a millenium earlier assuming that Psalm 72 had David for its author. There the endurance of the Davidic throne, a chief symbol of the salvation to be accomplished, is predicated on the unquestioned permanence of the sun and the moon (Ps. 72:5, 17).

But it is the trauma of the destruction of Jerusalem and the Babylonian captivity, where the work of salvation seemed to be in total collapse, that provoked emphatic and repeated recourse to cosmic solidity as the supreme court of appeal. In the arcane sequence leading from the Suffering Servant to exultation over the New Zion, one passage stands out by its matter-of-fact character. There (Isa. 55:10-11) reliability of Yahweh's promise is based on reference to the unfailing effect of rain and snow on the soil, a purely natural process. The same exilic period inspired Psalm 90, an extensive recall of the promises given to David. His throne is described there to be in the kind of ruined state that only the fall of Jerusalem could evoke. Hope is offered with a view on a circumstance of the promise given to David, namely, that the endurance of his throne would match that of the sun and the moon, "a faithful witness in the sky" (Ps. 90:37-38).

The chief witness is, however, Jeremiah, the prophet most existentially involved in the upheavals preceding and following the destruction of Jerusalem. His prediction of the Fall of Jerusalem is balanced with the assertion, repeated twice in the same context, that Yahweh's covenant with Israel would cease only if his covenant with the day and night, a chief sequence in nature, would ever be broken (Jer. 33:19-20, 25-26). Similar is the ray of hope offered by Jeremiah following Jerusalem's destruction. The passage (Jer. 31:35-37) is all the more noteworthy because there the breakdown of the alternation of day and night is spoken of as an impossibility since it cannot occur "in

6. *De Genesi ad litteram,* Lib I, cap. 19.

7. See S. A. Pallis, *The Babylonian Akitu Festival* (Copenhagen, 1926), pp. 292-97.

spite" of Yahweh. In view of this, anything but accidental should seem the sequence whereby reflection on creation precedes reflection on salvation history in several Psalms (19, 24, 33, 92, 95, 136, 148), with only Ps. 147 showing a reverse sequence, and the sequence of Ps. 104 and 105.

Apart from these evocations of the solidity of the universe that have added value in their existentially dramatic character, there are corresponding statements which, because they are so matter-of-fact, should seem no less impressive. The stars are spoken of as having a "duty that shall not pass away" (Ps. 148:6), of being an army drilled by the Lord himself (Isa. 40:26) and of not failing to answer His call (Isa. 40:26), an idea echoed by Baruch (3:35) in a more poetic style. The long encomium in Proverbs of God's wisdom begins with a reference to the wisdom whereby the earth is set on its foundation and the heavens are fixed firm (3:19-20).

The wisdom in question is, of course, broader than mere architectural planning. The universe is spoken of in the Bible as a proper dwelling place for man because God is "the designer and maker of the earth...not creating it to be a waste [chaos] but designing it to be lived in" (Isa. 45:18). Focusing on that habitability could turn into a celebration of coziness as if sunny skies and gentle rain alone were to be faced by man (Ps. 104). But there is also the more detached recognition, such as in Psalm 19, of a properly designed universe with no reference to man. Furthermore, the recognition is declared to be a matter of obviousness to be denied only by fools (Pss. 14 and 53).

Obviousness can readily invite oversight, as illustrated by the scant attention given to the implication of the expression God Almighty or Almighty God. Nothing less is implied there than the existence of an *all* or universe. The shortness of this English word (with its Hebrew equivalent hardly longer) is in striking contrast with the vastness it can convey including the very totality of things. The latter can, however, be evoked by enumeration of parts, a device skillfully used in Gen. 1 and also in Ps. 50 where God's ownership is recounted in reference to the animals of the forest, to mountain beasts, to birds and to whatever stirs in the plain. It is only then that the general statement is made: "for mine is the world and its fulness" (Ps 50:12).

It is on God's exclusive ownership of *all* that the author of the book of Wisdom bases God's love for all. The context (ch. 11) is noteworthy for more than one reason. First, it contains an emphatic declaration about the total absence of hatred on God's part for anything he made, precisely because all were made by Him. Not surprisingly, it contains an explicit reference to the "whole universe," though it is a mere "grain from a balance" when measured against God. Second, together with ch. 13, it shows a heavy dosage of unmistakably Greek expressions. A chief among them is the reference to the Creator who fashioned "the universe from formless matter" (11:17). Undoubtedly there is Greek influence behind the remark that the Creator "disposed everything according to measure, and number, and weight" (11:20).[8] No less Greek is the phrase "from the greatness and the beauty of created things their original author, by analogy, is seen" (13:5).

While the phraseology is Greek, the content is very un-Greek. No Greek philosopher, however well versed in the use of analogy, made an inference to the existence of a personal transcendental Creator who is meant in those chapters that are a mere

[8] This phrase was one of the most often quoted biblical passages in medieval writings, according to E. Curtius, *European Literature and the Latin Middle Ages* (London: Routledge and Kegan Paul, 1953), p. 504.

digression in a celebration of general and special providence. The latter has of course for its object the people of the Covenant. In the book of Sirach, also composed in Greek, genuinely Hebrew expressions abound in connection with the universe. Such are "the always punctual moon" (43:6), "the stars that never grow slack at their watch" (43:10), and the "marvels which the Almighty God has solidly constructed for the universe to stand firm in its glory" (42:17). There may be Greek influence behind the sweeping declaration that "all things hold together" (43:28) but no such suspicion can arise about the great assurance given in the first and longer part of the book dealing with moral precepts, many of them natural laws of morality. Their validity is predicated on the permanent and universal lawfulness of interaction among various parts of the created realm (16:24-26).

The "formless matter" in the book of Wisdom and the no less frequently discussed "made them out of things non-existing" in 2 Mac 7 are the kind of expressions which, when taken by themselves, can only generate futile arguments.[9] It is no less futile to ignore the perspective in which they stand. In both cases, and dramatically in the second, the perspective is about God with absolute sovereignty over the totality of everything else. One, therefore, could reasonably expect that in the same perspective the idea of creation out of nothing would have been quickly formulated, once adumbrated, to take the less generous interpretation of those expressions. Yet two hundred years after the redaction of Wisdom and 2 Mac., Philo's voluminous writings, filled with sincere monotheism, offered not a single explicit statement on creation out of nothing and only one passage out of many that logically implies it.[10]

There should seem, therefore, much more than what meets the eye in that creation out of nothing was enunciated in Christian ambience within one hundred years following Paul's great missionary journeys and within half a century following John's death.[11] Since creation out of nothing here is considered only inasmuch as it has a relevance to thinking about the universe, there should seem an added interest in taking a look at its New Testament doctrine. Jesus certainly assumed on the part of his audience plain acceptance of the regularity of natural processes, the basis for reading "the portents of the sky" (Lk. 12:56). This was his ground for taking them to task for not being ready to read the signs of spiritual times. His audience could sense that he had attributed divine authority to his words insofar as they were to survive even the heaven and the earth (Mk. 13:31, Lk. 21:33). His parting words, "all authority is given to me in heaven and on earth" (Mt. 28:17) revealed his consciousness of standing above the cosmos, a plainly divine prerogative. Apart from that he mostly took the world in a moral sense as the realm of sin, and so did John. But his strong denunciations of "the love of the world" never were tainted with Gnostic hostility toward matter. He defended no less energetically the reality of Incarnation. He did so with a cosmic connotation that had an intellectual significance which science, of all things, was to reveal in a distant future.

9. Instead of getting lost in philological hairsplitting, Christian exegetes should rather note that a shadowy matter, be it called "formless" or "nonexistent," could perfectly coexist with a shadowy god, be it Plato's "Good" or Plotinus' "One," but had to be looked upon as created out of nothing once God was spoken of as an absolute Sovereign over existence.

10. *De somniis*, I. 76, as cogently argued by F. V. Courneen, "Philo Judaeus and the Concept of Creation," *New Scholasticism* 15 (1941), pp. 46-58.

11. Mainly in the writings of Justin, Theophilus of Antioch, and Tertullian.

That cosmic connotation, tied to John's use of *monogenes,* comes into focus as soon as one recalls its foremost Hellenistic use. For Plato, Plutarch and Cicero, to mention only three chief spokesmen of classical pagan thought, the universe was *monogenes,* that is, the chief emanation from the divine.[12] John's use of the term dethroned the cosmos and saved it by the same stroke. By putting a flesh and blood being on the pedestal of *monogenes,* John erected a powerful barrier against pantheistic emanationism. That John also asserted the direct role of Christ in creation (1:3) was, of course, the same strategy which Paul had already followed. To strike at the root of Judaizing propaganda among the Colossians about dietary laws, sabbath, and sundry angelic powers, he held high Christ's role in creation (Col. 1:16). It was also through attributing the role of creation to Christ that Paul met the objection that the doctrine about Christ undermined monotheism.

The intellectual history made by his statement, "before anything was created he existed and he holds all things in unity" (Col. 1:17), is the one made by John's *monogenes.* It is a history about the repeated stillbirths and only one birth of science.[13] In all those stillbirths (witnessed in ancient China, India, Egypt, Babylon and Greece) the world was essentially a *monogenes,* an emanation from the divine. As a result the world was looked upon as an animated being and often subject to most contrary and capricious strivings. Emanationism also meant a gradual deterioration along the descending grades of being. Plotinus' system is a case in point and also an illustration of the scientific barrenness of that perspective. Even in the Greco-Roman world there were but a few halting steps, such as Cicero's remark about the cosmos as a clockwork,[14] toward a depersonalized view of the universe.

Why is it that only in the medieval Christian West did the clockwork perspective gain quick acceptance and in a scientifically fruitful way?[15] The only conceptual connection that can be traced out convincingly implies belief in Incarnation. It was only monotheism that was strong enough to assert the sovereignty of God and to face up to all rightful questions about the true measure of autonomy embodied in the universe. Within Muslim monotheism such questions were banished at the insistence of the orthodox Mu'tazalīes whereas in orthodox Judaism only such questions were considered that were explicitly contained in the sacred texts.[16]

Already from that vantage point - the high and late medieval centuries - it is possible to see a most important feature of the biblical view of the universe, crowned by the Incarnation. Its vital core remains creatively influential while its crust reveals more and more its time-conditioned character. The message that *all* is good, that is, solidly or consistently established because made by God, can be safely distinguished from talk about a tent-like cosmos and without discrediting the latter's veracity as a

12. The texts are quoted in Kittel under *monogenes.*

13. A detailed presentation of this is my *Science and Creation: From Eternal Cycles to an Oscillating Universe* (1974; 2nd enlarged edition, Edinburgh: Scottish Academic Press, 1986).

14. *De natura deorum,* 2:34. The reference is to an orrery reproducing the planetary motions.

15. Tellingly, Oresme used the clockwork-simile to illustrate the all-important idea of inertial motion (Newton's first law), first enunciated by his teacher Buridan with respect to the origin of the movement of celestial bodies. See my *Science and Creation,* pp. 240-41.

16. An illustration of this is E. E. Urbach, *The Sages: Their Concepts and Beliefs* (Jerusalem: Magnes Press, 1975), ch. IX on creation.

carrier of that message. One need not be a 20th-century Christian to have an enlightenment respectful of the light that shines in darkness without dissipating it. Indeed, late 20th-century Christians perform all too often far worse than their forebears six or seven hundred years ago.

For long before us a Copernicus remained supremely calm as he proposed the heliocentric universe. Spiritual hotheads called him first a fool and, on the other hand, set in motion a process that led to the condemnation of Copernicanism. This only shows that the vital core in question will not always enlighten any and all about specifics. The *magnalia dei* never acted and never shall act as if they were automated dispensers of spiritual snacks. They were and there will be always many Christians ready to think that "all coherence is gone"[17] when only a deeper coherence is emerging.

Unfortunately, what is taking place in science remains all too often the least publicized aspect of it. A major instance of this in our century is the flood of talk about relativity and quantum theory. As to the former, not one in a hundred books contain a hint let alone an informative chapter, about its most important result. It is not atomic energy, let alone atomic and hydrogen bombs, but for the first time in the history of science, a contradiction-free account about the totality of gravitationally interacting things.[18] Since all matter is gravitational, the result means a scientific grasp of the universe along one of its major parameters.

Were Psalms 14 and 50 to be rewritten today, they could contain the phrase: the scientifically uninformed and misinformed said in their heart, there is no God. Into this category would belong all who still grant a chief claim of Kant's *Critique of Pure Reason* that the idea of the universe is the bastard product of the metaphysical cravings of the intellect. For science at least, if not for pseudo scientific philosophers, the universe is not an illusion but a solid reality. A major fact still to be learned by many Christians is that the agnostic-pantheistic Einstein was very upset by the metaphysical perspectives opened up by his greatest achievement which he first offered under the title "Cosmological Consequences of General Relativity."[19] His information about the historical background of his achievement did not go beyond the times that witnessed Newton formulate the three laws of motion. It remained unknown to Einstein that the most important of these laws, the first about inertial motion, had by his time a more than 300-year-old history.Had he learned from the widely available publications about Buridan and Oresme,[20] he would still have done what many academics do today, refuse to appreciate the impulse which those two received from the view of the universe as created out of nothing and in time. By being Christian and of medieval provenance at that, such a look at scientific history is destined to remain greeted with scepticism if considered and pondered at all.

[17] A well-known phrase of John Donne and the title of V. Harris' monograph on the controversy raging around 1600 about the decay of nature (Chicago: University of Chicago Press, 1949).

[18] For details, see my *The Paradox of Olbers' Paradox* (New York: Herder and Herder, 1969).

[19] Particularly revealing are his letters to M. Solovine around 1950. For quotations from them, see my *The Road of Science and the Ways to God* (University of Chicago Press, 1978), pp. 192-93.

[20] Publications mostly inspired by the pioneering work of Pierre Duhem (1861-1916) on the medieval origins of Newtonian science. For details, see my *Uneasy Genius: The Life and Work of Pierre Duhem* (Dordrecht: Martinus Nijhoff, 1984).

The world-wide marketing of the nonsense about Einstein's relativity, that it proves the relativity of everything,[21] is matched only by the nonsense prevailing about quantum theory. The gist of that nonsense is that all interactions at the atomic and subatomic level are random, that is, partially if not wholly uncaused. Consistency is therefore merely statistical and valid only on the level of ordinary observations. Clearly, such a universe is very different from the biblical universe which, by being emphatically good, must be consistently reliable down to the very roots of its being. Almost a crude lack of perceptiveness is at work in a Christian who sees in that "quantum mechanical" world an ally of Christian faith,[22] a deliverance from iron clad mechanical determinism. For one, such a Christian fails to see that physical determinism, discovered freely and investigated freely, can never be any threat to human freedom. For another, such a Christian fails to see anything significant in the fervent espousal of that random world by a post-Christian world. The fervor is largely fueled by the "liberating vistas" of moral randomness, the worst counterfeit of true freedom.

That the universe is far from being random is stunningly revealed by the most significant work done in modern scientific cosmology. It is an unfolding of the vast implications of the discovery in 1963 of the 3° K cosmic background radiation, a remnant of a very early state of the expanding universe. Prior to 1963, and especially during the 19th century, only conjectures could be made about the early universe, but they were made profusely and often with an air of certitude. Laplace's nebular hypothesis formed the basis of most of those speculations that yielded only nebulosity, a sort of foggy state. Fog, if vast and uniform, can give to one within it the impression that it is a natural form of existence about which no further questions need be asked. Indeed, if a fog is perfectly homogeneous it will lack in specifics to which alone further questions can be attached. So much for the unwary steps that led many to believe that the nebular hypothesis dispenses with the need to ask questions about the origin of the universe.

Today the situation is very different. Cosmology has become a genuine science because of the many specifics, all closely interconnected, that are known about the early universe. In fact it appears that from its earliest stages on, the evolution of the physical universe runs along a narrowly defined track, a predicament far from being random.[23] That narrow, most specific, cosmological track leads in two directions. One is toward the present state of the universe, a journey purely for the science of physics. The other is toward the choice whereby this and not any other among the many possible cosmic tracks has become a reality. That direction leads beyond physics into the realm of metaphysics. Christians wary of metaphysics may cheat themselves out of a unique opportunity.

Christians, forgetful of the narrow gate into heaven, may not know what railroaders have always known, namely, that only a narrowly defined track is a good, reliable, usefully-built track. The world view of Genesis 1 will appear the most

21. For details on this cultural malaise, see my *The Absolute beneath the Relative and Other Essays* (Lanham, Md: University of America Press, 1988), in press.

22. An example is J. Polkinghorne, *The Way the World Is* (Grand Rapids, Mich.: Eerdmans, 1984). For a critique of its underlying presuppositions, see my *Chance or Reality and Other Essays* (Lanham Md: University of America Press, 1986).

23. The predicament lends itself to a very fruitful reformulation of the cosmological argument. See my *Cosmos and Creator* (Edinburgh: Scottish Academic Press, 1980) and "The Intelligent Christian's Guide to Scientific Cosmology," *Faith and Reason* 12/2 (1986), pp. 124-36.

creative world view even today provided one knows how good it is by its emphasis on goodness and what is truly good in modern scientific cosmology.

This world of ours, human world that it is, would not be true to itself if everything offered in modern scientific cosmology could be called good. Certain goods offered there with enormous fanfare are outrageously rotten. And just as in Paradise, where not the apple was rotten but its merchandising, here too it is not mathematical physics that is the culprit but the philosophy marketed in its wrappings. Tellingly, when almost four decades ago the steady-state theorists were held up to a major criticism before a prominent forum,[24] acknowledgment of their mathematical talent was certainly prominent. But why should one care about one's mathematics when the claim grafted on it is essentially philosophical and stunningly nonsensical at that? For there is no mathematics that can prove that hydrogen atoms, singly or in large numbers, are steadily coming forth out of nothing, let alone that they do so without a Creator. This is why, for instance, no attention should be given to headlines according to which the latest sightings of very distant galaxies give a glimpse of the moment of creation about 18 billion years ago. Science certainly can show that the universe is at least 18 billion years old. But the moment of creation, which is a transition from nonbeing into being, is as little a matter of observation as the transition itself. The latter can only be seen by meta-physical eyes of which no human being can permanently rid himself or herself.

Undoubtedly those eyes conjure up perspectives about man as not being his own master and can unmask the make-believe according to which ultimately all is randomness. Some of the steady-state theorists were honest enough to admit that their deepest motivation was not scientific but counter-metaphysical.[25] They tried to discredit the expanding universe as a too graphic reminder of transitoriness in general and of the words "heaven and earth pass away" in particular. In order to achieve their aim they were willing to be caught in the supreme irony that only a postulate of a supremely illogical steady creation out of nothing and without a Creator could keep the one and logical creation out of focus.

Such an irony does not seem to bother the spokesmen of inflationary theory of the universe, the latest rage in scientific cosmology. Trusting their mathematical formulas they claim to produce by mere speculation countless universes. Ten years ago a chief of them spoke glibly of this universe as possibly "the last free lunch." In the Spring of 1987, emboldened perhaps by the absence of philosophical outrage within the scientific community, he held it most likely that the universe was produced by a scientist (inflationary of course and unwittingly inflated too) in a cellar, of all places.[26] Cellars never have evoked clarity and order.

Order, which is coherence, is in fact the chief problem vexing the inflationary theorists. The source of their problem is not that the universe may, in its earliest phase, have been far more rapidly expanding than ever since. Nor is their problem due to their shifting from general relativity to quantum mechanics as a framework of cosmological analysis. The problem lies with the chronic oversight that quantum

24. Before the Royal Astronomical Society in 1953 by its president, H. Dingle.

25. Most outspoken in that respect was Fred Hoyle who a few years ago spoke of the universe as being God by definition, and vice versa.

26. See the interview of M. W. Browne with Prof. Alan H. Guth of MIT in *The New York Times,* April 14, 1987, pp. Cl-C4.

theory, which is a special form of statistics, is also philosophy. Reliance on statistical mathematics carries with it the acknowledgment that only aggregates of events can be quantitatively evaluated and that therefore one must rest content with numerical values which as such do not apply to individual events. But from this it does not follow that individual events have no strict quantitative values, let alone strict ontological status.

Using quantum mechanics about the whole of the universe means that universes in large numbers are to be postulated or else the application of quantum mechanics, which is always about averages, is meaningless. But then no two universes can be assumed to have the same properties, for if they are indistinguishable they are useless for the purposes of statistical evaluation. Hence the fragmentation of the universe into disconnected universes within the inflationary theory. Their spokesmen have recently spent much effort in trying to secure some coherence among those separate universes. This only proves that even scientists cannot live long without a single universe, the only universe worthy of its name. Theologians who have forgotten that their worship of almighty God makes no sense without the reality of a single *all* or universe, may now re-learn their basics from the latest in science. It brings in a post-Christian era an awesome witness to the vast fruitfulness of belief in Christ in whom all things are held in unity.[27] Such is a most recent lesson of a simultaneous look at the universe in the Bible and in modern science. This and similar lessons should seem particularly important to learn in an age that becomes more scientific with each passing day and in which, for better or for worse, science has become the language which is believed to be understood, and certainly needed day in and day out, by any and all.

[27] For a detailed presentation of the impact which orthodox Christology had on the development of science, see my *The Savior of Science* (forthcoming).

THE CONTRIBUTORS

PHYLLIS BIRD, Garrett-Evangelical and Seabury Western Seminaries, Evanston, Illinois

PEDER BORGEN, The University of Trondheim, Dragvoll, Norway

TERENCE E. FRETHEIM, Luther Northwestern Theological Seminary, Saint Paul, Minnesota

BRIAN GERRISH, The Divinity School, The University of Chicago, Chicago, Illinois

STANLEY L. JAKI, Seton Hall University, South Orange, New Jersey

J. GERALD JANZEN, Christian Theological Seminary, Indianapolis, Indiana

STEVEN KRAFTCHICK, Princeton Theological Seminary, Princeton, New Jersey

BENNIE C. OLLENBURGER, Mennonite Biblical Seminary, Elkhart, Indiana

PETER STUHLMACHER, University of Tübingen, West Germany

SHEMARYAHU TALMON, The Hebrew University of Jerusalem, Jerusalem, Israel